Between Transcendence and Historicism

SUNY Series in Hegelian Studies

Edited by William Desmond

Between Transcendence and Historicism

The Ethical Nature of the Arts in Hegelian Aesthetics

Brian K. Etter

State University of New York Press

Published by
State University of New York Press, Albany

Printed in the United States of America

For information, address State University of New York Press,
194 Washington Avenue, Suite 305, Albany, NY 12210-2384

Production by Judith Block
Marketing by Anne M. Valentine

Library of Congress Cataloging-in-Publication Data

Etter, Brian K.
Between transcendence and historicism : the ethical nature of the arts in Hegelian aesthetics / Brian K. Etter.
p. cm. — (SUNY series in Hegelian studies)
Includes bibliographical references (p.) and index.
ISBN 0–7914–6657–4 (hardcover : alk. paper)—ISBN 0–7914–6658–2 (pbk. : alk. paper)
1. Hegel, Georg Wilhelm Friedrich, 1770–1831—Aesthetics.
2. Aesthetics—Moral and ethical aspects. I. Title. II. Series.

B2949.A4E88 2006
111′.85′092—dc22

2005007685

ISBN–13: 978–0–7914–6657–5 (hardcover : alk. paper)
ISBN–13: 978–0–7914–6658–2 (pbk. : alk. paper)

10 9 8 7 6 5 4 3 2 1

Contents

Preface

This book is written out of the conviction that, after a century of modernist avant-garde artistic movements, the nature of the arts needs to be rethought. It is intended for those who are open to the possibility that the arts pose a problem within modern society; that criticism of the arts is a legitimate option; and that what philosophers and theorists of the past have said about art is potentially worthwhile. It argues, specifically, that what Hegel had to say about the arts is important for a perspective that is related to the characteristic attitudes of modernity, yet is able to ground criticisms of the arts both in his day and in our own time. It also argues that Hegel is important in the way he interprets artistic traditions as he knew them, transforming long-standing artistic theories into a genuine, philosophical understanding of the arts. While his aesthetic is not without problems of its own, these prove instructive for considering the problems posed by the arts in the modern world.

The argument in these pages, therefore, is not aimed at an exclusively Hegelian audience. Although it will be of interest to scholars of Hegel, the hope is that what it has to say will also be of interest to readers concerned with broader aesthetic questions. Whether I succeed in addressing what is of fashionable concern at the moment, the issues of the ethical nature of the particular arts and the role of tradition are serious and will not disappear. The tendency among philosophers to celebrate modernism and now postmodernism has worked to foreclose debate about fundamental aesthetic issues. I argue here that there are good reasons to see Hegel as pointing the way to a valid critique of these movements that are largely uncriticized in the academic community.

This book was undertaken out of a long effort to understand Hegel's aesthetic within the context of his larger philosophical system, and out of a sense of the need to rearticulate an aesthetic that would explain the legitimacy of the inherited artistic traditions of Western culture. Hence I have explored some of the topics in this book already in articles and essays. Permission to use them has been graciously granted in the following cases:

"The Sounds of the Ideal: Hegel's Aesthetic of Music," *The Owl of Minerva* 26 (1994): 47–58, appearing in chapter 5; "Beauty, Ornament, and Style: The Problem of Classical Architecture in Hegel's *Aesthetics*," *The Owl of Minerva* 30 (1999): 211–35, appearing in chapter 7; and "Hegel's Aesthetic and the Possibility of Art Criticism," a paper read at the 1996 meeting of the Hegel Society of America, published in *Hegel and Aesthetics*, ed. William Maker (Albany: State University of New York Press, 2000), 31–43, part of which appears here in chapter 3. Quotations from *Aesthetics: Lectures on Fine Art*, by G. W. F. Hegel and translated by T. M. Knox are reprinted by permission of Oxford University Press © 1975 Oxford University Press. I gratefully acknowledge this permission as crucial to the analysis and critique of Hegel's aesthetics. All quotations from the *Aesthetics* are from Knox's translation unless otherwise noted.

I would like to thank Professor William Desmond, editor of the SUNY series in Hegelian Studies, for his encouragement to pursue this project. I also thank Kettering University for its generous support of a sabbatical to make this book possible. Finally, I want to thank my wife, Linda, for reading the manuscript with an eye both for typographical errors and for nonsense masquerading as philosophy.

Abbreviations

English translations follow the German editions of Hegel's works. All quotations are from the English editions unless otherwise noted in the text.

*Enz.*1–3 *Enzyklopädie der philosophischen Wissenschaften im Grundrissen (1830), Sämtliche Werke*, vols. 8–10. Edited by E. Moldenhauer and K. Michel (Frankfurt am Main: Suhrkamp, 1970).

EL *The Encyclopaedia Logic*. Translated by T. F. Geraets, W. A. Suchting, and H. S. Harris (Indianapolis, IN: Hackett, 1991).

PM *Philosophy of Mind: Part Three of the Encyclopaedia of the Philosophical Sciences (1830)*. Translated by William Wallace and A.V. Miller (Oxford: Clarendon Press, 1971).

*VÄ*1–3 *Vorlesungen über die Ästhetik, Sämtliche Werke*, vols. 13–15. Edited by Moldenhauer and Michel (1970).

A1–2 *Aesthetics: Lectures on the Fine Arts*. Translated by T. M. Knox. 2 vols. (Oxford: Clarendon Press, 1975). Pagination is continuous; vol. 2 begins with p. 613.

GPR *Grundlinien der Philosophie des Rechts oder Naturrecht und Staatswissenschaft im Grundrisse, Sämtliche Werke*, vol.7. Edited by Moldenhauer and Michel (1970).

PR *Philosophy of Right*. Translated by T. M. Knox (Oxford: Oxford University Press, 1952).

VPG *Vorlesungen über die Philosophie der Geschichte, Sämtliche Werke*, vol.12. Edited by Moldenhauer and Michel (1970).

PH *The Philosophy of History*. Translated by J. Sibree (New York: Dover, 1956).

VPR 1–3 *Vorlesungen über die Philosophie der Religion*. Ed. Walter Jaeschke, in *Vorlesungen, Ausgewählte Nachschriften und Manuskripte*, vols. 3, 4a, 5 (Hamburg: Felix Meiner Verlag, 1984).

LPR *Lectures on the Philosophy of Religion: The Lectures of 1827*. Translated by R. F. Brown, P. C. Hodgson, J. M. Steward, and H. S. Harris. Edited by P .C. Hodgson (Berkeley and London: University of California Press, 1988).

WL 1–2 *Wissenschaft der Logik, Sämtliche Werke*, vols. 5–6. Edited by Moldenhauer and Michel (1970).

SL *Hegel's Science of Logic*. Translated by A. V. Miller (1969; Atlantic Highlands, NJ: Humanities Press International, 1989).

Abbreviations for works of other authors will be introduced as needed in the notes.

1

Introduction

The arts pose a paradoxical challenge to contemporary society. On the one hand, there is a general sense that the arts are an important constituent of civilization, and that the great achievements of the past ought to be preserved as a heritage for the future. That heritage is important enough to maintain at high levels of professional institutionalization. Major cities boast of their art museums and opera companies, both of which are successful in attracting audiences and donations. When a major city loses a symphony orchestra, for example, there is genuine regret and often renewed efforts in the business community to raise money to revive the orchestra. Finally, after the architectural ravages of the post-World War II era, there is now an admission of the legitimacy of historic preservation of older buildings and neighborhoods; the heritage of the past is necessarily a visual one.

On the other hand, there is a prevailing sense of irrelevance attached to the artistic heritage of our civilization among the artists and critics who define the world of art today. Instead, there is a preoccupation with the new, the absolutely original, as constituting the impulse of art since the advent of the modernist movements at the beginning of the twentieth century. This creates what may be called a presumed normativity of the present, in contrast to the normativity of the past that characterized Western art from the Renaissance through the end of the nineteenth century. The styles and forms once held up as models for aspiring artists no longer hold the same respect. Tradition has long since ceased to be the context for artistic creativity.

Since the time of Hegel, Western art has been understood as a historical phenomenon. Indeed, Hegel is largely responsible for casting the succession of styles in the form of a historical narrative in his *Aesthetics*. This belief in the historicist nature of art—that styles and approaches to artistic creativity are held to be profoundly shaped by history—accords each style its own dignity as the suitable product of that age's spirit or worldview. But such historicism easily slides over into a conviction that present efforts are the only ones that matter simply because they are of our own time. Thus, what was once creative can be retained in a museum but cannot be regarded as relevant to the present needs of art. The corollary, then, is what may be called "presentism"—the belief that only what is being done in the arts now is relevant to life in our time. Increasingly, museums, orchestras, and other cultural institutions are pressured by the art world, often through government funding agencies, to give as much weight to present artistic efforts as to the longer historical heritage. In this way, historicism serves to justify a radical presentism.

Accompanying the art world's presentism is a similar presentism within the academic world. Indeed, we find frequent disquiet at the artistic heritage of Western civilization in the academic curriculum. The literature, music, and visual arts which broader society still respects often appear to be held in contempt by precisely the educational institutions whose responsibility it is to serve as its custodians and transmitters to future generations. The presentist hostility to tradition affects the aesthetics of art as well: in the name of an up-to-date postmodernism, art is seen as having no rational content, no relation to an objective world that can be shared among observers.[1] But this form of academic presentism is merely the continuation of the impulse of artistic modernism, by which the authority and heritage of Western tradition is overturned to make way for what is radically new.

The attractiveness of the presentist thesis is the ability to justify the modernist avant-garde movements that have emerged since the early twentieth century. They define themselves most often by their rejection of traditional styles and approaches, claim to be of their own time, and insist on the irrelevance of tradition to supply norms governing artistic creativity.[2] The academy has long accepted this position and its artistic results uncritically, for to attempt a critique would necessarily involve asserting the relevance of standards arising outside the framework of the modernist project. It becomes impossible, therefore, to justify such a critique on modernist premises. In this way, the very existence of artistic effort in modernity appears to necessitate the presentist thesis if it is to maintain its uniquely modernist character.

Perhaps precisely as the result of the success of modernism in defining the contemporary art world, however, a profound ambivalence about the arts in contemporary society has emerged. The abstraction of modernist art, and now the ironic images of postmodernism, raise the question of what it all means: what significance does artistic creativity, so defined, really possess? To regard the arts as highly as did the nineteenth century—as elevating, ennobling, and purifying—seems altogether out of keeping with the tenor of our time. But without satisfactory answers to the question of significance, there can only be a deep ambivalence toward art and its institutions. Indeed, whether art is necessary to either an individual or a civilization is a question not guaranteed of a persuasive answer today.

In this situation, Hegel—when he is not ignored because his idealism seems irrelevant to modernity—is often used to justify the modernist project, precisely because he appears to sanction the historicist presentism essential to modernism. Theodor Adorno in particular has cited Hegel to justify his own Marxist inspired celebration of modernism (although such use of Hegel amounts to a misappropriation).[3] Yet in his own day, Hegel was astonishingly critical of developments in the arts, and unhesitatingly gave an affirmative answer to the question of the necessity of the arts. In these matters, his aesthetic merits much more attention than it is generally given. Hegel's aesthetic is cast in terms of both a transcendent dimension of art and a historical unfolding of each of the fine arts of his day: architecture, sculpture, painting, music, and poetry. (It should be noted that this does not preclude the extension of the underlying concepts to more modern arts such as photography and cinema, as simply employing a new technology does not necessarily create a new art.) While the element of transcendence proves the principal stumbling block for modern readers, the element of historicism appears more in keeping with the modern understanding of the contingency of human endeavor. In this aspect of Hegel's thought, it is tempting to see the origin of modernist historicism and its corollary of radical presentism. Nevertheless, it is important to recognize that Hegel sees art as neither purely transcendent nor entirely historicist in nature: art partakes of both, but occupies a middle ground, which is vital for understanding the significance of art on Hegel's view. It is in the context of art as lying between transcendence and historicism that Hegel finds art having its real value.

This point, which is crucial to the book's argument, demands some elaboration in order to clarify its significance. Certainly the thesis of historicism recognizes an obvious dimension of human experience: what Plato calls the world of becoming; what St. Augustine calls the temporal world; or what Hegel understands by history, all refer to the aspect of time that has a history because it can be remembered and therefore retained as a still-living present. In this sense, therefore, a sense of the historical nature of time need not imply presentism as its corollary, for it may yield traditionalism as its product just as easily. But radical historicism, understood as seeing historical time as the sole formative factor in human experience, jettisons the role of memory and the value of the past, and thereby results in presentism. What this new kind of historicism seeks, as exemplified in the work of Martin Heidegger, is a perspective on human existence oriented toward the future rather than the past, in which the present is merely preparatory, rather than the culmination of preceding efforts.[4] But this is because it lacks a crucial dimension which previous conceptions of human experience made central.

What is common to Plato, St. Augustine, and Hegel is a relation of the temporal, or historical world, to the eternal or transcendent. For Plato, the world of becoming is only a shadow of the eternal world of real being, in which are found the Ideas that alone endure and really matter.[5] For St. Augustine, the temporal world created by God exists for the sake of God; temporal goods are to be esteemed only insofar as they contribute to the love of the eternal good.[6] And for Hegel, who had a more positive appraisal of this world of temporality, history was the manifestation of the Absolute Spirit: it was neither accidental nor a product of human caprice, but rather a revelation of the divine will itself, as the Idea of Freedom (*VPG*, 32–33; *PH*, 19–20). How to interpret this is indeed problematic, for the relation of the Absolute to history in Hegel's thought is by no means free of ambiguity. But while Hegel's understanding of history may well be challenged as theologically unorthodox, his sense of history nevertheless resists a pure historicism stripped of transcendence.[7] Hence Hegel, together with the long philosophical tradition, understood history within the larger context of transcendence. Humanity occupies, on this view, the middle ground between the two poles of transcendence and a historicism devoid of evidence of the transcendent. Both dimensions are necessary for understanding our nature.

In spite of both the longstanding accusations of pantheism and the defenses of Hegel that see in his philosophy a doctrine of pure immanence, the now prevailing understanding of Hegel's theology recognizes in it a dimension of transcendence. More than a generation ago, Emil Fackenheim argued for the religious foundation of Hegel's philosophy, recognizing the tenuousness of the attempt to hold the absolute and the contingent together in one unified vision of the Whole.[8] More recent work follows this insight into the centrality of religion for Hegel. Bernard Reardon, for example, understands that all religion requires the perception of God as a transcendent being, so that philosophical understanding of the God of faith cannot evacuate the transcendent dimension.[9] Yet for Christianity, God cannot simply be wholly Other, but dwells also in the believer's consciousness. Thus Hegel remains faithful to this much of Christian orthodoxy: God cannot be wholly immanent, either. Quentin Lauer also defends Hegel against charges of pantheism, arguing for a more orthodox conception of God than most commentators.[10] For him, a philosophical understanding of God cannot negate the content of the Christian faith, but rather aims to show its rationality—a project not unfamiliar to readers of St. Thomas Aquinas. Charles Taylor, although more critical of Hegel's theology, sees Hegel as arguing for a God distinct from the world, yet needing the world to complete Himself.[11] Cyril O'Regan, with perhaps the clearest understanding of Hegel's departures from Christian orthodoxy, nevertheless emphasizes that, in spite of Hegel's heterodoxy, it is still possible to identify a distinction between the divine and the world God creates and to which He reveals Himself.[12] Finally, although both Stephen Houlgate and William Desmond see Hegel's conception of God as ambiguous, they also see it as being more than just the human spirit writ large: God is something more than simply immanent.[13] But then there is still an element of transcendence; the Absolute is not reducible to the workings of this temporal order.

The character of art will necessarily be seen quite differently if the transcendent dimension is forsaken. For in that case there will be no eternal warrant for the continuity of time, nor the eternal perspective on human activity, nor the conviction that the totality of history matters. Instead, the past will vanish from memory, its achievements cast to the winds, and its traditions banished from sight. Only the present and the future will matter: thus does pure historicism result in radical presentism, the condition of the modern age. Hence, the quarrel in the arts today is no longer what it was in the seventeenth century—no longer between the ancients and the moderns over which civilization is superior—but is rather something else. Today's quarrel is necessarily between tradition and its denial, and the latter assumes its force because of the presentist reconception of temporality and its relation to the transcendent. The only critical understanding possible of modern presentism, therefore, is from within a perspective that accepts historicism in its most basic sense, that is, seeing history as essential to understanding all human endeavor while justifying a perspective from transcendence as well; this Hegel supplies.

It is within the context of art understood as representing the middle ground of temporality, between transcendence and pure historicism, that the traditional value of art arises. This value lies in its ethical substance and function. For Hegel, this is cast in terms of art's vocation of representing "the Ideal," the state of character that embodies the bliss and serenity religions articulate as their ideal of life. It is important to emphasize that Hegel describes both a classical Ideal and a Christian Ideal: the Ideal is not simply a relic of Greek classicism, as it was for artists and critics from the Renaissance through the eighteenth century. Even in the case of the Christian Ideal, however, it is not otherworldly for Hegel. Its attainment does not wait for heaven, but is the aim of all development and action in this life. Therefore, this is an ethical ideal in the classical sense of the ethical: it is an ideal of character.[14] But, Hegel insists, it is particularly the task of art to represent this ideal. Such an ethical substance of art is concretely what it means for art to be this-worldly, yet conscious of the divine, to lie between historicism and transcendence. Art therefore has a high ethical function.

The ethical nature of art according to Hegel will certainly prove a stumbling block for modern readers. Surely it appears paradoxical: art has been sundered from moral purposes and ethical ideals for at least a century. It is axiomatic that art in the modern world, and perhaps in any era, cannot be limited by moral constraints. Certainly, much art of the avant-garde in the last century, as well as today, shocks or offends our moral sensibilities. Even without an intent to do so, however, art is held to be free; it is autonomous and expressive of the artist's deepest feelings, even in the most abstract forms. The pleasure to be taken in the aesthetic is therefore a pure pleasure, a confrontation with the most exalted efforts of the human spirit. On either view, therefore, the ethical seems far removed from the concerns of art today, and it has been largely banished from the discourse of aesthetics.

The reason for the banishment of the ethical from consideration in modernist art lies in the nature of time as radical historicism conceives it. For if there is no transcendent dimension, there can be no "Ideal" as Hegel describes it: no Ideal of character or state of being found in the divine and represented in the arts. Nor will the ethical, in the more secular (and narrowly Hegelian) sense of customary duties, fare well, either, for custom is a species of tradition—and tradition is forsaken in radical historicism's presentism. Thus it is no surprise to find a lack of moral teaching in the most characteristic of modern philosophy, indeed, a celebration of amoral will to power in Nietzsche and of ruthless resoluteness in Heidegger. But Hegel's aesthetic implies that without ethical norms, there can be no aesthetic norms, either. The ethical nature of art springs from an ethical order that lies between historicism and transcendence—that, in other words, flourishes in a conception of temporality informed by transcendence. Hence the title of this book locates the ethical nature of art precisely between transcendence and historicism.

In discussing the questions which motivate this book, I have thus far relied on intuitive notions of words such as "modern" and "modernity." It is time to attempt to bring some clarity to their use, however, since the concern with history and historicism necessitates conceiving history as having an endpoint not just in the present, but in a modern age generally. Modernity is notoriously ambiguous: it may be distinguished from the classical, the medieval, the Renaissance, the early modern period, or the whole tradition up to the advent of an artistic modernism which defined itself in the twentieth century by the rejection of tradition. If we add to this confusion the difficulties introduced by the concept of the postmodern, we find that postmodern may mean anything from post-Nietzschean philosophy to post-1980s artistic movements. In this range of reference, some postmodern approaches to architecture may appear relatively conservative, reviving a few elements of the classical past, while other visual arts appear just as radically innovative as the earlier avant-garde. In this situation, postmodern functions like post-Impressionism: it identifies a chronological period, not a stylistic or conceptual unity. The same problem may be found in the root concept, "modern."

For the sake of clarity, I will employ the term "modern" to mean a period of time capable of including the present; the meaning of the word simply does not allow us to say we are living in postmodern times. The beginning point of modernity, however, must remain ambiguous: for Hegel, the worldview which informed his day began with the advent of Christianity, so that ultimately the modern had to be distinguished from the pagan civilization of classical antiquity. By the seventeenth century, however, the quarrel between the ancients and the moderns rested on the sense that the Renaissance had resulted in a new civilization, in spite of its beginnings as a revival of the culture of classical antiquity. Yet what made Hegel's day—and ours—decisively different were events even more recent: the Reformation, the Enlightenment, and the French Revolution. If we add subsequent historical developments to the list, doing so does not alter the fundamental point. Modernity has, in fact, multiple beginnings; if we wish to understand the present age, we cannot define the beginnings of it too precisely or uniquely, lest we lose the complexity inherent in our present historical position. For we are not the creatures simply of the present time, but rather creatures of all the inherited past. If Hegel's historicism has anything to teach us, it is that lesson of indebtedness to the past.

It is otherwise with the case of modernism in the arts; here the term has a definite meaning, referring to the avant-garde movements of the twentieth century. Although there are multiple styles that can be distinguished, such as Expressionism, Surrealism, Cubism, and Abstract Expressionism in the visual arts, the International Style in architecture, and Expressionism and Serialism in music, they are all defined by their self-proclaimed rejection of the styles and approaches of the past. Thus modernism in the arts has a definite historical beginning in the decade before World War I. It also may have a definite historical end; most critics see modernism as having come to an end beginning in the 1980s. This raises the question, however, of what has replaced modernism, and what the relation of the replacement is to what has gone before. The term "postmodernist" is generally used to refer to those styles which have arisen in the last two decades. Thus, it may appear that postmodernism suggests a new chronological period, after modernism, which on analogy with the modern might be called the postmodern age. Yet this would be to conflate the self-conscious historicism of the arts with the larger issues of our self-awareness of history.

Accordingly, I reserve the term "postmodern" for those self-proclaimed movements which call themselves by that name. This means restricting the term to movements in philosophy and the arts, not as a chronological designation, but as a label of particular movements. Although these see themselves as occupying a chronological position in history, it is difficult to endorse their view of themselves. Moreover, it raises a host of unruly questions concerning the end of history or the end of art, which are ultimately solipsistic and unfruitful. Much has been written about Hegel's sense of living at the moment of the completion of history, or at least the end of the Christian era. But neither Hegel nor anyone else has been able to say what would transpire in the future; Hegel was aware that he could not be a prophet, even if in retrospect much of what he describes appears prophetic. Thus a conception of postmodernism, which sees itself as essentially and chronologically postmodern, has the impossible consequence of seeing itself as presently occupying the time after the period which includes the present. Instead, it is a position best understood as dependent on the prior conception of modernism. However, both modernism and postmodernism have succeeded through radical presentism in raising the question of the significance of the arts in the modern world. It is this position that I challenge through a reconsideration of Hegel's aesthetic.

In order to carry out this project, it is necessary to turn to sources other than Hegel, for philosophical reflections on art do not exist isolated from the objects of their reflection or of their history. Indeed, a crucial component of the practice of the arts has been the history of theoretical reflection on art by artists themselves. From Vitruvius through the most tendentious modernist, the articulation of an aesthetic by a practitioner has been the most important means of advancing the artist's cause. Thus any discussion of the relevance of Hegel's aesthetics of the arts must take into account both the tradition of artistic practice and more specifically the tradition of theoretical reflection by artists themselves. Thoughout this book, therefore, Hegel's discussion of the arts is placed in the context of the artistic traditions he sought to explain—either as a confirmation of Hegel's understanding, or as a corrective.

Equally, however, Hegel's aesthetic cannot be assessed adequately apart from the tradition of philosophical reflection on the historically important topics of aesthetics: chief among these are beauty, truth, and goodness. These categories have been so dismissed from aesthetic reflection in the twentieth century that they now appear quaintly naïve and largely irrelevant to the modern practice of the arts. But emphasizing their traditional importance to aesthetics will contribute to a better understanding of Hegel, for the ways in which he uses terms such as beauty, the Ideal, and the ethical life are critical to making sense of his system of the fine arts. To see these terms as peculiar to Hegel's usage is to miss the meanings they import from more traditional contexts, thereby missing much of the potential richness of Hegel's aesthetic.

If it can be shown that Hegel's aesthetics is coherent within the categories he both develops elsewhere in his philosophy and assumes from the tradition of theoretical reflection on artistic practice, then the case will be much stronger for considering his aesthetics as relevant to the dilemmas art faces in our world. The modernity of which we are so acutely conscious appears to demand an art and an aesthetic uniquely suited to it. Yet efforts to produce such an art and a suitable aesthetic have failed signally to satisfy the deepest yearnings of the human spirit. If Hegel's conception of the arts and their role in society prove persuasive, then the ground will be prepared for a revival of an artistic practice that matters and will merit our attention in a renewed civic life. What is required is to rise above the contentious dialectic of traditionalism and modernism to reacquire the opening of temporality to the beauty of transcendence and the ethical life.

Part I

Art between Transcendence and Historicism

Chapter 1

Is Art Necessary?

The challenge that modernist art posed at the beginning of the twentieth century lay in its uncompromising rejection of what had been central to the artistic traditions of our civilization. Sensuous charm, the representation of intelligible content, and the nobility of thought and feeling were now banished from sight and hearing, with the effect of forcing a reconception of art. To accept the modernist enterprise meant that coherence, recognizability, and beauty could no longer be insisted upon without appearing to reject all that defined artistic creativity in the modern world. But the result is that, a century later, this challenge has produced not just skepticism about the ideal of beauty that art was traditionally to embody, but skepticism about the nature and function of art itself. Although artistic modernism is founded on the faith that art is one of the highest of human callings, its success is bound to call into question whether art is indeed necessary when it becomes incomprehensible, sensually unappealing, and deliberately provocative. The conviction of art's necessity cannot be divorced from the nature of its form and content.

Postmodern art shares with modernist art this effect of calling its own significance into question; although making use of elements of various historical styles of art, including modernism, it does so without a sense of historical narrative. The diversity of approaches to painting that are considered compatible with postmodernism, from neorealism to neoexpressionism, raises questions about the significance of these approaches themselves.[1] Even the return to unabashed representation in neorealism fails to portray a significant content, and certainly not a narrative content such as was traditionally considered essential to painting. Postmodernist architecture, like postmodernist painting, also embraces a wide variety of styles and approaches. But in the most characteristic cases, the return to some elements of traditional form, such as pediments and gables, occurs without a corresponding return to classical ornament in the forms of identifiable orders and entablatures. The effect is more of an ironic commentary on formal possibilities than a coherent approach to architectural design: again, the question of the artistic significance of such a style cannot be avoided. Finally, the advent of a less dissonant music rooted in a rudimentary tonality is often hailed as a return to some semblance of tradition by those weary of the atonality of modernist composers. But again, there is a gulf separating the postmodernist minimalism from the premodernist tonal tradition, for there is no melody, only a monotonous rhythmic repetition or static chords as the focus of attention. Such music, too, raises the question of the significance of the art in the absence of beauty.

This sense of the loss of significance through the exhaustion of possibilities in the arts is what underlies the growing perception that art has reached its end. The museum of art may now include anything because there is no criterion defining art.[2] Yet today a deep skepticism reigns regarding the highest values of truth, beauty, and goodness that once defined art: this is the essence of philosophical postmodernism. Although it seems to have little explicitly in common with artistic postmodernism, it has clear consequences for how art is regarded, and in particular for whether art is held to have any compelling purpose or significance. This new skepticism is rooted in the philosophy of Nietzsche and Heidegger; it begins from the point of view that there is no rational truth, no absolute good or moral virtue, no transcendent source of authority.[3] There is therefore no beauty, no compelling argument for art such as the traditional doctrine of beauty once supplied, and no tradition that can still be asserted. Indeed, it sees the death of art as the characteristic of the postmodern era.[4] The new skepticism strips ideals (both moral and aesthetic) of their presumptive rightness, and decries—in a line of thought inherited from Marxism—the attempt to maintain a culture that displays such ideals publicly as an imposition of the values of one class on another, or of one social group on all others. But this postmodern skepticism regarding the arts is an outgrowth of the earlier modernist aesthetic, in which traditional categories of beauty and moral purpose for the arts were decisively rejected.

In this condition, it is well that we take a step back to the era when the arts were held in unquestioning esteem: for the nineteenth century's faith in the power of art in the lives of both individuals and civilizations stands in stark contrast to the ambivalence with which the twentieth century has come to regard them. In this respect, the *Aesthetics: Lectures on Fine Art* by G.W. F. Hegel constitutes the most systematic and influential source for understanding the nineteenth century's attitudes toward art. Delivered in 1823, 1826, and 1828–29, and published after his death in 1835 in the collected works edited by H. G. Hotho,[5] Hegel's lectures were an attempt to integrate what would today be identified as largely separate concerns about beauty and the nature of art with the history of the individual arts. For Hegel, however, the philosophy of a contingent enterprise such as art was necessarily concerned with understanding the nature of its contingency, that is, with its history. But for the question, whether art is necessary in any sense, Hegel's historicism may be put to one side temporarily in order to discover the answer he gives. Doing so permits us to place the postmodern insignificance of art in a clearer light.

Hegel on the Necessity of Art

The traditional explanation of the significance of the arts was in terms of beauty, by which was understood a transcendent good pointing to the eternal nature of the Platonic Good itself. But this no longer convinces; the modern world has no use for Platonic Ideas or for beauty as a transcendent quality. For the modern world, art appears designed purely for aesthetic contemplation, and in its divorce from all utilitarian motives, it thereby loses the sense of significance that comes from being enmeshed in a network of needs and satisfactions. In contrast to both the traditional Platonic account of art as the imitation of beauty and the modern world's commitment to artistic autonomy, Hegel's aesthetic enmeshes art in a network of human needs and satisfactions and yet argues against all merely utilitarian justifications of art. Thus it avoids Platonic transcendentalism as well as utilitarianism: for these reasons, it should appeal to modern sensibilities. On the other hand, precisely because it employs the traditional language of beauty, and accords to the historicity of art the value of each age—and particularly of the classical era—it has been as suspect as other, more Platonic aesthetics have been in the twentieth century. That it has not received the attention it deserves is largely due to its having so little in common with modern preoccupations.

Like many of his contemporaries, Hegel's high estimation of the value of art rests on the conviction that art is an expression of the human spirit. The need to produce art, however, is not just a matter of spiritual self-expression or a desire to be creative. Rather, it arises from the rational nature of the human spirit. Human nature is a "thinking consciousness," so that necessarily "man draws out of himself and puts before himself what he is and whatever else is." This general remark may indeed explain both philosophical and artistic activity, but the unique impulse to create art resides in the particular need for the sensuous recognition of what we are and what the world is: "The universal need for art . . . is man's rational need to lift the inner and outer world into his spiritual consciousness as an object in which he recognizes again his own self" (*VÄ* 1, 50–52; *A* 1, 31). In other words, the need for art originates in the need to surround ourselves with reminders of who we are and what kind of world we truly live in; the emphasis on re-cognition rather than on original cognition is crucial to avoiding utilitarian didacticism, which Hegel repudiates. But neither is art a purely intellectual means of perception: the need for art arises precisely because we have a sensuous nature, and art is directed to that side as well as to our intellectual or spiritual side by its union of the sensuous and the spiritual. We seek sensuous reminders of the human condition rather than exclusively theoretical knowledge.

Hegel goes further, however: art is necessary because of a need to impress on external things "the seal of his inner being," so that we make these things our own. We do this "in order, as a free subject, to strip the external world of its inflexible foreignness and to enjoy in the shape of things only an external realization of himself" (*VÄ* 1, 51; *A* 1, 31). That is, we need to create art fundamentally as a means of making the world our own; by art we come to feel at home in the world. Hegel is emphatic: "man in his worldly environment must be domesticated and at home," in both nature and social relations, so that the individual's character and "the objective totality of external existence . . . harmonize and belong together" (*VÄ* 1, 327; *A* 1, 252–53). The importance of this feeling at home cannot be emphasized enough at this point, for the peculiar situation of the last century has been for man not to feel at home in the world. Martin Heidegger, in particular, describes the human condition as "throwness" into nowhere. It is only when we are removed from "entanglement" in the world of ordinary affairs that we have revealed to us the true condition of "not being at home" in the world.[6] Hegel's aesthetic, therefore, stands in stark contrast to the assumptions of recent modernity: in his view, we require feeling at home in the world, and art is the principal means by which we bring into effect what we so sorely need. But what we need is precisely, according to Hegel, knowledge of the true condition of humanity. Hence Hegel defines the high purpose of art's vocation: "to unveil the truth in the form of sensuous artistic configuration . . . " (*VÄ* 1, 82; *A* 1, 55). Art, in this view, is called to the highest possible purpose in representing the truth of who we are and the kind of world in which we live.

The Aesthetic of Modernism

From this brief consideration of Hegel's clear vindication of the necessity of art, it is possible to see why his aesthetic has largely fallen into disfavor and neglect. He understands humanity to have a given nature, out of which emerges certain definite needs. The need for sensuous recognition of our nature is what gives birth to art in the first place; to this is added the need for the sensuous recognition of our world. But the modern perception is instead that we have no nature: human existence emerges out of Nothingness, and the world in which we live is one in which we cannot possibly feel at home. If this indeed be the human condition, the case for art would have to be entirely different. For if humanity have no nature, art itself would have no given nature; we would neither expect to recognize in it our nature, nor the nature of the world into which we have accidentally come. In such a situation, the contemplation of art as a product of human activity divorced from any conception of human nature would have to answer to whatever purpose art might have. Indeed, the contemplation of art would have to be divorced from any conception of an overarching purpose rooted in human needs. Art would necessarily be as autonomous as human existence itself.

Without pretending to offer a complete survey of all aesthetic theories current in the philosophical literature, it is useful to seek out the principal, most characteristic theories of the modernist period.[7] The modern conceptions of art can be reduced to four essential positions, taken as representative types for the purpose of this analysis. These reveal both the aesthetic positions fundamental to the modern period and the degree to which they form the foundation for a common modernist enterprise:

1. Art has a peculiarly aesthetic value to the spectator, listener, or reader that arises principally from the formal properties of the work.
2. Art attains its significance as the product of a creative act that is the artist's expression of his inner self.
3. What is of principal interest in art, to either the creator or the spectator, is the materiality of the medium.
4. Art has legitimacy only as the expression of the alienation of art, and the artist, from society as a whole.

Although these positions are essentially contradictory, all four establish art as autonomous from moral, religious, or social ends.[8] All of them, therefore, contribute to the paradoxical character of modernity's simultaneous celebration of art and ambivalence towards the arts as actually practiced. The result is that art becomes an end in itself, the object of an aesthetic contemplation whose value must be taken for granted.

The modern concept of aesthetic contemplation is rooted in precisely this autonomy: it severs art from the fulfillment of human needs. Textbooks tell students to notice the significant elements of form and the handling of the medium employed, but the justification of artistic creation is almost always cast in terms of the artist's self-expression, and the therapeutic exercise of the usually unidentifiable emotions that stir his or her soul. What matters is originality: we are asked to perceive the wholly new, and to see the value of what has never been done before. What is not admitted in aesthetic contemplation is the apprehension of objects or truths represented in art, even in traditional styles. This is the essence of the modernist enterprise; it has succeeded thoroughly after a century of artistic militancy. As a result, however, the value of the contemplation of such originality becomes mysterious.

These four distinct views share, moreover, a common hostility to the traditional conception of art as a good that is perceived as a good because its sensual beauty is understood as a reflection of a higher intellectual purpose. More precisely, they reveal a refusal to consider art as having an ethical purpose that ennobles the viewer or listener in cultivating and participating in painting, music, drama, or literature. It is because ethical justification has shrunk that the exaltation of art as an end in itself has grown commensurately with the paradoxical consequence of its trivialization. That the concept of aesthetic value has become the most common substitute for the older language of beauty appears to suggest an equivalency that allows for a broader range of aesthetic responses than beauty suggests. Thus the aesthetic of contemplation of artifacts autonomous from any other purpose depends on having a category of appraisal such as "aesthetic value." Nevertheless, an examination of these four modern conceptions of art must raise questions concerning the adequacy of the concept of aesthetic value and, more broadly, the success of the larger modern project of an autonomous art meant purely for disinterested contemplation. Hegel's clear vindication of the necessity of art stands in the sharpest possible contrast to these four positions.

Form as the Source of Aesthetic Value

The prevalence of the concept of aesthetic value as the term for the significance of autonomous art should be problematic. For the assumption that there is such a value makes it imperative to identify its nature. In practice, aesthetic, or artistic value is a unique type of pleasure taken in the disinterested contemplation of works of art that are displayed solely for the purpose of such contemplation.[9] The nature of such a pleasure, however, is a problem: the solution that satisfies the criterion of artistic autonomy requires an escape or separation "from the real world of our practical affairs."[10] What then gives pleasure? The engagement of all our mental capacities is posited as an activity that produces a pleasure intrinsic to the contemplation of art. It requires art to be totally absorbing, an alternative to life rather than a part of life.

The concept of aesthetic value is most often held to originate in the formal properties of an artwork. Thus Monroe Beardsley, for example, finds the three canons of aesthetic value to be completeness, coherence, and intensity: the criteria of completeness and coherence are clearly formal properties of the work, while intensity recognizes a subjective component of the spectator's or reader's experience of the artwork.[11] Like most other twentieth-century analytic philosophers, Beardsley dismisses the traditional concept of beauty as an account of the value of art on the grounds that to imply that something is judged to be good, just because it is beautiful, seems neither self-evident nor capable of convincing demonstration.[12] Beardsley also rejects any intrinsic moral effects of art, so that there is no necessary moral value attendant on an artwork taken to be beautiful.[13] All that is left is the set of general canons of aesthetic value, which are not demonstrated in any deductive way, but are taken to arise from the general practice of art criticism. In this way, the value of the experience of art is reduced to a stimulation of the spectator's perception of formal properties with a certain intensity.

But if formal qualities have often been taken as the object of aesthetic "appreciation," it is perhaps less clear what this means in practice for each art. Hence, recent defenders of the concept of aesthetic value seek its origin in multiple kinds of artistic properties. Goldman finds that expression and representation are as important as form, and Malcolm Budd finds that each art has its own species of artistic value.[14] Budd, in particular, seeks such artistic values as intrinsic values in any work of art. The more the concept of aesthetic or artistic value is pluralized, however, the more it risks becoming incoherent. It becomes difficult to say what exactly such artistic values are beyond generalities such as meaning and worth. In the case of music, for example, there is no identifiable meaning or emotional content.[15] Thus, what constitutes aesthetic value, and what gives rise to it, remains problematic in the modern concept of art. In particular, attempts to locate the vale of "serious art" in its formal qualities ultimately fail to convince.[16]

The origins of the problems in the concept of aesthetic value lie in the legacy of Kantian philosophy. The principle of autonomy can be traced back to the late eighteenth century, when it attained its codification in Immanuel Kant's *Critique of Judgment*. Kant argues that judgment of taste is not pure if it is subject to a definite concept, so that ideas of morality and the mimetic fidelity to reality are equally threatening to the purity of aesthetic judgment of what he calls "free beauty."

> There is presupposed no concept of any purpose which the manifold of the given object is to serve, and which therefore is to be represented in it. By such a concept the freedom of the imagination which disports itself in the contemplation of the figure would be only limited.[17]

Even though Kant speaks in the traditional language of beauty, what matters is the ability of the viewer to allow his imagination to "disport" itself freely. Natural beauty is "free," and so is "foliage for borders or wallpapers," and anything else that does not represent something "under a definite concept." The beauty of a human being, a horse, or a building, however, is "adherent beauty," because it presupposes "a concept of the purpose which determines what the thing is to be, and consequently a concept of its perfection"; thus the judgment of this kind of beauty is less than pure, and in that measure inferior (*CJ* §16, 66). Mimetic art is therefore less valuable than the arts of abstract design or of themeless music, or than nature itself.

What is called in modern terminology "aesthetic value," therefore, is for Kant a pleasure arising from the free play of the faculties of understanding and the imagination (*CJ* §35, 129). This free play is aroused by purely formal qualities having no inherent purposiveness; hence the formalism of the modern conception of art arose in the first place as a necessary consequence of the autonomy of the judgment of beauty. Kant concedes that adherent beauty has a place in the fine arts, but art is in general purposive and thus inferior (*CJ* §44, 148). The greater danger in the arts, however, was sensory charm, and against this corrupting influence Kant recommends a "more or less close combination with moral ideas," as giving the kind of self-sufficient pleasure that pure form would otherwise provide (*CJ* §52, 170). But, although moral concepts have a natural association with mimetic art, they too are a source of corruption to the purity of aesthetic judgment. Thus the autonomy of aesthetic judgment in fact devalued art itself according to the Kantian view. This remains the heart of the problem with the formalist theory of aesthetic value in art and the source of the modern paradox of the exaltation of art founded on an aesthetic of insignificance.

Expression as the Value of Art

Twentieth-century aesthetic theory has not, however, restricted the concept of aesthetic value to simply the formal properties of an artwork; there has also been a powerful current of thought focusing on both the subjective experience of the spectator and the subjective motivation of the artist. These two foci combine in the theory of expression as the source of aesthetic experience, exemplified cogently in the philosophy of John Dewey. Dewey's aesthetic is founded on the psychological experience of the subject who beholds art. Aesthetic perception involves enjoyment; it is an active rather than a passive role because it involves the surrender of the self to the process of perception.[18] But this is not unlike the experience of the artist in creating art; for the artist must in fact begin with an aesthetic perception of what he wishes to create. The psychology of perception, then, is used to vindicate the autonomy of art:

> An object is peculiarly and dominantly esthetic, yielding the enjoyment characteristic of esthetic perception, when the factors that determine anything which can be called an experience are lifted high above the threshold of perception and are made manifest for their own sake.[19]

As in Kant's aesthetic, there is a peculiar pleasure attached to the category of the aesthetic—which here replaces the older term of beauty—and which is taken to be autonomous from any other concern. Yet a pleasure so autonomous would be justified as significant only on hedonist grounds unless there were something deeper in art itself. It is to avoid the peril of insignificance that Dewey joins to the doctrine of Kantian autonomy that of expressivism.

For Dewey, art is fundamentally emotional expression—but expression understood not as mere emotional "discharge," but rather as an ordering through the lens of prior experience, the resistance of the environment, and the artistic medium itself.[20] Thus Dewey's doctrine of expressionism is not crude:

> ...the expression of the self in and through a medium, constituting the work of art, is itself a prolonged interaction of something issuing from the self with objective conditions, a process in which both of them acquire a form and order they did not at first possess.[21]

Form and order are here made central to the work of art and indeed to the working of the artist. But the self that is expressed is the "emotivist self" of Alasdair MacIntyre's description; ultimately, then, the self that is perceived in the work of art is just this emotivist self.[22] Thus Van Gogh depicted a particular object, for instance, a bridge over the Rhône, as "a new object experienced as having its own unique meaning." That meaning was created by the fusion of the artist's own emotion of "utterly heart-broken" desolation with the object; thus the depiction of the bridge became an "expression" of the artist.[23] The aesthetic value of the work of art, therefore, becomes precisely the perception and enjoyment of such expression of the artist, in which the artist's self and his object are thoroughly fused. This has become a firmly rooted dogma in the teaching of art appreciation.

Dewey also, however, conceived art as the making of something entirely new, endorsing the modernist project of creation as rejection of tradition while at the same time defending the thesis of art's autonomy. Dewey writes: "Impulsion beyond all limits that are externally set inheres in the very nature of the artist's work." He specifically denies moral limits for art, and asserts that "one of the functions of art is precisely to sap the moralistic timidity that causes the mind to shy away from some materials. . . ."[24] This position relies on Clive Bell and Roger Fry, the two art critics of Bloomsbury who did much to advance the cause of modernist art through their attention to its formal qualities rather than its objective content. Thus the modern conception of artistic autonomy is fundamental to both formalism and expressivism in modernist aesthetics.

The modern conception, however, is not rendered more coherent for having combined the elements of formalism and expressivism. For if the weakness of Kantian formalism lies in the potential insignificance of an autonomous art, that potential is not alleviated by the insertion of the artist's expression of himself into the account. Rather, significance is attached to an activity precisely in the degree to which it addresses the deepest needs of life, whether cognitive, moral, religious, or social. In that sense, art is a derivative activity, and the doctrine of autonomy will always risk trivializing art. Hence it is no surprise that even aesthetic theories which remain formalist in defining art attempt to find some redeeming effects that make aesthetic experience important.[25] But why the artist's emotion would appear to be significant enough to merit anyone's attention, much less enjoyment, is not explained in Dewey's account, nor is the necessity of pleasure taken in artistic form. The insistence on the radical originality of art, indeed, only makes such pleasure surely more difficult. Thus neither formalism nor expressivism secures to art the significance which the doctrine of autonomy fails to justify.

The Aesthetic of Materiality

Formalism and expressivism, however, do not exhaust the varieties of modern aesthetic theory which seek to account for the value of art a subjective value to the spectator. Nor do they exhaust the possible points of view artists often hold; in particular, artists frequently cite the material of their medium as the primary focus of their attention. Even in explaining their work to others, they assume that the real interest in their work must lie in the way they handled the material medium. This is so striking that it must be curious, but in fact there is ample philosophical precedent for it in the work of Martin Heidegger. Situated within his existentialist analysis of the condition of modern life to which we have already referred, Martin Heidegger's study, "On the Origin of the Work of Art," is perhaps the most sophisticated attempt at an aesthetic of modernity. Heidegger provides the greatest continuity with previous aesthetics, while searching for an answer to the question of what is art that will be well adapted to the modern social condition. He maintains the concept of the work of art and, like Hegel, he retains a link between art and truth: "Art is truth setting itself to work."[26] Such a conception of art is essentially poetic: "Art, as the setting-into-work of truth, is poetry"; poetry thus becomes the model for all the arts (*PLT* 72). But in saying this, Heidegger inverts the traditional responsibility of poetry to a preexistent truth; instead, poetry becomes the making of truth. Indeed, in *Being and Time*, he had already rejected the concept of objectivity and truth.[27] Finally, like Hegel, he argues that whatever beauty art has is precisely the appearance of truth in the work of art: beauty is something conceptual, not a merely surface quality or an external formal property (*PLT* 79). But in spite of such superficial continuities with Hegel, who Heidegger admits has the most comprehensive treatment of the question of art, Heidegger's aesthetic in other ways is strikingly modern. It is these ways of thinking about the nature of art which are of most importance to us.

Heidegger takes a particular work of art—Van Gogh's still life representation of shoes—as his example to show what truth art can reveal. The portrait of the shoes reveals the essential nature of the shoes as they lie in repose: we perceive that they are "equipment," possessing the quality of "blank usefulness" (*PLT* 34). Shoes themselves do not reveal their nature so transparently, because in a real pair of shoes, we see their "thingness." But art portrays not the thingly nature of the thing, but their character in their use as equipment, which is intermediate between "thing" and "work" (*PLT* 31). This does not mean, however, that art must be representational, the adequacy of which might be decided by the recognizability of its imitation. Rather art is simply "the reproduction of the thing's general essence" (*PLT* 36). For Van Gogh, certainly, that did not require careful attention to the details of any of his subject matter; in fact, Van Gogh agrees with Heidegger on the purpose of art as the representation of general essences.[28] As a consequence, it makes sense to say that for Heidegger not only does art reveal truth; but rather, it is only in art that we see truth revealed. For the fact that shoes in real life do not reveal their true nature as equipment, but instead contaminate our perception with the material of which they are made, means that we must turn to art to discover the truth even about shoes.

It is of course not the case that we turn to art in order to learn something as trivial as the nature of shoes. But, Heidegger argues, this simple example reveals the nature of art and the nature of the truth found in art. The work of art isolates the nature of the thing it presents for perception: thus the artwork is purely autonomous from any context or any larger purpose. Indeed, Heidegger notes that "[t]o gain access to the work, it would be necessary to remove it from all relations to something other than itself, in order to let it stand on its own for itself alone." This, however, is precisely what every great artist intends for his work. "The work is released by him to its pure self-subsistence" (*PLT* 39). Again, Heidegger gives an example. Architecture, the most nonrepresentational of the arts, produces works which reveal a truth, not in the context of other works, but in creating a world as a context for human life. Thinking perhaps of both Greek and Catholic statuary inside sacred precincts, he notes that the temple provides the place where the statues are set up, so that the god himself will be present in this place. Thus the work of art is set up "in the sense of dedication and praise" (*PLT* 42). But the praise is specifically not of the divine, but rather of the world created by the artwork itself. The function of art, then, is to reveal the truth in the deep sense of unveiling a world. "Towering up within itself, the work opens up a world and keeps it bidingly in force" (*PLT* 43).

The concept of the world opened up by art, however, is counterbalanced by what Heidegger calls "the earth"; the work of art also lets the matter of the earth be itself, as in the quality of the stone used in architecture, or the splendor of the gold used to adorn the moldings in a church. The artwork, therefore, lets the material of nature shine forth in itself, not as something to be used as equipment. But there is a tension, then, between the attention to the earth and the attention to the world in the work of art. Hence, "[t]he work-being of the work consists in the fighting of the battle between world and earth" (*PLT* 48). Art "sets forth" the earth and "sets up" the world, and in doing both of these, "lets truth originate" (*PLT* 75). Thus art is a mode of knowing, not merely a craft or a skill in making, and the work of art emerges as utterly unique in the way it establishes truth (*PLT* 60–61). We need art to know both the earth and the world in their essential natures, that is, the material and the world created by the work itself.

Heidegger's aesthetic, therefore, insists neither on representation nor on beauty, and therefore it seems well suited to the artistic conditions of the twentieth century. It has a high view of the purpose and autonomy of art. But the truth that Heidegger finds in art is a presentation of the genuine character of the materials used in the work of art—again, a perception more suited to the twentieth century's preoccupation with the medium employed in the artwork—as well as a creation of a world in itself. Because such a world is essentially unique to each work of art, the truth thus created is a truth unique to each work. It is nonobjective, because "the world" in general is not an object in any case: the paths of our lives are perceived through their subjective effects on our being (*PLT* 43). The work of art, therefore, in "setting up" a world, is an opening into the subjectivity of human existence. There is no need here, then, for art to concern itself with a moral or ethical content as the reason for its existence; in this, it conforms to the canons of contemporary artistic practice. Heidegger validates the sense of autonomy and subjectivity of art in the modernist era, in the course of constructing an aesthetic of materiality. For just that reason, however, Heidegger's aesthetic deprives art of any objective significance arising outside of its own narrowly constructed world.

The Aesthetic of Alienation

If Heidegger's aesthetic proves able to justify the significance of an essentially subjectivist art in the modern world, the Marxist aesthetics of Adorno and his postmodernist successors articulate much more clearly the alienated character of art and the artist as underlying the phenomenon of modernism. According to this view, the self-representation enclosed in modernist art is of the self as alienated from the possibility of the ideal: the artist, in this view, becomes emblematic of the universal condition of humanity. Thus, although the social realization of truth and of an ideal of moral goodness is denied, postmodernism depends for its interpretive stance on the very categories it denies. In this way it embodies the alienation it sees as characteristic of modernity.

Theodor W. Adorno, one of the most representative philosophical apologists for the avant-garde, links this alienation explicitly with the condition of modern bourgeois society, in which art's autonomy withdraws art from a society that is "ever less a human one." Thus does art become "the social antithesis of society," having for its aim not the contrast of an ideal held up against the commercial spirit of the capitalist world, but the persistent critique of the inhumanity of that world.[29] Hence art is left with the task of directing aggression against established norms, of shattering the ideology of decoration which, in reflecting "the world in a positive light," in calling "for a better world, became a lie which legitimated evil."[30] The aesthetic ideology of the beautiful must be dismantled by art itself.

The alienation expressed in art may also be described in terms of an inevitable feature of advanced industrial society, a sociological fact of the diremption of the individual and society. The avant-garde, then, "claims to be the model for a privileged mode of knowledge of the real, a moment of subversion of the hierarchized structure of the individual and society, and thus an instrument of true social and political action."[31] It rejects (and therefore the defender of the avant-garde must also reject) the traditional aim of art in aspiring to embody the ideals of truth, goodness, and beauty. The work of art will become ambiguous, defining "its success fundamentally in terms of rendering problematic such a set of values, and in overcoming—at least momentarily—the limits of the latter."[32] The alienation of the individual, therefore, is fundamentally an alienation from the values of society: the postmodernist apologist for the avant-garde must call into question all determinate notions of goodness and truth in defense of the individual.

This position has several consequences, which have been realized in more recent postmodern critics. One is a calling into question of artistic institutions, such as museums and theaters and concert halls, which collect and display the artistic canon of great works, either literally in the case of museums or figuratively in the case of theaters and concert halls. The museum, on this view, ceases to be an institution where the great works representing the best artistic achievements are kept on display to allow the public to view them. Rather, the museum becomes a metaphor of capitalist possession, an instrument of the ideological domination that "allowed its visitors symbolically to possess objects that were inaccessible . . . and as such invested with high cultural prestige."[33] The "imaginary museum" of music is even more suspect, as the avant-garde of totally serialized and aleatoric music have both brought a disappearance of the traditional concept of a work that is self-contained and developmental. Hence, critics of the concept of the work look to the dismantling of the ritual of the concert, with its traditional focus on European classical music, as a necessary step to opening up musical institutions to other kinds of music—especially the avant-garde, which has rarely been successful in the concert hall.[34] To destroy the institutions preserving the inherited artistic traditions becomes the means of destroying the ideals and values exhibited and represented therein. It is the concommitant of the avant-garde's wish to destroy the normativity of the artistic styles and forms inherited from the past.

The second consequence, however, is to call into question the very notion of what constitutes a public for art. The perspective of many postmodernist critics is to see artists and audiences as representatives of specific sociological groups, denying the category of a larger "public" altogether. In this view, marginalized peoples of different races and societies, or a marginalized gender or orientation, become the objects of solicitude, as the artistic culture of the majority becomes illegitimate simply through being portrayed as an imperialistic abuse of power.[35] But the error here lies in reducing an art to its originator, the values expressed in it to its class of creators, and the audience to a collection of fragmented social groups. What is lost entirely is the concept of the public as a universal body: the fallacy of the sociological dissection of society thus intrudes into the dimension of artistic taste and activity.

A third consequence therefore emerges: the reduction of art to perpetual insignificance. For even more radically than the positions already examined, deconstructionists such as Jacques Derrida seek to dismantle the claim of rationality as it applies to the arts. Viewed in this light, art becomes something entirely separate from the already suspect realm of rational argument and truth claims; it becomes a perpetual challenge to reason precisely because of its autonomy and sovereignty. Art can never be integrated into life; it can only be a catalyst of problems, productive of a crisis for reason, never a solution of problems or a reconciliation of opposing sides in a conflict.[36] But this is precisely to render art a suspect category altogether. Without discrete works embodying ideals of truth, beauty, and moral goodness, institutions that preserve those works in identifiable narrative traditions, or a coherent public sharing the ideals embodied in art, it is difficult indeed to argue for the relevance of art to life. The arts pale into insignificance as they are severed from the domain of reason.

The postmodernist critique suggests, therefore, that the position of the arts in the modern world is peculiarly problematic: there appears to be no consensus that ideals should be represented in individualized works, that those works should have a public role, or that a canon of works should be publicly preserved as the historical embodiment of any ideal. The double alienation of the individual from the possibility of the ideal and from the larger society leaves art as only the expression of that condition of alienation. It is, of course, not only the artist who is thus estranged, but ostensibly every individual. Such a condition is at once pathological and paradoxical: pathological in its universality, and paradoxical if society can be composed of none but individuals who find themselves never at home in it. In such a condition, as Jacques Barzun argues, the tradition of an art that sought knowledge and representation of truth appears to be at an end; the devaluation of the world must inevitably diminish the need for art as traditionally understood.[37] But this will mean the end of art as we know it from the historical tradition.

Having examined four principal philosophical positions from the modernist and postmodernist schools of the twentieth century, it is clear that what unites them in a common enterprise is hostility to any kind of moral, ethical, or spiritual ideal as the content of art. Thus, although the importance of art generally, and new art in particular, is assumed, it appears to have little justification outside of the subjective experience it affords the spectator, or the expression of the artist's alienation which is asserted to be the properly universal experience of modern humanity. The Kantian thesis of art's absolute autonomy, therefore, dissolves three elements that were once considered together as vital to all art:

1. the ethical content as the intelligible substance of art;
2. the responsibility to intelligible norms of form as the transparency of artistic content;
3. and the concept of a beauty that is at once of this world and yet transcendent in origin.

The dissolution of these three elements, taken individually, accounts for the rise of formalism, expressivism, and materialism as aesthetic stances. But taken together, they define the modernist enterprise generally and guarantee the alienation of the artist from the larger society, as well as the trivialization of art. Indeed, if critics as divergent in their assumptions as Arthur Danto and Jacques Barzun share a deep pessimism regarding the present and future significance of art, it should be a sign that the premises of the modernist enterprise must be reconsidered. Given the inadequacies in modernist aesthetics, as well as the sense that the course of art history has come to an end, it is essential to return to the earlier aesthetic tradition for a better understanding of art. Hegel's aesthetic, with its vindication of the need for art arising from the purpose of unveiling the truth, as well as its understanding of art's historicity, appears as the best prospective alternative to the modernist aesthetic of absolute autonomy. However, Hegel also recognizes the unique condition of modernity, so that his argument for the need for art turns out to be more attuned to the sense of alienation characteristic of the twentieth century than we might expect.

Hegel on the Need for Art in the Modern World

The alienation characteristic of the modern world was diagnosed already by Hegel, who had no illusions about the actual relation of the individual to the larger society. A person's actions arise, he argues in the *Philosophy of Right*, as the fulfillment of social roles prescribed by custom, law, and institutions in which individuals maintain their freedom, but modern civil society is ruled by economic motives. The result is a loss of independence through the development of a thorough interdependence among the individuals comprising society. One's activities are mechanical and one's requirements are largely not fulfilled through one's own labor (*GPR* §198; *PR* 129). In language that may seem astonishingly prescient, Hegel describes modern society even more harshly in the *Aesthetics* as consisting in "mutual exploitation" with extremes of both poverty and wealth. But poverty and distress create a permanent condition of alienation as the inevitable consequence of a life economically determined, while the wealthy individual's withdrawal from this condition of "endless dependence" fails to cancel his alienation: "for this reason the individual is not at home even in his immediate environment, because it does not appear as his own work" (*VÄ* 1, 337; *A* 1, 260). Modern economic life, therefore, has the character of universal alienation from the products of individual labor.

Such a paradoxical pathology of modern life is ill suited to representation in art, but it goes far to explain the difficulties art faces in the modern world. Hegel claims that we need art, in order to make ourselves feel at home in the world, by representing to ourselves what we most truly are—as not alienated from either the ideal or society. Yet the fact of modern life is that the individual is not at home in the world. What is required, then, is an ideal represented in art that will be other than the actuality in which we necessarily find ourselves living:

> Therefore what is most fitted for ideal art proves to be a third situation which stands midway between the idyllic and golden ages and the perfectly developed universal mediations of civil society. This is a state of society which we have already learnt to recognize as the heroic or, preferably, the ideal Age. (*VÄ* 1, 337; *A* 1, 260)

It is the age described by Homer, in which the heroes kill their own food, make their own armor, and inherit their families' symbols of authority. The feeling portrayed, Hegel says, is one of joy in possession that can come only from the satisfaction in one's own labor, and the identification of the individual with his family.

It is not only in the products of individual labor, however, that the heroic age presents us with an ideal to which we can no longer aspire; it is also a matter of moral action in the larger ethical life of the community. The modern world is bureaucratized and interdependent, so that the individual appears as insignificant, having no action he can call his own. Individuals must be ruled by the state through law, whether by compulsion or by their free assent to the laws, and the punishment of a crime is necessarily assigned to the proper authorities, but all this removes a large field of action that was important to heroic times. What is required above all in art is the representation of individuality "in which the authority of the ethical order rests on individuals alone, who, by their private will and the outstanding greatness and effectiveness of their character, place themselves at the head of the real world in which they live" (*VÄ* 1, 242; *A* 1, 184). This condition is found in art from heroic times; for heroes "are individuals who undertake and accomplish the entirety of an action, actuated by the independence of their character and caprice" in carrying out "what is right and moral" (*VÄ* 1, 243–44; *A* 1, 185). The absence of a state provided the condition for the model of moral action that most fully represents the true potential of individuality in making law and enforcing it by private action.

In yet another way ancient society in the Heroic Age differed from modern conditions: in spite of the individuality Hegel emphasizes in contrast to the modern state, the individual in heroic society knew himself to belong undividedly to his family and clan. A hero's actions were never merely the defense of his own private interests, but always the assertion of the rights of his family. Thus it is not only the presence of a fully developed economic life in civil society, or a state that punishes crimes and thereby precludes revenge that distinguishes modern society, it is also the restriction of individual activity to the arena of the family and domestic affairs. In contrast to the ancient hero's defense of the family's rights:

> A father's care of his household, and his honesty, the ideals of decent men and good women, are the chief material here, where their willing and acting is restricted to spheres in which the human being, as an individual subject, still operates freely . . . in accordance with individual choice. (*VÄ* 1, 253; *A* 1, 193)

Yet actual action is quite often so restricted that what remains is mere disposition to choose, because what is required in action is dictated by circumstances. This was the prosaic state of affairs in Hegel's day; it is ill suited to representation in art because it is so far from the ideal of decisive moral action. But it is also another reason why art from earlier, more heroic times becomes all the more necessary, and why Hegel praises the dramatic works of Schiller and Goethe as an attempt to revive the heroic point of view (*VÄ* 1, 255–57; *A* 1, 195–96). To be sure, Hegel later states emphatically that no "Homer, Sophocles . . . or Shakespeare can appear in our day" (*VÄ* 2, 238; *A* 1, 608)—thus creating the impression that the creation of truly great art is impossible in the prosaic modern world. Hegel finds no reason to lament the rise of a modern, integrated, interdependent society, but only the preservation of art grounded in the ideal of individual independence can sustain it by providing the necessary recognition of the moral life.

This is to say, however, that the modern world needs an artistic representation of a way of life it is no longer permitted to enjoy. Hegel would agree with the postmodernists that the individual is alienated not only from society, but from such an ideal, in the sense that we are permanently estranged from the heroic ideal as an actual way of life. But he insists, against the postmodernists, that just because of that alienation, we require the artistic representation of the ideal: it is only through the preservation of the ideal of life in art, and specifically in heroic art, that we can feel at home in the world in spite of the actual social conditions in which we live. Thus Hegel begins from the same premises as the postmodernists, but arrives at precisely the opposite conclusion. Art ought not be antagonistic, seeking to destroy ideals simply because society does not live according to them, but rather portray the ideal in order to allow humanity to feel at home in the world.

The analysis Hegel provides in the passages cited above explains not simply the importance of the category of art, but also the imperative of the preservation of a canon of works embodying the heroic ideal. Those works which have most perfectly represented the ideal of morally active individuality in substantive unity with the family are those that will be preserved for posterity, and will be most necessary to modern society. These are, first and foremost, the poems of Homer. Moreover, art will be in the character of an adornment of social life: a decoration that will always be more splendid than the actual conditions of life. The impulse to ornament arises from the desire for "contemplative satisfaction," and even in the beautiful things from nature such as gold and jewels: these "have no interest for him in themselves," but acquire their significance from belonging to man, and "to what he loves and venerates," whether his kings or his gods. In the same way, too, art is an adornment, as are the institutions of the art world such as museums and theaters. Art, therefore, honors and venerates even more than the beautiful things of nature. It creates the splendor of a civilization, and "it can but redound to the fame and supreme honour of every people to devote its treasures to a sphere which within reality itself, rises luxuriously above all the distress of reality" (*VÄ* 1, 335; *A* 1, 258–59).

The splendor of the arts, then, is fundamentally a publicly displayed activity. "But however far the work of art may form a world inherently harmonious and complete, still, as an actual single object, it exists not for itself, but for us, for a public which sees and enjoys the work of art." Hegel adduces theatrical performances as his illustration, but musical performances could be added easily, as concerts are public affairs (*VÄ* 1, 341; *A* 1, 263–64). Had he elaborated further, he could have pointed to the creation of art museums, such as the one in Berlin in his day, as precisely the institution that was finally able to create a public for the visual arts.[38] Heretofore, paintings and drawings might be created for royal or aristocratic patrons, or for a bourgeois art market after the seventeenth century: but now such works of art were placed on specifically public display. Moreover, the institution of the salon (as in Paris) helped to make even new art the subject of public display, as new works were exhibited in first the bienniel and later annual competition. Finally, he might have pointed to the public character of the city itself, both in the architecture adorning the public buildings on squares such as the Alexanderplatz, and in the more mundane buildings in which people dwelt and lived their private lives: all these combined to create a public realm.[39] Hegel was correct, therefore, in claiming the principle of the public nature of the arts.

Yet Hegel's argument for the necessity of a public, canonical art is weak: what modern society needs most it cannot produce, and must in fact preserve from the earliest days of recorded history. The heroic poetry of Homer may indeed be timeless, but it must also be an anachronism. Hegel's argument, therefore, runs the serious risk of being a kind of false consciousness, preserving the heroic morality of another era for a modernity that not only does not produce such artistic representations, but cannot allow such a lawless moral impulse to exist. Hegel's aesthetic may indeed be accused of partaking of the same problem as is often perceived to afflict nineteenth-century art and aesthetics in general: admitting but decrying the essence of modernity, it seeks refuge in an irrelevant past. Yet to do so would be to miss the larger point he raises for understanding art in the modern world. When the conditions of social life assume a form that dehumanizes the individual person, this cannot be taken as the ultimate truth of the human condition. Rather, art becomes all the more important as the representation of what human nature is called to be. Without art, in other words, we would have no reminder immediately before us of the truth of what we are and what kind of world in which we ought to live.

It is imperative, therefore, to turn to a deeper consideration of the problems of aesthetics and Hegel's response to them in order to get beyond his well known and quite traditional esteem for the Greek classics. To understand Hegel on the need for art aright, we need to understand his concept of the ethical content of art and its relation to artistic form and the traditional concept of artistic beauty. For it was in the nexus of the good and the beautiful that the philosophical tradition understood the significance and need for art. Although Hegel rejected any kind of crude didacticism such as had been common in the eighteenth century, he did see a profound connection between beautiful art and the ethical order. The beauty of the Ideal is essential to his conception of art.

Chapter 2

Beauty and the Transcendence of the Ideal

The character of art in the modernist period, when considered in the context of the prior tradition, ought to raise serious questions regarding the nature of art itself. Does art in general need to be beautiful? Do the visual arts need to be representational? Do music and architecture, lacking a clear representational content, have other similar, expressive requirements? And if beauty be necessary to the aim of art, what would be the definition of beauty? Similarly, if significant subject matter is necessary to the purpose of art, of what should it consist? But if the answers to the questions about the necessity of beauty and the significance of content in art are negative, then what is the significance of art at all? The questions posed by the modernist enterprise are, therefore, of the utmost seriousness for the future of art itself.

The originators of the modernist avant-garde rejected the concept of beauty in its traditional conception as a quality of visual (or in music, aural) appeal as part of their denial of traditional content in the arts. That is, they developed a concept of abstraction which necessarily entailed a loss of one or more of the components of beauty: intelligible harmony and charm. Wassily Kandinsky justifies the abstract forms of his expressionist art as a necessary loss of external harmony in order to procure a new kind of "internal harmony."[1] The notion of visible beauty in the sense of coherent form, then, became a restriction of the essence of art; the "canceling of conventional and obtrusive beauty" was the requirement of the new art.[2] But the exterior harmony of which he complained was that which resulted from the representation of recognizable elements of the real world, and especially the narrative content of traditional painting. Similarly, in the case of music, Arnold Schoenberg proclaims "the emancipation of the dissonance" on the ground that musical harmony did not really matter; only the motivic and thematic material was important to the coherence of what he called the "idea" of a piece of music.[3] But the overruling of harmonic coherence grounded in consonance and tonality seriously undermines the ability of the listener to discern the motivic unity Schoenberg sought, so that the new music is apt to sound as chaotic as abstract painting looks. For both Kandinsky and Schoenberg, the motive was the expression of their "inner need," a heightened emotional content that surpassed the traditional limits of their arts. Thus they maintained a kind of content, but at the cost of the restraint imposed by the criterion of beauty in both the sense of intelligible harmony and charm.

The other arts have also been affected by the modernist hostility to charm. Le Corbusier, one of the founders of the International Style in architecture, likewise rejected the nineteenth-century aesthetic of elaborate ornamentation and decoration of the interior of homes; the home was to be a "machine" for dwelling, in which simplicity and austerity of the furnishings and surroundings would be more comfortable and peaceful. In both the interior and the exterior, visual detail was banished in the name of an unarticulated harmony, and in explicit rejection of visual charm.[4] In the case of poetry, a similar hostility to the charm of meter and rhyme became the defining condition of the modernism of Ezra Pound and T. S. Eliot. Thus, although modernist poets often retained a commitment to poetic content, the traditional character of poetic form largely disappeared. What these examples show is that the conventional concept of beauty was rejected as an inhibition of the artist's self-expression or truthfulness. But although painting, music, and poetry maintained a concept of artistic content, however foreign its expression might seem in comparison to the prior tradition of intelligible representation, many of the new styles still raise the question of the significance of that content. For it is not immediately clear that we should care for the self-expression of shattering emotional pain in Schoenberg's music, or in Kandinsky's paintings, or the solipsism of Pound's self-absorption. The nonsense of Dada, the provocations of Duchamp, the surrealist psychology of Breton all raise the question of both the significance of content and the significance of art in the absence of beauty even more forcefully. Modernism is a dogmatic refusal to see the reality around us, to participate in the beauty of this world, and to recognize the dignity of the familiar.

The connection between art and beauty, therefore—a connection which was once taken for granted—has been severed by a century of artistic modernism. Indeed, the very concept of beauty has long been dismissed from the philosophical vocabulary as a historical artifact that cannot be resurrected.[5] The term "beauty" now denotes a mere surface quality; it appears easily dispensable because it is rarely applicable. Yet in the longer tradition, beauty in the arts was never simply a judgment about appearance; rather, it was deeply connected with a moral or ethical content. This was so even from the beginning, because the word for "beautiful" in ancient Greek is *kalón*, which also carries the meaning of "noble" or "fine," which are fundamentally moral categories.[6] The concept of beauty was therefore already linked in the language and thought of ancient Greece with an ethical category; it was never simply an aesthetic idea, although it could apply to sensuous things as well. The Latin *pulchritudo* also bore similar meanings. But the connection between art and ethical content has been rejected in the twentieth century. In these respects, it is difficult to make sense of earlier aesthetic theories or to appreciate their integrity. It is essential, however, to reexamine the connection between art, beauty, and the ethical in light of the inadequacy of modern aesthetics. For their close relationship defined the long tradition before the advent of modernism.

Hegel belongs to that long tradition, even as he makes important distinctions in some of the traditional aesthetic concepts. But he also justifies the necessity of art as the sensuous representation of the absolute Idea by transforming this aim of art into the representation of an ethical content. This representation, in its unity of form and content, he renames "the Ideal" and identifies as the "Idea of the Beautiful." But this emphasis on the ethical content receives much less attention than his claim for the truth of art (which is itself a matter of controversy for the modern world).[7] Thus it is necessary to examine seriously the arguments by which Hegel seeks to link truth, goodness, and beauty.

Hegel on the Purpose of Art

In order to consider Hegel's logic in connecting art specifically with a moral or ethical purpose, it is helpful to return to his original treatment of the purpose of art generally in setting forth truth. There, he made large claims for the nature of the truth represented in art, so that art is a presentation of the absolute Idea as the totality of truth in which the Concept is united with actuality. Many traditional aesthetic theories also connected art straightforwardly with truth, particularly in imitation and didacticism. But in discussing the purpose of art, Hegel rejects traditional formulations such as the imitation of nature or any kind of didacticism. Against imitation, he observes that the mere copying of natural forms appears superfluous and is indeed an inadequate representation of nature; it makes the sole concern of art the degree of correctness of the imitation, rather than the artist's own power of synthesis and creation. Certainly not every art can be assimilated to the model of the imitation of natural forms; Hegel identifies architecture and poetry as obvious examples (*VÄ* 1, 65–69; *A* 1, 42–45), although certainly traditional aesthetic theories of these arts attempted to justify them by this ancient formula.

Hegel also rejects the other traditional concept of the representation of everything human, although admittedly this seems closer to a comprehensive account of the arts. On this view, the aim of art is essentially to awaken human passions of all sorts, to make us aware through feeling of "the splendour of the noble, eternal, and true: moreover to make misfortune and misery, evil and guilt intelligible, to make men intimately acquainted with all that is horrible and shocking, as well as with all that is pleasurable and felicitous . . ." not only in what is a representation of the world of reality, but also through the realm of the imagination (*VÄ* 1, 71; *A* 1, 46). But he argues that this constitutes no single purpose of art, for the awakening of all possible passions through all possible contents empties art of any true purpose. While art has a wide variation of content, something is missing from such a formulation of the purpose of art as a creative activity and product. What is missing is precisely the sense of a higher end for which all artistic content is ordered.

Reason demands such a higher end, and as it pertains to human needs regarding the contents of art, it must inevitably be an ethical end. Yet it is important to be clear about the precise nature of such an end. Again, Hegel rejects common doctrines of his day, that art ought to "mitigate the ferocity of desires," or purify the passions, provide moral instruction, or generally effect a moral improvement. These were doctrines inherited from the eighteenth century, and they had wide currency even in the nineteenth. But they are inadequate as conceptions of the purpose of art. For the first, the mitigation of the passions, Hegel notes that as an external representation of an object, art necessarily mitigates the passion attached to that object. Hence, art, "while remaining in the sensuous sphere, liberates man at the same time from the power of sensuousness." This, however, fails to specify the aim of art, for it pertains to the power of any sensuous representation, whether its purpose is for good or evil. Thus, the purification of the passions would require the artistic content "to be brought into consciousness in accordance with its universality and essentiality" (*VÄ* 1, 73–75; *A* 1, 48–50). That is, there would have to be an additional specification of the content of art in order to accomplish such an aim, and that content must be presented in such a way that it is perceived as part of what we truly are as human beings. What might be accidentally a passion or a failing shared among many or even most of humanity is not who we are essentially.

Whereas the doctrine of purification appears inadequate, however, Hegel finds the demand for art to provide moral instruction ludicrous. If such instruction is supposed to be blatant and explicit in the work of art, so that the content can in effect be reduced to "an abstract proposition, prosaic reflection, or general doctrine," then the sensuous aspect of art "becomes a useless appendage," a veil masking the didactic content—and therefore a distortion of the concept of art itself. "For the work of art should put before our eyes a content, not in its universality as such, but one whose universality has been absolutely individualized and sensuously particularized" (*VÄ* 1, 77; *A* 1, 51). To make the sensuous aspect of art superfluous converts art into something else: a crude kind of philosophy, but devoid of the rational argument that is crucial to that endeavor of the human spirit. Moreover, to banish pleasure in the sensuous side of art is surely to impoverish our experience of art.

Thus, although Hegel defends art as a representation of ethical truth, it cannot be a didactic presentation of moral duties. He allows that moral betterment may indeed result from the contemplation of art, but what was often intended by advocates of this doctrine in his day was a limitation of the content of art to nothing "but moral subjects, moral characters, actions, and events." In this way, the demand for moral betterment becomes much more than a demand for a story to have a moral, for example—which is common enough—but becomes a curtailment of the field of possible moral lessons that could be drawn. For a lesson about the evil of sin—whether Mary Magdelene's or Oedipus'—necessarily requires the representation of that sin in order to achieve moral betterment. Moreover, as Hegel notes, for a person to be moral, one needs "reflection, the specific consciousness of what accords with duty," and then action in accordance with this reflection. By duty Hegel understands the moral law as Kant had described it in the *Critique of Practical Reason*: "the duty chosen for duty's sake as a guide out of free conviction and inner conscience," to which indeed human nature, in its "sensuous impulses, selfish interests, passions," and feelings is opposed (*VÄ* 1, 78–79; *A* 1, 52–53). Thus, duty cannot be moral unless it is chosen out of opposition to our natural inclinations; this is a restatement of the Kantian position, but it recalls the Augustinian doctrine of the two wills, in which the good will is now defined as that which chooses duty over self.[8] This conception of morality cannot allow an art that seeks moral betterment to be restricted only to morally good characters and actions. Instead, we must see precisely the moral battle inside the character of the hero in order to discern the goodness of will that is capable of overcoming selfish inclination and temptation.

The opposition between duty and inclination, however, is fundamental to a correct understanding of the aim or purpose of art. For, as Hegel notes, this opposition is intrinsic to the human condition; it is not invented by modern philosophers such as Kant, even if modern culture has made the sense of opposition more acute than before. Yet Hegel senses keenly the spiritual tension defining modernity in this contradiction between human nature and the demands of duty:

> The result is that now consciousness wanders about in this contradiction, and, driven from one side to the other, cannot find satisfaction for itself in either the one or the other. For on the one side we see man imprisoned in the common world of reality and earthly temporality, borne down by need and poverty, hard pressed by nature, enmeshed in matter, sensuous ends and their enjoyment, mastered and carried away by natural impulses and passions. On the other side, he lifts himself to eternal ideas, to a realm of thought and freedom, gives to himself, as will, universal laws and prescriptions, strips the world of its enlivened and flowering reality and dissolves it into abstractions, since the spirit now upholds its right and dignity only by mishandling nature and denying its right, and so retaliates on nature the distress and violence which it has suffered from it itself. (*VÄ* 1, 82; *A* 1, 54)

Such a stark contradiction, however, cannot go unresolved, for if the temporal side of humanity is oppressed by passion, the moral side of pure duty unduly denies the temporal element. It is the task of philosophy, in particular, to seek the reconciliation of these oppositions.

Similarly, however, the aim of art demands just such a reconciliation, for it too yields contradictory demands, from the representation of the passions on the one side to the aim of moral betterment on the other. The key lies in abandoning the notion of utility, that art is somehow supposed to set before us something outside of itself which has "independent validity." Rather, the aim of art must lie within itself. Thus Hegel concludes in the passage "that art's vocation is to unveil the *truth* in the form of sensuous artistic configuration"—but goes on to specify that truth: "to set forth the reconciled opposition just mentioned, and so to have its end and aim in itself, in this very setting forth and unveiling" (*VÄ* 1, 81; *A* 1, 55). That is, the aim of art is the representation of truth, but not for didactic purposes. Rather, it is for the purpose of recognition of who we are and what kind of world we live in. Yet in this passage, Hegel has gone further than this recognition: the truth of who we are is twofold, involving both a sensuous nature and a moral will. And the world we live in is also, therefore, twofold, involving both the temporal earthly reality that often oppresses us and the spiritual world of ideas and freedom of will. This is the opposition "just mentioned," which it is the task of art (as for philosophy) to reconcile. But art is uniquely suited to represent such a reconciliation, since art is already the reconciled union of sensuous form and spiritual content. The opposition that lies at the heart of the human condition, therefore, is what gives rise to art in the first place. What demands this places on the moral content of art remains to be seen.

Beauty, the Ideal, and the Reconciliation of Art

Hegel's aesthetic rests on the premise that the Concept of human nature must be understood as freedom—a freedom of will inhering in every human subject (*VÄ* 1, 201; *A*, 1, 151).[9] This is the truth about human nature that is fundamental to all of Hegel's philosophy. Such freedom is in fact both defining Concept and actual reality, and this union of Concept and actuality, as we have seen, is what Hegel calls "the Idea."[10] We have already encountered the Idea as the totality of truth about who we are and the world in which we live; the Idea of Freedom, therefore, is the truth of the absolute Idea applied to the human realm. Similarly, Hegel defines the Beautiful as "the Idea as the immediate unity of the Concept with its reality"—but "only in so far as this its unity is present immediately in sensuous and real appearance" (*VÄ* 1, 157; *A* 1, 116). Hence he can define art in terms of the Beautiful: for art presents precisely this sensuous appearance of the Concept or essence of human nature as artistic beauty. Thus, a most important requirement for art follows from the sensuous nature of the representation of the Idea: "that the Idea and its configuration as a concrete reality shall be made completely adequate to one another" (*VÄ* 1, 104–5; *A* 1, 73–74). Such artistic configuration, united perfectly with the Idea it represents, constitutes for Hegel "the Ideal." It is synonymous with the beauty of art.

However, the Idea found in art pertains to the realm of human freedom, so that the Ideal becomes that of human freedom in its focus as well. Thus it is the Ideal, rather than the totality of the truth of the Idea about the world in which we live, which is determinative for the treatment of art in Hegel's aesthetics. It is the Ideal which is beauty, and—to emphasize the crucial point—the Ideal is not simply an intellectual construct, but rather the artistic representation of the Concept of human freedom. It has both an intellectual content and a sensuous representation. Hegel explains that it "treads into the sensuous . . . but at the same time draws this, like the sphere of the external, back into itself," so that the Ideal exists "in externality, self-enclosed, free, self-reliant, as sensuously blessed in itself, enjoying and delighting in its own self." This makes the Ideal a "ring of bliss" (*VÄ* 1, 207; *A* 1, 157). That is, the Ideal is a representation of subjective freedom that, in being the ultimate good, constitutes an ideal of character, in which the quality of bliss becomes the defining aspect. The Ideal, therefore, is specifically artistic in its representation of the ideal of bliss, a unity indeed of content and form, of Concept and artistic realization.

The Ideal as the central concept for art is thus related to the Idea in this sense: art brings the inner and subjective into harmony with the outer and sensuous. But this is related to a more traditional concept of art and ideal beauty, which required the artist to select only the most beautiful parts of the reality he sought to imitate in order to produce the greatest artistic beauty: the imitation of nature was subordinate to the production of beauty. As Hegel puts it, art brings into "harmony with its true Concept what is contaminated in other existents by chance and externality," so that by a process of purification, it produces the Ideal (*VÄ* 1, 205–6; *A* 1, 155).[11] The Ideal, therefore, like the Idea, is also a union of the Concept with actuality, but with a purified actuality: art will exhibit an ideal of freedom that "real life" does not, due to the "contamination" of chance and other exigencies. The Ideal is unique to art, and art uniquely has the mission of representing this Ideal. Hence, to emphasize the earlier point, art is central to life precisely as the only purified representation of the Ideal of life.

The relation of representation to the Ideal requires clarification, however. It is easy to cast this relation in terms of the familiar terms of form and content, and indeed Hegel himself uses those terms in demanding that for art to be a harmonious union, "the content must be qualified for such representation," and the sensuous form must itself be similarly concrete and individual (*VÄ* 1, 100–1; *A* 1, 70–71). What form means for Hegel, therefore, becomes critical for understanding his concept of the Ideal: for some commentators, Hegel's usage appears slippery, and form can mean either the sensuous structure of an artwork, or the genres of art, or the historical styles to which Hegel seems to point in his notion of "art-forms."[12] But Hegel carefully makes historical artforms the locus of the unity of form and content: the Ideal has particular historical manifestations in the double sense of particular ways of representing the Ideal of freedom, and the particular ways in which that Ideal of freedom is conceived and realized according to its religious foundations.

Hegel therefore emphasizes the historical nature of the Ideal as the immanent realization of its divine dimension: for classical art in particular, as the art in which the perfection of beauty subsists above all as "serene peace and bliss":

> For the blessed gods [of Greek art], that is to say, there is no final seriousness in distress, in anger, in the interests involved in finite spheres and aims, and this positive withdrawal into themselves, along with the negation of everything particular, gives them the characteristic of serenity and tranquillity.

Here Hegel gives the gods a description in terms of the ideal of character they embody, which is also the ideal for humanity to emulate. Hence, even in Greek tragedy, the heroes "are so portrayed that they succumb to fate, still the heart of the hero recoils into simple unity with itself when it says: 'It is so'" (*VÄ* 1, 208; *A* 1, 157–58). Acceptance of fate and the renunciation of the ends initially pursued preserve one's freedom, even in death. The tragic hero thus accepts his fate with tranquillity: the serenity of the gods becomes the model for the serenity of man.

If classical art has a particular Ideal, so too does the romantic art, as Hegel calls it, of the Christian era: but the romantic Ideal differs in the degree that Christianity differs from classical paganism. Because the fundamental experience of Christ lay in His suffering and death on the cross, the art of the Christian religion explores the depths of passion, the "dissonance of the heart." The Ideal will even be lost from sight at times, for the disunion between suffering and the Ideal may well result in genuine ugliness. Hegel insists, nevertheless, that:

> Even in romantic art, however, although suffering and grief affect the heart and subjective inner feeling more deeply there than is the case with the ancients, there do come into view a spiritual inwardness, a joy in submission, a bliss in grief and rapture in suffering, even a delight in agony.

The result is a paradoxical union of opposites, of "smiling in weeping," of "tranquillity amidst agony and suffering" (*VÄ* 1, 209; *A* 1, 158). Thus the essential identification of the Ideal with serenity and tranquillity is preserved, but Christian art forces the Ideal to coexist with more acute suffering than in classical tragedy. It does not deny the reality of suffering or renounce the ends that suffering achieves, but it transfigures suffering and ennobles it as the expression of freedom. Once again, the Ideal, originating in the realm of the divine, becomes the archetype for human emulation in the confrontation with evil and sin. The romantic Ideal is still an ideal of character precisely because it has its origin in the character of the man who was God incarnate.

Art therefore has the mission of representing the truth about the reconciliation of the demands of moral duty with the demands of sensuous nature. It is an essentially cognitive, but not merely didactic mission. It is an ethical function without being narrowly moralistic in its demands on artistic content. Concretely, therefore, the reconciliation depicted takes the form, according to Hegel, of serenity and tranquillity even in the midst of woe and agony. This is an ethical ideal of character; its representation is the goal of art. Only art, not real life (aside from the singular instance of Jesus Christ), can show this as the true reality of who we are.[13] But in an important way, this restricts art's original characterization as the representation of the totality of the absolute Idea, the truth of who we are and in what kind of world we live, to the human dimension of the reconciliation between duty and passion. This is why the ethical content of art is the crucial category for understanding Hegel's aesthetics.

For Hegel, the Ideal, with its ethical import, is the form of artistic beauty. It is an objective quality residing in the artwork, not a subjective perception on the part of the beholder, as beauty (when it is spoken of at all) today is held to be. As Hegel phrases it, "the beautiful must be grasped as Idea," that is, as the unity of the Concept of beauty with its real existence in a work of art (*VÄ* 1, 145; *A* 1, 106). The Concept of the beautiful may be given an abstract definition, but it is the concrete realization of it that constitutes the perceptible Idea of beauty. This is why the Concept of the beautiful demands artistic treatment rather than merely philosophical elucidation. Hence Hegel remarks that "the beautiful is characterized as the pure appearance of the Idea to sense" (*VÄ* 1, 151; *A* 1, 111). An aesthetic following this conception of beauty will necessarily issue in a critical assessment of the beauty of individual works of art and an inquiry into their depiction of the Ideal as the specific form of the Idea in art. But this equation of beauty and the Ideal makes Hegel's aesthetic all the more difficult.

It is perhaps easier for us today to speak of the beauty of nature rather than the beauty of art; that is the context where it seems "natural" to retain the traditional language of beauty. Hegel, however, in common with that same tradition, places higher value on artistic beauty than on natural beauty; only Kant placed natural beauty higher than the artistic. Nevertheless, Hegel finds it essential to begin his discussion of beauty with the "beautiful in nature," for it reveals the basic elements of the Concept of beauty. But this raises the question of what constitutes the Idea embodied in natural beauty; what Concept or essence is united with its real existence? Hegel argues that only life constitutes such an Idea, for the traditional division of the living being into body and a principle of life, called the soul, conforms exactly to the requirements of the Idea (*VÄ* 1, 160; *A* 1, 118). More particularly, it is subjective life that determines itself and causes its own motion; that is the Idea in nature. Indeed, the human being is the highest Idea in nature, although the animal may also be said to have a degree of beauty.

Since the Idea appears in nature, it is possible to speak of the beauty of life in nature: natural beauty can exist only where there is a living organism. But the nature of beauty is such that it is a property to be apprehended only by the human mind; in this sense, beauty depends on the perception of the beholder. However, this is because the Concept itself must be apprehended as part of the appearance of the Idea to sense, and this can occur only for us as living beings who have minds (*VÄ* 1, 173; *A* 1, 128). What we perceive, of course, is not the Concept or the living principle itself of the animal in nature, but rather the outward harmony that results from the inward (nonrational) soul. Thus we judge some animals ugly and others beautiful. Furthermore, we judge inanimate landscapes beautiful by analogy when they have "a pleasing or impressive external harmony which interests us"(*VÄ* 1, 176; *A* 1, 131). Finally, we speak of the beauty of nature in cases such as a moonlit night or a pastoral scene, because of the emotional moods such scenes arouse, but this is entirely derivative: it is a matter of the apparent harmony of nature with the emotional life of human beings. In none of these examples is there a manifestation of human self-consciousness or rationality in nature itself, so that the beauty of nature remains inferior to humanly created artistic beauty. Natural beauty, therefore, cannot participate in the beauty of the Ideal as Hegel presents it, although art can make use of nature for the depiction of beauty.

Although Hegel goes on to give criteria for the "external beauty of abstract form," pointing to regularity and symmetry, conformity to law, and harmony (*VÄ* 1, 178ff.; *A* 1, 133ff.), it is clear that for him there is no possibility of a reduction of the Concept of beauty to a quality simply of sensuous form, as was true for Kant. Since beauty pertains as much to the intelligible content of art as to the nature of its sensuous form in the representation, it cannot become a merely formal property. But this makes the concept of beauty even more confusing to us than as a formal property. To speak of a beauty of content, or an intellectual beauty, is to speak in a language that seems utterly remote from even the sense we take as the core meaning of the word "beauty." It is therefore necessary to examine the philosophical tradition of the concept of beauty, in order to learn what sense can be made of such a concept, and to what extent Hegel was indebted to that tradition. Hegel's aesthetic has turned out to rest on unfamiliar terms with their own peculiar import, such as "the Idea" and "the Ideal." Given the more common understanding of ideas and ideals as purely intellectual and usually subjective in nature, these terms, with the emphasis he gives them on the union of Concept with reality, make his aesthetic difficult enough. The connection he makes between these and the concept of beauty in art is essential to understand the traditional concept of beauty in order to understand Hegel's more peculiar terms correctly. The apparent peculiarity of Hegel's usage can then be put into a philosophical perspective that shows the relevance of these terms to artistic practice and aesthetic judgment.

Transcendence and the Metaxological in the Traditional Concept of Beauty

Any investigation of the concept of beauty as it came to be applied to the arts must begin with the idea of beauty as it was defined and employed by the Greek philosophers. The concept of beauty, however, was not a unitary concept even for Plato and Aristotle, for it embraced not only the moral connotations already noted for *kalón*, but a combination of formal properties consisting in harmonious proportions and a more elusive radiance that remained intangible. For example, in the *Metaphysics* Aristotle remarks that "the chief forms of the beautiful are order, symmetry, and definiteness, which the mathematical sciences especially investigate,"[14] while the beautiful, as the noble or the fine, is the governing object of choice for virtuous actions in the *Nichomachean Ethics* and the *Eudemian Ethics*.[15] Close attention to Plato, however, reveals the reason why the concept of beauty mattered so much to the long tradition of artistic theory and philosophical aesthetics. Contrary to the assertions of modern critics, the concept of beauty in Plato's sense is not hopelessly idealistic: it signifies both the goodness of this world of becoming and its origin in the transcendent world of being.

The most important text for understanding Plato's concept of beauty is the passage in the *Symposium* in which Diotima describes the nature of beauty and the hierarchy of beautiful objects that are loved. Diotima begins by correcting Socrates on the nature of Love: Love is neither divine nor mortal, beautiful or good, nor ugly or bad. Rather, Love is spiritual: it lies between (*metaxù*) the divine and the mortal and between the beautiful and the ugly. The concept of the spiritual is crucial to explain the nature of Love, in order to explain the nature of the love of wisdom that is philosophy. A spirit such as Love desires what it does not have in all its perfection, yet knows enough to know that it desires it. Hence a philosopher, neither wise nor ignorant, seeks wisdom because he loves it in the middle between the divine and the human. But it is the status of the beloved that is important here, for what is loved is beautiful, and is loved because it is beautiful: "The lovable, indeed, is the truly beautiful, tender, perfect and heaven-blest. . . . "[16] The locus of beauty, however, is not between the human and the divine, like Love, but rather is found spanning the full range from the human to the divine.

The famous ascent passage describes the range of beautiful objects that are loved; they comprise a hierarchy that forms the education of the soul toward the love of beauty-in-itself. One begins to love beauty by loving the physical beauty of one body: such beauty is particular and tangible. But then one realizes that the beauty in all bodies is the same. Thus physical beauty is immediately generalized to a universal quality of all human beings. Such beauty is much less important than the beauty of character, however: the next step is to "set a higher value on the beauty of souls than on that of the body, so that however little the grace that may bloom in any likely soul, it shall suffice him for loving and caring . . . "(*Symp*. 210b). From this perception of the beauty of character one begins to perceive "the beauty in our observances and our laws"—those practices, in other words, that help shape an individual's character (210c). Thus for both physical beauty and ethical beauty (in the Greek sense of ethical), there are two separate stages in the ascent toward a more perfect contemplation of beauty, the second stage being in each a generalization of the first. Beauty in itself must be common to all beautiful objects.

The description of the ascent of the lover of beauty is not finished, however: for next, he must come to see the beauty in the different branches of knowledge (210c). This knowledge is what philosophy itself pursues, until the ultimate goal is reached, the vision of beauty in itself. This beauty is "ever-existent and neither comes to be nor perishes, neither waxes nor wanes; next, it is not beautiful in part and in part ugly. . . , nor so affected by position as to seem beautiful to some and ugly to others." It will not show itself as resting in anything, "but existing ever in singularity of form independent by itself" will be the beauty of which all beautiful things partake (210e–211b). The contemplation of this ultimate vision of beauty is what makes life worth living, by providing an object for the quest for an ever more abstract conception of beauty. The soul, having progressed from the love of sensuous beauty to the love of ethical beauty, and then to the love of knowledge, ends by loving the beauty-in-itself that provides the unity underlying all the directly perceivable, and apparently incommensurate, kinds of beauty. Thus, beauty is a property of mortal things, both physically and ethically, and it is also a property of human institutions; but it is also an Idea (in the Platonic sense) that subsists in the realm of the eternal. The lover of beauty dwells in the spiritual realm between the mortal and the divine, but beauty for Plato is a category that ranges from the human all the way up to the divine. Plato, like Hegel, vindicates the intellectual nature of the types of beauty found in this world.

The poetry of the ascent passage, however, not only cannot conceal the abstractness of the concept of beauty-in-itself, but emphasizes it. Diotima offers one more clue about the nature and purpose of the contemplation of beauty, in which she connects the vision of beauty-in-itself with the inspiration to give birth to real virtue by teaching (212a). But the modern world is not accustomed to speak in terms of ethical beauty, just as it has largely forgotten the language of virtue, and we do not often speak of the beauty of knowledge except in the case of elegant mathematical proofs. Thus, what meaning can the love of beauty itself have, when beauty is so abstract a quality that it covers the most diverse conditions? The idea of beauty as articulated in this fundamental text from Greek philosophy utterly lacks definition. For what the *Symposium* presents to clarify the unity of all beautiful things, physical and spiritual, is simply "being by itself with itself always in simplicity." This is hardly adequate.

The *Symposium*, however, is not the only description in the Platonic corpus of a beatific vision of beauty. In the *Phaedrus*, Plato employs the mystical imagery of light in a passage wherein Socrates recalls the soul's original vision of beauty before the soul came to inhabit a body. All glimpses of beauty in this life awaken the memory of this original vision:

> But beauty was once ours to see in all its brightness, when in the company of the blessed we followed Zeus as others followed some others of the Olympians, to enjoy the beatific vision and to be initiated into that mystery which brings, we may say with reverence, supreme felicity. Whole were we who celebrated that festival, unspotted by all the evils which awaited us in time to come, and whole and unspotted and changeless and serene were the objects revealed to us in the light of that mystic vision. Pure was the light and pure were we from the pollution of the walking sepulchre which we call a body, to which we are bound like an oyster to its shell.[17]

Here beauty shines in brightness. It is transcendent and divine, seen most clearly when the soul is not yet corrupted by being joined to the body, but only rarely glimpsed in this life after the mystical manner of the *Symposium*. Nevertheless, in this world beauty is perceived more clearly than knowledge, for "ideal beauty" is reflected in physical forms such as beautiful faces.[18] Thus beauty is not only simple, pure being itself; it shines forth and is a brightness capable of being reflected—like the light of the sun in the simile for the good-in-itself of the *Republic*.[19] This image of beauty as light is one of the most enduring descriptions of beauty in the tradition of Platonism, for it makes the concept immediately intelligible in a way that the more abstract definition of the *Symposium* does not. Hence for Plotinus, and later Ficino, beauty is the ray of divine splendor illuminating all it shines upon.[20] This is what came to inspire the Renaissance concept of beauty as an immaterial grace shining through the material preparation of beauty.

Nevertheless, the shining brilliance of beauty was not the only aspect of beauty that Plato described in the later dialogues. The ideas of proportion and order were closely associated with beauty in the *Timaeus*, giving rise to the equally strong emphasis on harmonious proportions as essential to beauty in the motions of the heavenly bodies and the elements of matter (*Tim* 30, 92). This aspect was closely connected with the relation between beauty and goodness: "The good, of course, is always beautiful, and the beautiful never lacks proportion." Proportion in the human body is essential to its beauty, and a fitting proportion between the mind and the body is, according to Plato, essential to the overall beauty of the human being.[21] Indeed, the entire account of virtue in the *Republic* is based on an analysis of the proper role of each component of the soul in order to establish the overall harmony of the soul based on the proper proportion of each in determining action. If virtue constituted ethical beauty, as the *Symposium* argues, then proportion is certainly a vital element in it just as in physical beauty.

The dichotomy of harmonious order and radiant splendor emerged as important in Renaissance artistic theory but had its origin in Plato's own treatment of the idea of beauty. Although he employs both conceptions of beauty, it appears that perceptible beauty is created by order, whereas beauty-in-itself is conceived as radiance from the realm of the eternal. But if beauty-in-itself is that in which all beautiful objects participate, then the two require a deeper connection. For Plato, order, harmony, and proportion are necessary but not sufficient conditions of beauty in the visible world: beauty cannot exist without them. But there is something more, captured most clearly by the language describing beauty shining brightly: it is most like the sun.[22] Beauty, then, is an intangible quality shining through the whole of something, whether a body, a soul, the cosmos, or knowledge. Beauty is not identical with the goodness of a thing, but may be defined, according to Plato's conception, as the instantiation of goodness: that which makes the goodness of being intelligible and perceptible. Beauty, therefore, contains both a transcendent and an immanent dimension.

This sense of beauty as the instantiation of goodness is the key to understanding Hegel's identification of artistic beauty with the Ideal. According to Plato, simply because we inhabit the metaxological realm, we are not without a glimpse of the divine or the Infinite, and that glimpse is precisely the beautiful. For Plato, beauty-in-itself is transcendent in a way that makes its radiance the source of serenity and felicity; its unity is the source of all love. For Hegel, beauty also has a transcendent component: the Ideal of bliss or serenity, although taking different forms in classical paganism and Christianity, must always be understood as rooted in a conception of the divine nature. Its religious origins are therefore more concrete than the Idea of beauty was for Plato.

Nevertheless, beauty is also perceived in the things of this world, the quality of this life; this Plato emphasizes as well. This kind of beauty is one of the characteristics of the "betweenness" that William Desmond has called the metaxological.[23] Human beings inhabit the realm between the purely mortal and the divine, or as Pascal phrases it, between nothingness and the Infinite. Hence the beauty of character and customs—ethical beauty—is crucial to Hegel as well as to Plato. The Ideal for Hegel, visible in art, is never simply transcendent; it is also found quintessentially in the metaxological realm. The continuity of beauty, then, bespeaks the continuity of the metaphysical domain that humanity inhabits in the domain of temporality.

Hegel preserves this crucial insight from Plato. But it is the beauty found in this world through the medium of art that is most important for Hegel: for art, more than nature itself, brings beauty into the reality we experience by making the Ideal sensuously perceptible. In so doing, art makes beauty a living part of this world, not simply otherworldly; that is, art makes beauty metaxological. Thus the necessity of art lies precisely in making the ethical Ideal visible in the metaxological realm. The ethical purpose of art is integral to the necessity of art.

By emphasizing the ethical nature of art, Hegel provides a coherent challenge to modernist theories of art, which cannot relate art to life except in terms of angry alienation. Hegel reminds us that an ideal of character is indeed vital and provides justification of why art matters. His aesthetic is important, not only for raising questions that challenge us to rethink prevailing assumptions, but also for suggesting a way out of the impasse created by modernism in all its forms. In particular:

1. Hegel articulates a deeper vision of ethical substance in art than the idealism of Plato. Attention to his discussion of both the history of the Ideal and the individual arts will reveal the complexity of his account.
2. Hegel offers a historicist account the modern world often uses to justify developments that led to the triumph of modernism. Yet he manages to respect tradition, unlike his modernist heirs (such as Heidegger and Adorno) who invoke his authority. Close attention to this aspect of his aesthetic will show that Hegel's view of art history lies between a pure traditionalism born out of a conception of the past as the locus of transcendent revelation and a pure historicism born out of a total rejection of such transcendence. Thus Hegel's conception of art history turns out to be metaxological in the sense that art occupies the middle between the purely divine and the merely mortal aspect of human nature that measures time by the passage toward death.
3. Finally, Hegel sees art as a public representation of who we are as members of the several levels of community to which we belong. Thus, precisely because his philosophy of history is dialectical in its dynamic, informed by the tension between the divine and the human, he vindicates implicitly the metaxological character of human existence as lying between the divine and the possibility of nothing transcendent informing human affairs.

Given these elements of importance in Hegel's aesthetics, it is imperative to examine them at length for their illumination of the problem of the arts in modern society. The historicist nature of the Ideal, however, requires immediate attention, since it threatens to disrupt the transcendence that serves to ground the Ideal in Hegel's thought. A proper understanding of Hegel's historicism will correct the common impression that it is merely a dialectical movement celebrating the emergence of the modern present.

Chapter 3

The Historicity of the Ideal and the End of Art

For Hegel, the task of art was the sensuous representation of the Ideal, which was at once an ideal of character and an intelligible content of artistic beauty. The Ideal demanded adequate artistic form; the content and form together constituted the beauty which was the aesthetic goal of art. For modern critics, however, the concept of beauty is both too idealistic and too narrow to serve as a criterion of artistic judgment. Today, art is severed from both moral and intellectual content, and its forms are not restricted to judgments grounded in the perception of what is visually or aurally pleasing. But there is also the conviction that the traditional aesthetic, whether cast in Platonic or Hegelian terms, is a thing of the past; the march of history is assumed to have definitively abandoned the aesthetic of beauty in art. The attitude of presentism precludes the extension of historical criteria to the arts.

Yet for Hegel the Ideal is also conditioned by its historicity: it takes different forms with different conceptions of character and the relation of bliss to woe in the classical and the Christian eras. Hegel's aesthetic thus raises the question of whether the historicity of artistic practice does not simply record the contingency of human subjectivity, leaving the grounding in transcendence as only an accidental characteristic of earlier times. In this case, the historicist critique of the concept of beauty would attain force. But there are deeper reasons to be skeptical of Hegel's concept of artistic beauty, for even he acknowledges that art may not always present what is pleasing; it can depict the ugly and the hateful, as well as powerful intimations of the divine itself in the category of the "sublime." If these departures are fitted into the category of beauty, then modern critics are right in claiming that it is both too idealistic and too narrow. This would be a fatal flaw, however, in Hegel's concept of art as the realization of beauty.

A closer reading of Hegel's historical dialectic of art shows an awareness of this tension between the theory of beauty and the demands of art even in his day. Already by the mid-eighteenth century, the beautiful had ceased to be the exclusive aesthetic category. Edmund Burke's *Philosophical Enquiry into the Origin of our Ideas of the Sublime and Beautiful* of 1757 definitively established the category of the sublime as the second pole of the aesthetic, defined by danger or the threat of suffering.[1] This means that at the very moment when the fine arts were being integrated as a system by means of the concept of beauty, beauty itself was no longer the only category available to artists. However, the richness introduced into aesthetics by the concept of the sublime is purchased at the price of an incoherent aesthetic theory; a dichotomy of concepts no longer provides a unitary account of the purpose of artistic endeavor.

Yet the sublime can also be cast as the representation of the magnificent or the infinite as well as the powerful or the terrifying. This was the step taken by Schiller, who thereby added to the complexity of the concept of the sublime.[2] The sublime, as that which inspires awe or terror, could therefore also be employed as the representation of the power of Nature or of the transcendent power of the divine. Indeed, the German word for the Sublime, "*Erhaben*," is derived from the verb "*erheben*," "to elevate." The sublime is elevated above ordinary experience and ordinary beauty. It breaks the bounds of mere harmoniousness, and by its lack of symmetry brings the intimation of a transcendent power into art. It is apparent, then, that the concept of beauty can no longer be taken as the ruling paradigm of art. Logically, the link between art and beauty can no longer be maintained, unless the concept of beauty is so substantially modified that it ceases to retain the original sense of a pleasing visual appeal together with the implication of ethical nobility.

One of the principal tasks of Hegel's aesthetic is to attempt to integrate the sublime into his account of the aesthetics of art. He does so by means of a historical dialectic, which is also a conceptual dialectic. Therefore, his theory of the arts incorporates the sublime as the contrast with beauty but argues for a synthesis of the two as the central explanation of the art of Christian culture. In doing so, Hegel points to the significance of art as the representation of the infinite and transcendent in the human condition of finitude and mediated being. But because the dialectic of the sublime and the beautiful is explicitly historical for Hegel, his historicist aesthetic also raises the question of the condition of art at the end of history, that is, as he understood it at the point of his own time. Taken broadly rather than literally, the effect raises the question of the role of the arts in the modern world. Thus, precisely because Hegel links the development of aesthetic categories with the unfolding of the history of artistic forms and styles, the same development, which appears to encompass the breadth of both the sublime and the beautiful, ends by rendering suspect the nature and function of art itself. This corresponds exactly to the condition of the arts in the modern world. In order to address these intertwined concerns of the end of art in the modern world and the nature and function of art that is to be both sublime and beautiful, it is necessary to retrace Hegel's development of these aesthetic categories.

The Sublime as the First Principle of Art

Hegel considers the emergence of art in the first historical stage of artistic development, the symbolic art form. There, the sublime rather than the beautiful emerges as the essential content of art; the Ideal does not appear in this first stage. The symbolic art form depends, however, on the form of the symbol, which Hegel understands as a sign: "the content of the idea which it brings into appearance" (*VÄ* 1, 395; *A* 1, 305). That is, it is capable of suggesting a property it already contains. This symbolism, Hegel argues, is found particularly in some Eastern religions, such as Zoroastrianism and Hinduism, yet without yielding a symbolism of the sublime. Indeed, the symbolism essential to art itself is fundamentally negative: that is, it must make the meaning "become explicitly free from the immediate sensuous shape" (*VÄ* 1, 448; *A* 1, 347). The sensuous or the natural, then, becomes negative, superseded by the transcendent meaning it suggests. Hegel finds such a conception of the symbolic quintessentially in the Pyramids of the ancient Egyptians, where the sensuous artistic shape of the burial vaults symbolizes the immortality of the soul without representing the nature of immortality itself (*VÄ* 1, 457; *A* 1, 354). The sublime, however, is a purification of the concept of the Symbolic, and is in particular a representation of the Absolute itself.

There are two ways in which the Absolute can be represented sensually through symbolic means: one is pantheistic; the other is monotheistic. In the former, all of the natural world is regarded as belonging to the substance of the divine, whereas in the latter, the absolute transcendence of God over His creation becomes the crucial characteristic represented in art. Hegel finds the two principal examples in, respectively, Indian poetry and Hebrew poetry. The art of the sublime is found only in the latter. There, the justice and goodness of God establish the existence of the created world. Such art, Hegel claims, represents the transcendence of God by degrading the existence of this world (*VÄ* 1, 479; *A* 1, 372). Thus the sublime has nothing in common with the beauty of the Ideal because the Ideal concerns the inner character of spirit. But here the Spirit of God so transcends the external world that it cannot be represented in itself; only the subordination of the world to God can be shown. Therefore, sacred poetry, as found in the Hebrew Bible, provides the purest example of the sublime.

For Hegel, then, the sublime is removed from the ambiguity inherent in earlier conceptions of the category. Instead of being either terrifying or magnificent, here it intimates the absolute transcendence of a God infinitely powerful, separated from the finite world; the finite world merely suggests the power of God, but not His presence. The human individual, in this context, finds his satisfaction "in this recognition of the nullity of things and in the exaltation and praise of God" (*VÄ* 1, 483; *A* 1, 375). The mind is elevated in such praise, but humility before God is the essential attitude, the condition for obedience to God's law. Such obedience is the condition for all satisfaction of life in this world, and disobedience is the occasion of trial and punishment (*VÄ* 1, 485; *A* 1, 377). Thus, the divine law itself emerges as the best evidence of God and the highest example of the sublime. But the Ideal does not yet appear in art.

The Emergence of the Ideal in the Classical Form of Art

As we have seen, Hegel maintains the Ideal as the representation of the concept of inward freedom from the contamination of chance and externality. He finds it came into existence with the art of classical Greece, and he distinguishes the classical Ideal from the Christian or romantic. The former emerges in "serene peace and bliss," whereas the latter acknowledges suffering and grief while finding joy and bliss in submission to the often cruel demands of externality. Thus the romantic Ideal is more complex, even paradoxical, than the classical, and therefore more profound. It seeks a transfiguration of suffering and death as the highest subject of representation in art. Our understanding of both of these Ideals requires deepening, for Hegel does not merely present them as distinct historical entities, existing only accidentally, but rather as arising in a particular order for reasons having to do with the inadequacy of first the sublime and then the classical Ideal itself. The relation between these two, in turn, is crucial for understanding the dynamic of the romantic Ideal and the course of modern artistic history.

The classical Ideal is the first time there is a harmonious unity of form and content; it brings the Idea of the beautiful into appearance. Humanity, purified, constitutes the essence of the classical Ideal, so that external reality and the human spirit are mutually adequate to each other (*VÄ* 2, 19–20; *A* 1, 432). Hence the classical Ideal is one of harmony and repose: there is

> only the untroubled harmony of determinate free individuality in its adequate existence, this peace in that real existence, this happiness, this satisfaction and greatness in itself, this external serenity and bliss which even in misfortune and grief do not lose their assured self-repose. (*VÄ* 2, 24; *A* 1, 436)

Hence the classical art form does not know any opposition within itself; there is no disharmony between the individual and the Absolute, but only complete identification. There is no disunion between the human spirit and the external reality such that the ugly and hateful would be the result. These latter conditions are obtainable only with the advent of the romantic art form under the influence of Christianity's conception of the human spirit.

Three questions arise in connection with the identification of this Ideal of absolute harmony with the practice of Greek classicism. First, why did the ancient Greeks first produce the classical Ideal? Second, how is it that the classical Ideal, seen here as fundamentally a human Ideal, is a reflection of the divine? Third, how does the classical Ideal yield to the romantic?—what was the logical process by which the romantic was compelled to emerge and triumph, according to Hegel's conception of historical development?

The answers to these questions will help us to understand the conception of artistic beauty which Hegel finds clearly present in the classical art form.

In answer to the first question, Hegel argues that the ancient Greeks had a concept of the divine that must be distinguished sharply from the sense of absolute transcendence characteristic of the sublime deity of Judaism as well as the purity of spirit characteristic of Christianity. For the Greeks, "the Divine in general is to be apprehended essentially as the unity of the spiritual and the natural" in belonging to the Absolute; there is not yet a differentiation between God and either the human spirit or nature (*VÄ* 2, 46; *A* 1, 453). While this may be doubted as an accurate characterization of the Greek concept of gods who could be present in this world, he explains more fully in the *Lectures on the Philosophy of Religion* that the Greek sense of the divine was precisely the "free subjectivity" that is also the essence of humanity (*VPR* 2a, 533–34; *LPR* 329–30). Thus the shared unity of the Concept of freedom resulted in an Ideal that was free from tension: the Ideal of repose entered into art for the first time because there was no disjunction between God and humanity such as characterized other religions.

With regard to the second question, Hegel argues that the Greek gods possessed genuine individuality precisely because of their polytheistic nature. Hence the gods were conceived along essentially human lines and given a fundamentally human shape. Because of this absolute unity between individuality and the universality of the divine, there arose in "the genuine ideal figure of classical art infinite security and peace, untroubled bliss and untrammelled freedom" (*VÄ* 2, 82; *A* 1, 482). Sculpture became the quintessential classical art because it alone represents the ideal character of peace, bliss, and freedom. This spiritual nobility that is the Ideal must be the subject of representation in a way that renders the divine form intelligible under a human figure. This does not mean that sculpture is the only art that manifests the Ideal, for the other arts also have classical phases, and there is also the romantic Ideal. But this raises the question of why the perfect unity of the classical Ideal fell apart and yielded to the Christian.

Hegel understands the transition from the classical to the romantic art form not simply as a new religion displacing the old, but more deeply as the dissolution and exhaustion of the classical art form in preparation for the appearance of the Christian Ideal. The lack of conflict within inner subjectivity was an inherent deficiency of the classical Ideal, but it was the decadence of classical Roman society that exposed this deficiency. The development of satire provided the ground for the repudiation of the Ideal (*VÄ* 2, 110–12, 123–26; *A* 1, 504–6, 514–16). Once satire became the prevalent mode of artistic representation, the conflict between the Ideal and the actual became stronger than the requirements of the Ideal in itself. Hence the need for an Ideal that could encompass the sinful, the ugly, and the hateful, and depict their overcoming by the activity of the divine itself. This was achieved concretely by the Christian faith: it was able to understand God as not removed from human suffering, but able instead to participate in it and thereby to redeem it for His own purposes.

The Christian Ideal and the History of Romantic Art

Hegel describes the Ideal as the representation of a state of character—as serenity, bliss, or (in the Christian manifestation) rejoicing in weeping. In this, he conforms to the tradition of taking the ethical as the essential quality of beauty, rather than seeking to locate beauty simply in physical form. Nevertheless, the Ideal is specifically a spiritual ideal that is sensuously represented; it is a union of physical form and ethical content. Thus, it is closer to an Aristotelian form that is always united to matter rather than to a purely transcendent Platonic Idea, for it is not an abstract universal. The Ideal is always dependent upon specific historical circumstances, which are religious in nature. Hence the Christian romantic Ideal differs from the classical. But in common with Plato, Hegel understands beauty to be grounded in the divine even as it is manifested representationally in the temporal world.

Unlike Plato's conception of beauty, however, Hegel's is not a mystical vision. He concludes Part I of the *Aesthetics* with an extended discussion of "the determinacy of the Ideal." Noting that the divine as pure unity and universality can only present itself to the intellect as indeterminate, classical pagan polytheism became the first example of the determinate representation of the divine; Judaism and Islam forbid such visual representation, so that only poetry in praise of God's power and glory is appropriate in those religions. But Christianity affords the widest scope for artistic representation. It is not, as in classical paganism, a case of man representing the gods, but rather God become a specific, historical man in Christ. God's involvement in earthly affairs both fills pious men with the spirit of God and validates all of the earthly sphere of life. But precisely because the Divine is now known to be concerned with all the affairs of human life, beauty of character attains a divine sanction it did not have in classical times: nobility and virtue (to use the classical terms) do not arise merely from the life of the *polis*, but are rather the expression of the truth of God. Thus the modern criticism of the vague idealism of the doctrine of beauty cannot apply to Hegel.

The Ideal in the Christian conception yields an art of a specific ideal of character. Certainly the conceptions appropriate to earlier ages can no longer obtain: in the symbolic age, impersonal abstractions or an animist nature; in the classical age, the unification of the natural and the spiritual in the perfection of the Ideal of beauty. But Christianity regards the human spirit as not entirely reconciled with the sensuous world, so that the classical unity of the Ideal is dissolved into subjectivity and externality, and the spirit seeks reconciliation with itself instead of with the external world (*VÄ* 2, 128; *A* 1, 518). Beauty, therefore, becomes the specifically spiritual beauty of the inner life. But this is only a development of the original Platonic doctrine of the beauty of character.

Nevertheless, there are implications of this new relation of the spiritual with sensuous externality that stretch the category of beauty beyond the classical connotation. For if on one side there is the peace of God, on the other is the pain of Christ's suffering and death as the redeeming activity of God. Moreover, because now the human spirit understands itself as torn within itself between infinitude and finitude, as having to choose between good and evil, it must seek a reconciliation that can only come about from a struggle, in the process of which "grief, death, the mournful sense of nullity, the torment of spirit and body enter as an essential feature" (*VÄ* 2, 133–34; *A* 1, 522). Only in Christianity, therefore, does death acquire its meaning; only in romantic art does suffering appear in the aspect of necessity. This profoundly alters the sense of beauty.

Romantic art must renounce the classical ideal of beauty as the representation of the tranquillity of the soul; "on the contrary. . . , it intertwines its inner being with the contingency of the exernal world and gives unfettered play to the bold lines of the ugly" (*VÄ* 2, 139; *A* 1, 526–27). The spirit becomes indifferent to the subject matter of the external world: elements of the natural world, the commonest scenes of everday life—these become acceptable to art, without the need for idealization or transfiguration. But even beyond this indifference, the ugliness of genuine evil becomes an element of the external world which may find its representation in art as the context of the spirit's activity. It is this that makes the theory of beauty appear so contrary to the full potential of art, even before the advent of modernism.

Hegel organizes the discussion of the subject matter of romantic art into a paradigm that is both historical and developmental, a story of the unfolding of the tension latent within the romantic Ideal. The first group of subjects is supplied by the content of divine revelation and the response of the faithful to it. The second group concerns the human realm itself, as it is informed by the affirmation of the Christian ideal of character, with "the virtues of this affirmative subjectivity, namely honour, love, fidelity, and bravery, the aims and duties of romantic chivalry." Finally, there is the representation of spiritual independence itself, or the free treatment of "external circumstances, situations, and the complexity of events" in all their contingency, in which the tension within the romantic Ideal falls apart into its twin opposing poles of subjectivity and contingency (*VÄ* 2, 141–42; *A* 1, 528–29). But it is not pure contingency, subjectivity, or ugliness which exemplify the romantic Ideal, for these elements represent the disintegration of the romantic Ideal. Rather, the romantic Ideal reveals itself most clearly in its religious and chivalric modes in which the tension between the divine and the world is maintained.

Because romantic art is concerned above all with the reconciliation of God with the world, it is spiritual rather than physical beauty that is the goal of art. The beauty of subjectivity becomes the beauty of deep feeling, and this is shared necessarily with others as the feeling of love. Thus the Absolute manifests love for the world in the life, suffering, and death of Christ, by which reconciliation with the world is accomplished. The love this awakens is the summit of the romantic Ideal, and it elicits humanity's attempt to appropriate the reconciliation which God has already brought about, which may indeed demonstrate the most acute suffering and penance in the process. This is the way, then, that Hegel explains the main divisions of the content of purely religious romantic art: the redemptive story of Christ's life and sacrifice; the love of Christ for others, Mary's love for her child, the love of the disciples for their Master; and finally the love of Christians for God (*VÄ* 2, 147; *A* 1, 533–34). But this last division witnesses a return to suffering: for the love of Christ produced martyrs to the faith, and converts who were acutely conscious of their sin. Yet painters depict the martyrs and saints as expressing "the bliss of torment," so that grief is overcome in knowledge of God's presence in the life of the faithful (*VÄ* 2, 163; *A* 1, 546). Thus the romantic Ideal is an ideal of feeling and character having Christ Himself as the exemplar.

The romantic Ideal is manifested more, however, in its elaboration as chivalry. Hegel argues that in spite of the absolute claims of religious love, to remain in the Absolute is to have only an "abstract" love, failing to satisfy the demands of life itself. "The heart which is only now perfected in its simple bliss has therefore to leave the heavenly kingdom of its substantive sphere, to look into itself, and attain a mundane content appropriate to the individual subject as such" (*VÄ* 2, 170; *A* 1, 552–53). Hegel, therefore, places a much higher valuation on the world as such than Christian theology has the reputation for allowing. He justifies it by the necessity for the Kingdom of God to win a place in this world, rather than be relegated solely to the next; Christians must be part of a community of believers, and communities are part of this world. It is in fact part of Hegel's understanding of Christian theology that the Holy Spirit exists immanently within such a community and the worldly realm itself conforms to the freedom of the Spirit, and thereby becomes "the ethical realm" (*VPR* 3, 252, 264–65; *LPR* 470, 483–84). Thus faith must lose its negative attitude toward human affairs, and art will come to have other subject matter besides the purely religious. Once again we see Hegel's emphasis on the metaxological character of human existence.

The content of romantic art centers first of all on the "forms of the romantic self-filled inwardness of the subject," that is, on the chivalric feelings of honor, love, and fidelity. Hegel notes that these "are not strictly ethical qualities and virtues," for they are only feelings, rather than feelings united with actions. Thus the sense of honor is not bravery defending the common good, nor even one's own individual rectitude; "on the contrary, honour's struggle is only for the recognition and the abstract inviolability of the individual person." So too, love "is only the accidental passion of one person for another," rather than the ethical relation of marriage. And finally fidelity, that is, loyalty to one's earthly master, although an actual tie between two people, remains only intersubjective and removed from the life of the state (*VÄ* 2, 169–72; *A* 1, 553–54). The poetry of the Christian Middle Ages concerns these three subjects as the romantic Ideal in the world and begins already to secularize the originally transcendent Ideal of the Christian faith.

The higher valuation of the secular world, as a consequence of the chivalric mode, results in a withdrawal from the domain of the religious altogether. For while the feelings of love and fidelity find their exemplars in religious love and devotion—and indeed medieval poetry referred constantly to Christian models—the domain of feeling expands as a subject of art into the treatment of individual character. The Ideal, then becomes independence of character, and the task of art is the examination of self-determining character. This, Hegel finds, is the great genius of Shakespeare. *Macbeth, Othello*, and *Richard III* are examples of tragedies which depend on characters who set their own ends, which they accomplish "with the unshakeable logic of passion, without any accompanying reflection or general principle, solely for their own satisfaction" (*VÄ* 2, 200; *A* 1, 578). The heroes of these tragedies are utterly without moral principle: here Hegel identifies plays that are acknowledged as among the greatest, yet which lack the moral dilemma of a *Hamlet* or the portrayal of folly and its attempted correction such as in *King Lear*. In contrast, another kind of play presents characters who are not developed much inwardly, yet who suffer at the fate of external circumstances, as in *Romeo and Juliet*, or Miranda in *The Tempest* (*VÄ* 2, 205–6; *A* 1, 581–82). Hegel explains the importance of this latter kind of character study, however, as in reality a study of the destiny of restricted yet deeply inward characters entangled in circumstances (*VÄ* 2, 209–10; *A* 1, 585). But there is always a danger that such art will become empty: both spiritual independence and the realm of pure contingency constitute only restricted sides of romantic art. Thus, in spite of our greater familiarity with Shakespeare and post-Renaissance art, the romantic Ideal remains best understood in terms of its first two categories, religious art and chivalry. For these modes, even the ugliness of suffering and sin is subordinated to the beauty of reconciliation.

Nevertheless, the latent potential of the romantic Ideal poses substantial problems for a theory of art cast in terms of beauty and divine transcendence. If the history of romantic art is held to issue in the spiritual emptiness Hegel discerns already in some of the greatest Elizabethan drama, and which he finds characteristic of some of the literature of his day, then this antithesis to beauty is difficult to incorporate into the concept of art defined in terms of beauty. More seriously, the withdrawal of art from its religious origins signals a collapse of the content of the Ideal itself. This is the origin of the frequently held belief that Hegel prophesied the end of art.

But an Ideal emerging explicitly from religious origins and then in the course of its development withdrawing altogether from those origins in the divine not only poses a contradiction in the Concept of the Ideal; it also makes the whole historical schema of the unfolding of the Idea through art a conundrum. Thus the conceptual difficulty to which modern critics of the aesthetics of beauty in art point—that art must be defined in terms broader than beauty to account for the totality of artistic practice—is related in Hegel's aesthetics to the historical problem of the secularization of the Christian Ideal and the possibility that art will indeed come to an end. It is helpful, therefore, to consider the problem of Hegel's historicism first, before facing the more abstract question of the relation of late romantic art to the theory of beauty.

The Question of the Supersession and End of Art

One of the most frequent readings of Hegel's historicism is the notion that he prophesies the end of the romantic art form as a result of an inevitable secularization. As the divine content of the Christian Ideal is emptied out, the romantic era will come to an end, just as had the classical. But if the divine content is altogether absent, then the Ideal will have disappeared, and with it, art itself. This thesis of the end of art, moreover, is often joined to an understanding of Hegel as arguing that philosophy—specifically, in his system—supersedes art as the means of knowing the truth about ourselves.[3] In this view, art becomes unnecessary at precisely the moment it ceases to exist. In a crucial passage from the introduction to the romantic art form, after outlining the split of the romantic art form into the pure subjectivity of spiritual independence and the contingency of external circumstances, Hegel states:

> Therefore we acquire as the culmination of the romantic in general the contingency of both outer and inner, and the separation of these two sides, whereby art annuls itself [*sich aufhebt*] and brings home to our minds that we must acquire higher forms for the apprehension of truth than those which art is in a position to supply. (*VÄ* 2, 142; *A* 1, 529)

This makes both what is often taken to be the "funeral oration" of art and the case for the supersession of art by religion and philosophy.

Yet to see this as support for either the funeral oration thesis or the supersession thesis would be a hasty overreading of the passage, for two reasons. First, there is the difficulty of the German term *aufheben*, which may mean "to raise," "to preserve," or "to annul"—a profoundly plural ambiguity that Hegel exploits as the central explanatory term of his dialectical sense of history. But the sense of the passage as the annulment of art arises in the context of the disintegration of the romantic Ideal into its separate parts of the inner and outer. The only question is whether anything of art is preserved, or if it completely disappears as it yields to those higher means of knowing truth, religion, and philosophy. If the role of art as the sensuous representation of truth were preserved, then this passage might more plausibly be read as simply stating that there are higher means of knowing truth—and that art begins to make us aware of that fact. Second, if there is a problem with art at a particular moment of history, then other forms of knowledge such as religion or philosophy might indeed come to the fore at that point—but it need not be a permanent state of affairs. That Hegel evidently sees the romantic art form disintegrating in his own time is implicit in the passage, and the forces which led to that disintegration can be seen as underlying the emergence of modernism in the twentieth century: in particular, the tendency toward individual autonomy and complete subjectivism in regard to truth. Nevertheless, the sense of the inevitability and irreversibility of history may well be questioned. A deeper understanding of Hegel's position on both the supersession thesis and the concept of the end of art shows why.

Hegel's treatment of the relation between art, religion, and philosophy in the *Aesthetics* appears to lend support to the supersession thesis. All three are concerned with knowledge of the Absolute: they are the means by which the human spirit appropriates and becomes absolute spirit. But art is representation for "sensuous knowing . . . in which the Absolute is presented to contemplation and feeling." Religion is a higher means of knowing, in which worship of God is essentially "pictorial thinking," while philosophy, the highest mode of knowledge, "is the free thinking of absolute spirit" (*VÄ* 1, 139; *A* 1, 101). This hierarchy of modes of knowledge makes art a preparatory step to the religious, and the religious to the philosophical. Yet Hegel rejects, as elsewhere, the notion that art is to be understood simply as in service to other functions, including the religious, although it is true that religion often enough makes use of art. But art in itself is not to be understood merely as an adjunct to worship, for indeed he believes that in ancient Greece, the poets themselves gave the people "a definite idea of the behaviour, life, and effectiveness of the Divine." In the larger sense, religion was the consequence of art (*VÄ* 1, 141; *A* 1, 102). Art, therefore, not only had its own dignity and integrity; it was absolutely fundamental to ancient Greek worship. The Ideal of art is intimately religious in nature.

Nevertheless, Hegel finds the domain of art limited, and this condition is reflected in the way art is used in the modern world: "For us art counts no longer as the highest mode in which truth fashions an existence for itself." This happened early in the history of art, and then as each people matures, judgment condemns the representations of the divine in art: hence Plato's strictures against art as imitation, and Judaism's forbidding of images. Even Christianity, since the Reformation, has retreated from the use of images in worship. Here, Hegel acknowledges the historical importance of statuary and painting in Catholic and Orthodox churches but regards the Protestant Reformation as offering the truer point of view because it is more inward and more spiritual. Thus he concludes that "the form of art has ceased to be the supreme need of the spirit." To even the most exquisite of Christian art, "we bow the knee no longer" (*VÄ* 1, 141–42; *A* 1, 103). Religious worship, then, is for Hegel entirely a matter of inwardness and subjectivity, albeit within a community of believers, in which the Absolute is grasped by both intellect and feeling. Finally, philosophy makes knowledge of the Absolute self-conscious, uniting and transforming the objectivity of art and the subjectivity of religion (*VÄ* 1, 143–44; *A* 1, 104). But the images of art appear to remain superseded by the higher developments of both religion and philosophy.

The structure of the *Aesthetics* further appears to confirm the thesis of the end of art and its supersession by philosophy. There, the concept of the decline of art in each of its historical forms is a structural component of the argument. The classical art form dissolved due to two factors: (1) the inner deficiency of its anthropomorphism and (2) the rise of satire, which revealed the decay of the pagan system of gods and mores. Hegel also sees the romantic art form growing out of the Christian faith as lapsing into a state of decay already by the Elizabethan age owing to the development of art away from earlier religious and chivalric themes. Instead, post-Renaissance art was characterized by both an independence of character stripped of moral restraints and the merely realistic description of contingent circumstances oppressing individuals. Thus, combining Hegel's conviction of the development of philosophy to a point of its completion of the project of self-understanding with the concept of the end of art in the end of the romantic art form yields the thesis of the supersession of art by philosophy.

Nevertheless, any claim that philosophy displaces art must be understood in the context of Hegel's entire philosophical system, and concentration simply on the *Aesthetics* is not sufficient to accomplish such a purpose. Even in this work, he argues that the connection between art and the other modes of knowing the Absolute is one of complementarity, in which the limitations of the subordinate modes are supplemented by the higher out of their own inner demands (*VÄ* 1, 131–32; *A* 1, 95). Thus art is produced within a larger hierarchical framework embracing law, the state, religion, and philosophy. As we have seen, the spiritual condition of humanity is freedom and its struggle against the inner condition that denies us spiritual freedom in the forms of passions, grief, and torment. In our need to reconcile this opposition, art and religion emerge as the modes of knowing the Absolute that address our senses and our feelings, respectively, while philosophy addresses our thought (*VÄ* 1, 134–35; *A* 1, 97–98). This does not suggest that art must be superseded simply because we demand an intellectual understanding of truth. Rather, it implies that all modes of knowing retain their essential validity and necessity.

Hegel's understanding of the place of the arts in the various enterprises of the human spirit finds its most succinct expression in the *Philosophy of Mind*, the third part of the *Encyclopaedia of the Philosophical Sciences* of 1830. Here Hegel identifies art as the first manifestation of the consciousness of the Absolute, that is, of God as self-knowing Spirit. In the construction of human knowledge of the Absolute, then, art has priority, followed by religion and philosophy. The priority of art here is not a chronological priority, but rather a conceptual beginning: art is "the form of immediacy," in which God is represented by creative work. The sensuous representation of God in the artwork unites, therefore, nature and spirit in artistic beauty (*Enz* 3, §557; *PM* 293). What Hegel identifies as revealed religion, however, is the revelation by God of Himself to humanity. It is the second manifestation of the Absolute, and it is a movement in the opposite direction from art, in which humanity seeks the knowledge of God. The opposite directions in which these spiritual manifestations move, then, become reconciled in the third manifestion, philosophy. Hence, Hegel says philosophy "is the unity of Art and Religion," for it completes the dialectical movement by raising the spiritual consciousness of the other two moments to self-consciousness (*Enz* 3, §572; *PM* 302). Here the human knowledge of God approaches God's knowledge of Himself, because God has now revealed Himself. Just as God has complete knowledge of Himself in self-consciousness, so too does human knowledge of God and the world approach completeness in self-consciousness.

The *Philosophy of Mind*, therefore, should suggest a corrective to the supersession thesis, for art here is expressly the first moment in the dialectic of our knowledge of God. The first moment of the dialectic remains intact and retains its validity even as the second comes into being. Hence art did not cease when God revealed himself in the person of Christ and suffered death on the cross, but rather flourished as first an adjunct to worship and later for explicitly secular purposes within a Christian society. It is only as its secularity grows that Christian society comes under threat of losing the essence of what makes it distinctively Christian, and the role of art, therefore, becomes problematic. But this is a question of the dialectic of the romantic art form rather than a matter of the end of art altogether.

The End of Romantic Art Reconsidered

If art as a whole was not coming to an end in Hegel's view, nevertheless, the possibility of romantic art coming to an end now must be considered. The implication of Hegel's theological understanding of history for his aesthetic theory is that the arts of his day were the culmination of the Spirit's manifestation in humanity. Hence, the arts were strongly marked by subjectivity and inwardness: the individual human spirit was now the locus of the divine Spirit (*VÄ* 2, 128–33; *A* 1, 519–21). Yet, in lamenting that no Homer, Sophocles, Dante, or Shakespeare could appear in his own day, Hegel further states that "what was so magnificently sung, what so freely expressed, has been expressed; these are materials, ways of looking at them and treating them which have been sung once and for all" (*VÄ* 2, 238; *A* 1, 608). A failure of the romantic art form would appear, then, at precisely the moment of the attainment of philosophical self-consciousness according to Hegel's understanding of the progress of philosophy.[4]

But surely this would be the greatest irony if art came to an effective end just when artistic clarity of purpose ought to be at its highest.

As we have seen, Hegel saw romantic art falling apart into opposition already in the Renaissance. For the romantic principle of inwardness allows the external world to be represented as subsisting in its own manner, but the same principle allows the subjective world of the heart and spirit its own inherent dignity, so that the specific representation is equally accidental. In other words, the first consequence for romantic art is a far greater degree of realism than obtains in classical art: "everything has a place, every sphere of life, all phenomena, the greatest and the least, the supreme and the trivial, the moral, immoral, and evil . . . " (*VÄ* 2, 221; *A* 1, 594). But what Hegel could praise in the plays of Shakespeare had come by Hegel's day to constitute "the collapse of romantic art." For carried to an extreme, the portrayal of the prosaic world ended in stripping ordinary life of both its ethical character and its connection with the eternal. The second consequence, however, is the exaltation of the subjectivity of the artist in his expression of opinions, feelings, and originality (*VÄ* 2, 222; *A* 1, 595). That is, the endpoints of romantic art are either a pure realism with no ethical truth, or a pure subjectivism lacking in both reality and ethical truth. This is not necessarily a pronouncement of the end of all art, but the collapse of romantic art would mean the end of an artistic culture founded on Christian principles. It was not a prospect Hegel approved.

Hegel's observation is perceptive of trends already in evidence in the literature and art of the 1820s; the future course of the nineteenth century would confirm the dominance of realism as the first pole of development for romantic art. This was not a matter of being simply "portrait-like" (as he argued all romantic art was more or less), but rather a dissolution of representation into portraiture or an imitation of nature, "to an intentional approach to the contingency of immediate existence which, taken by itself, is unbeautiful and prosaic. Therefore the question soon arises whether such productions in general are still to be called works of art" (*VÄ* 2, 223; *A* 1, 596). Indeed so, as earlier in the *Aesthetics*, Hegel decisively rejects any definition of art in terms of the mere imitation of nature, on the grounds that such imitation is always superfluous, inadequate, uncreative, and unbeautiful (*VÄ* 1, 64–67; *A* 1, 41–44). Hence, purely realist art cannot be regarded as a further development of style within the general category of romantic art; it has to be rejected altogether as not being art. Only if the artist remained "faithful to the manifestations of spirit and also to the inherently substantial life of nature" could his work be seen as art (*VÄ* 2, 223–24; *A* 1, 596). That is, realism would have to be tempered with fidelity to human freedom as the essential life of the spirit, and that freedom would carry with it all the moral and ethical implications which he discerned to be missing in the realist approach to the arts.

The second pole of development for romantic art, toward subjectivism, lay in the emergence of humor or irony as an essential ingredient in art. Hegel notes that the intrusion of the artist's own personality risks destroying the unity of form and content that is the essence of artistic beauty, so that in that case art quickly loses its seriousness and dignity. In Hegel's day, the preeminent practitioner of humor in the novel was Jean Paul Richter, and Hegel makes clear that he had little use for his endless "drawing together and concatenating material raked up from the four corners of the earth and every sphere of reality," without development or substantive aim (*VÄ* 2, 230–31; *A* 1, 601–2). But the technique of an author's intrusion into the narrative in a deliberately ironic way was not limited to the novel; it is also found, for instance, in Pushkin's poem, *Eugene Onegin*. Thus the development of extreme subjective domination of the material by the writer constitutes both the end of romantic art—as the pole toward which the artistic spirit was moving—and its nadir.

Hegel's criticisms of contemporary artistic trends merit attention all the more for being rooted in his historicist view of art history. They reveal that he was not complacent in accepting whatever had developed historically as an inevitable state of art. Rather, both realism and subjectivism in their most radical modes can be judged harshly as departures from the romantic Ideal and indeed from the goal of art itself. This is possible because Hegel retains a conception of the Spirit as divine and transcendent even though it was also manifest in history and in the Christian community.[5] In this, the religious origins of the Ideal serve to ground a perspective that must call into question any thoroughgoing secularism.

To claim this, however, seems controversial. So familiar is Hegel's sense of the immanence of the Absolute Spirit in the history of the human spirit that any claim for transcendence seems suspect. Certainly Hegel himself is ambiguous: he makes God's self-knowledge a matter of "a self-consciousness in man and man's knowledge of God, which proceeds to man's self-knowledge in God" (*Enz* 3, §564;

PM 298), so that it appears that God's mind is nothing other than the human mind. Moreover, Hegel makes God's creation of the world, in which evil is a consequence of its finitude, the self-positing of God as other, as a matter of his "own essential determination" (*VPR* 3, 235; *LPR* 454). Hence the frequent charge since Hegel's day that he was really advancing a species of pantheism. If the world is nothing other than an extension of God's being, and the human spirit the being of God's Spirit, then there is no true transcendence built into Hegel's philosophical system, and the unfolding of the romantic Ideal in secularity becomes the necessary end of romantic art.

Nevertheless, Hegel's actual position is more subtle than these passages suggest. For he emphasizes that the Absolute is freely self-determining, that is, not acting out of necessity, so that the creation of the world was a matter of releasing the world as other to exist (*VPR* 3, 217; *LPR* 434). Indeed, Hegel is emphatic that "The world is something other than God" (*VPR* 3, 202; *LPR* 419). Even his claim that the divine and human nature must come to unity is to be understood not as a general proposition, but as a statement regarding the uniqueness of the Incarnation (*VPR* 3, 237–38; *LPR* 454–55), in which salvation is effected. Thus it is not inaccurate to speak of Hegel's concept of God as being transcendent as well as immanent. Indeed, Christian orthodoxy recognizes both transcendent and immanent aspects of God, the latter crucial for divine revelation in general, the Incarnation in particular, and the indwelling of the Holy Spirit in the Church. What is troubling is that Hegel is never entirely clear that the Absolute is absolutely Other. Too often, it appears rather as the Whole, of which the temporal realm of history is simply a part. Nevertheless, to the extent that Hegel insists the world is other than God, or even that the Whole has its origin in a principle that is not identical with the world, then he is acknowledging some residue of transcendence. For the world to be not identical to God is indeed to acknowledge a measure of divine transcendence.

Hence, the present for Hegel is not to be judged by a purely immanent standard. As long as the present is subject to a transcendent principle, however implicated in historical development that principle may be, there is the possibility of genuine criticism of both the present and the past on the grounds of metaphysical and ethical truth. In this case, however, the end of art is far from inevitable. Hegel's ability to criticize the arts of his day suggests that the future of art is open so long as we, too, remain receptive to the possibility of art requiring criticism. Hegel shows that radical presentism must be rejected if art is to be subject to the criticism needed to remain viable.

There is another reason for not reading Hegel's analysis of the decay of romantic art as a verdict pronouncing the dissolution of art altogether. For Hegel was not without hope or evidence to support that hope—a point frequently overlooked by his commentators. If the romantic form of art had dissolved into the apparent antithesis of realism and subjectivism, then the antithesis might yet be resolved dialectically. Hegel was properly cautious in envisioning that resolution, but he saw as one possibility "an inner movement of the spirit devoted entirely to its object and retaining it as its content and interest," that is, by a union of deep feeling with the object (*VÄ* 2, 240; *A* 1, 609). This is indeed the principle underlying what we call popular, rather than ironic, Romanticism in poetry, music, and painting—here, "Romantic" is capitalized to refer to the nineteenth-century movement. This is the better known heritage of the Romantic movement that was only emerging in Hegel's day and which he could discern only imperfectly. Lacking a term for it, Hegel could only point to Goethe and Rückert as the leading poets of the new movement. Their poetry relied on the pathetic fallacy to project moods onto nature, so that human feeling could be specified by natural metaphor and at the same time nature be revivified through the representation of its sympathy with human spirit. The result was to rise above the merely subjective feelings of the poet: such poetry possessed "a depth of feeling and a cheerfulness of the inwardly self-moving heart which through the serenity of the outward shape lift the soul high above all painful entanglement in the restrictions of the real world" (*VÄ* 2, 242; *A* 1, 611). Although Hegel does not explicitly say so, this accomplished precisely the goal of all true art: it embodied the Ideal (*VÄ*, 207–8; *A* 1, 157). Hence, the decadence of the romantic form of art was not necessarily the end of art's history; in fact, during the nineteenth century art would enjoy a substantial renewal in some genres simultaneously with the decadence of others. Recognizing this vindicates the whole history of romantic art as the unfolding of the potentialities inherent in the Christian Ideal. A better understanding of the relation of romantic art and the Ideal becomes imperative.

Romantic Art and Metaxological Beauty

The difficulty of reconciling romantic art, with its deliberate inclusion of the ugly and sinful in its scope of content, with an aesthetic that defines art in terms of beauty now becomes the central problem for Hegel's treatment of art in the Christian era. For the apparent contradiction within the Christian Ideal, of an emphasis on the sinful and the requirements of an art that is to be beautiful, is resolved in the ultimately beautiful reconciliation it depicts. The disintegration of the romantic art form Hegel describes as a falling apart of the Ideal into pure subjectivity and pure contingency is not necessarily a permanent state of art. The Concept of the Ideal remained intact in Hegel's day as a standard of criticism and might once again be perceived as having force in artistic production. But the problem is not in Hegel's conception of art history or in his aesthetic of beauty, but rather in a simplistic reading, on our part, of what an aesthetic of beauty implies for history. It does not have to be the case that such an aesthetic must account for all works produced in a given historical era. Classical tragedy was full of crimes of the worst possible sort, yet Hegel and all other defenders of the aesthetic of beauty saw in Greek drama the confirmation of the aesthetic of classical beauty. Therefore, a fuller understanding of the role of beauty in art is needed.

What is relevant here is precisely the character of the metaxological: if it has the nature of sinfulness and ugliness in large proportion it is nonetheless not devoid of evidence of transcendent beauty. But the metaxological realm is not altogether orderly; an art that wishes to represent the possibility of beauty within it must also represent the ugly, sinful, and hateful elements characteristic of life, but in such a way that there is an ultimate reconciliation with transcendence. Thus the romantic Ideal, although an apparently paradoxical expansion of the Platonic concept of metaxological beauty into both ugliness and beauty, turns out to be a necessary consequence of Hegel's requirement of art. In this way, Hegel's concept of the Ideal escapes the modern criticism of beauty as being too narrow. For Hegel's Ideal of beauty is complex enough to include even the ugliness of the metaxological as long as it is governed by reconciliation to the divine aspect of beauty.

Furthermore, it is evident that the Christian Ideal bears within it essential characteristics of the preceding two moments of the Ideal. For the emphasis on the Divine in the first historical phase of purely religious art corresponds most closely to the sublime, even as the Christian conception of the Divine ceases to be exclusively sublime because, in the Incarnation, it cannot be regarded as purely and simply transcendent. To this is joined the other aspect of beauty more characteristic of the classical Ideal, for the beauty of the reconciliation effected in the Incarnation partakes of the same quality of serenity and bliss. Yet as we have seen, this reconciliation is the result of a dynamic process that recognizes the reality of sin together with the ugliness it brings. Hence, the romantic Ideal always has a tension between the beautiful and the ugly that only a final reconciliation can resolve into the purely beautiful itself. In this, it partakes of the unique character of the Hegelian middle: it is located between transcendence and historicity, not reducible to either, but reconciling them into an affirmation of beauty.

With such a tension, it is possible to see that the dynamic of the history of the romantic Ideal is much more complex than that of the simpler classical Ideal. Although Hegel draws parallels between their historical developments, the stages of the romantic Ideal's development articulate a much more nuanced course. The secularization of the Ideal will always be one possible outcome of the romantic recognition of the reality of sin in this world. But the art that results from an emphasis on this world, whether realist or subjectivist in its orientation, will always threaten to mark the end of art unless some kind of reconciliation with a transcendent order is maintained. If the arts in Hegel's day did not mark the end of art after all, then we might well conclude they have indeed come to the end of their potential in the emergence of the radical subjectivity characteristic of modernism. Nevertheless, this is not because of any inevitable historical development, since we have noted evidence of artistic renewal to which Hegel gave his approval in his own time. The emergence of modernism must simply be understood as the radical rejection of genuine transcendence, the ethical life, and traditional norms. In Hegel's view, art founded on the rejection of these principles cannot be regarded as art. To repeat the crucial point: for Hegel, art is the representation of the truth of the ethical nature of human existence. This truth justifies challenging any art that rejects it.

Yet in speaking concretely of art in the metaxological realm between its historicity and the transcendent origin of its truth, as a concept art remains only abstract. We want to understand art more deeply: how the individual arts of architecture, sculpture, painting, music, and poetry (and prose literature) spring from the general concept of art. But this is indeed the most problematic aspect of Hegel's *Aesthetics*. For the Ideal, which has loomed so large in Hegel's definition of art as a general category, and which is crucial in connecting art to the traditional concept of beauty and making sense of its metaxological character, tends to disappear in his discussion of the historical artistic practice he observes and approves. Accordingly, much of what is of interest in Hegel's aesthetics lies in his treatment of the broad history of arts, yet his discussion of the actual aesthetics of those five arts has received comparatively little attention. It is necessary, therefore, to devote considerable attention to his treatment of each of the arts individually, to examine the extent to which his apparent departure from the aesthetic of the Ideal is actually true, and what corrective needs to be added to make Hegel's aesthetics a coherent and persuasive approach to the nature of the arts.

Part II

The Ethical Nature of the Arts

Chapter 4

Beauty, the Ideal, and Representational Art

Hegel discusses the individual arts in a manner typical of his contemporaries, arranging their treatment according to a hierarchy of dignity. Architecture, as the least representational, is first, while poetry, as the most intellectual, is last. In between lie sculpture, painting, and music—in that order. Moreover, each art is classified according to its essential nature within the historical art forms: he sees architecture as fundamentally symbolic, sculpture as classical, and the rest of the arts as romantic. This makes architecture explicitly the "foundation" of all the arts, revealing the essence of art itself, in spite of its nonrepresentational nature; this is because architecture gives shape to the objective world of nature (*VÄ* 2, 267; *A* 2, 631). Although the other visual arts rely on representation, architecture does not. Music and poetry are not representational in the same sense as the visual arts, but they are held to express something vital to the human spirit. Yet in what sense architecture could be the foundation of the rest of the arts becomes a mysterious assertion if its power lies not in its spiritual nature but in its capacity to present nature itself. To approach Hegel's treatment of the individual arts as a potential source of enlightenment regarding the nature of art seems, therefore, fraught with difficulties. Perhaps for this very reason commentators tend to give only cursory consideration to the individual arts in Hegel's aesthetics.[1] Certainly given Hegel's insistence on the necessity of intelligible content in the arts, one of the representational arts would be a far more likely candidate to reveal the essence of art.

It appears best to begin our examination of Hegel's treatment of the individual arts with those arts that most clearly depend on the prior concept of the Ideal: sculpture and painting. How architecture functions as the foundation of all the arts is best left to the end of the discussion, once the essence of each art has been clarified. Although this order appears to violate the order in which Hegel builds up his discussion of the arts through the art forms, it is the easiest way to understand Hegel's point in identifying architecture as the foundational art. Moreover, it makes it possible to see why Hegel appears not to rely on the Ideal in his discussion of this art in particular, and why it tends to disappear into the background in his treatment of music and poetry. Indeed, the striking characteristic about his discussion of the visual arts of sculpture and painting is that, in spite of the importance he attaches to the classical Ideal and the concept of ideal beauty in sculpture, ideal beauty disappears from his treatment of painting and the romantic Ideal becomes lost in the historical development of the art. Instead, they are replaced by the concept of "characteristic beauty," but at the price of ignoring the long tradition of art theory emphasizing the role of ideal beauty in painting. Attention to the visual arts first takes us to the heart of Hegel's aesthetics in a way clearly connected to the representational nature of those arts. It enables us to confront, at the outset, the issues posed by modernism's denial of beauty and representation.

Hegel's account of sculpture and painting makes their place in historical development central. In his view, sculpture is a classical art; painting is a romantic one. They have not only different aims in the materials employed, but different principles in their representations of the Ideal characteristic of the different eras during which their cultivation captures the essence of the age. Taken together, the history of sculpture and painting offer a complete history of the Spirit from classical times down to Hegel's own day. Shifts in the subject matter reveal the movement of the Spirit from the serene paganism of classical Greece to the Christian paradox of divine bliss in the midst of woe. But while Hegel does not offer any commentary on the development of abstraction, which is the central issue in the wake of modernism, he does point to the unfolding of the romantic spirit in the history of painting in a way that identifies the problem at the core of romantic art. For the original romantic content of the mimetic art of painting, Christ and the saints, gradually gave way to increasing emphasis on secular subjects such as landscape and everyday life. But this increasing secularization of art, beginning already in the Renaissance at the time of the emergence of the art into social prominence, had by the nineteenth century necessarily raised the possibility of the trivialization of subject matter. And in that case, the problem of what kind of art is appropriate to the modern world became a central consideration for aesthetic theory.

It is the development of abstraction that now forces the issue of what kind of art is appropriate in the modern world. In the analytical tradition, modernist aesthetic theories have focused on the passive "appreciation" of form, rather than the active engagement with content. On the one hand, Malcolm Budd, for example, rejects any role of cognition in the pleasure derived from viewing a painting.[2] The subjectivism of artistic value so conceived leaves no room for the cognition of an objective content. On the other hand, Richard Wollheim finds a content in even the most apparently subjectless, nonrepresentational style of the twentieth century, abstract expressionism. What matters for Wollheim is the artist's intention to create artistic value, which is the task of the viewer to discern from the painting and other relevant sources.[3] What makes the artist's intention valuable to the spectator, however, remains mysterious. This is the price paid for the abandonment of the concept of beauty in art, especially the kind of intelligible beauty found in Hegel.[4] For this reason, Hegel's aesthetic of the representational arts has much to recommend it over the modernist approaches of contemporary philosophy.

Hegel's Account of Sculpture as the Quintessential Classical Art

Hegel considers sculpture as the art in which the spiritual is known corporeally in the perfect union of soul and body (*VÄ* 2, 362; *A* 2, 710). This captures the essence of the classical Ideal, which is why Hegel considers sculpture the quintessentially classical art. The spiritual in its complete purity is divinity; the human spirit necessarily retains enough of the particular and accidental that it cannot become purely objective. The task of sculpture, therefore, is the representation of the spiritual in its perfection, and to do that, it must first of all be the representation of divinity "in its infinite peace and sublimity, timeless, immobile, without purely subjective personality and discord of actions and situations" (*VÄ* 2, 364–65; *A* 2, 712). The human spirit, although always consisting in subjective inwardness and self-knowledge, must come to understand itself as just this self-knowledge without inner discord. A representation of the human figure ought to imitate the divine as closely as possible, focusing on what is unalterable rather than the accidental and the transient. Therefore, the figures represented in classical sculpture, whether divine or human, must appear in repose, devoid of relation to anything in the world (*VÄ* 2, 365; *A* 2, 712–13). But this impassivity also follows from the permanence of the sculpted form in its classical material of stone, which suggests the unchanging nature of eternity and the divine. Thus individuality, facial expressions, and any reflection of the inner life of feeling and willing are forbidden to the classical Ideal of absolute repose.

The classical Ideal, therefore, is fully realized in the art of sculpture. The unparticularized character of the spirit, cast in perfect union with corporeal form, creates the Idea of beauty that is the true spirit of classicism (*VÄ* 2, 372–73; *A* 2, 718). This ideal had already been resurrected in the mid-eighteenth century by J. J. Winckelmann in his famous treatise on the superiority of the ancient Greek arts, *Reflections on the Imitation of Greek Works in Painting and Sculpture* (1755). Winckelmann argues that the Greeks portrayed men with "noble simplicity and quiet grandeur" even in the midst of situations of great suffering and agony.[5] The character of unity and calm is the quality of virtue; it is the essential beauty of content which informs and creates the beauty of form. Hegel acknowledged his indebtedness to Winckelmann (*VÄ* 2, 378; *A* 2, 723), although there was one essential difference in their arguments. For Winckelmann, the reason to study the Greeks was to learn from them in order to imitate their soundness of method and beauty of result for the benefit of contemporary culture. For Hegel, however, there could be no such revival; the spirit of classicism could only have been truly realized in the age when the pagan gods were anthropomorphic personalities, so that sculpture embodied the spirituality of the divine in its anthropomorphic form. In this way, the beauty of the classical ideal possessed both universality and individuality (*VÄ* 2, 413; *A* 2, 751).

Hegel emphasizes the placement of sculpture within the larger architectural context of buildings and monuments. Therefore, the characteristic function of classical sculpture conformed to its task as the representation of the classical Ideal: its task of representing the divine to the *polis* meant that it was placed in and on the classical temple. Thus, the single figure of a god was placed inside the temple, whereas a grouping of figures was placed outside as the decoration of the pediment. In the latter, there was action, or indeed, as in the *Laocoön* group, signs of struggle and grief, in spite of which nobility and beauty are preserved (*VÄ* 2, 433–34; *A* 2, 768–69). Thus, Hegel's contention that classical sculpture could not exhibit any subjective emotion is suspect on the basis of one of the most famous examples from antiquity. But since the sculpture appears not to have been of Hellenic, rather than classical Greek provenance, perhaps this excuses it from Hegel's strictures.

Although there are symbolic and Christian stages of the art, the essence of sculpture was best revealed in the classical era. Indeed, Hegel is quite dismissive of Egyptian sculpture in spite of its prefiguring Greek achievements; it lacked the "truth, life, and beauty whereby alone the free work of art becomes ensouled" (*VÄ* 2, 452; *A* 2, 783). Christian sculpture, on the other hand, suffers from a serious inner contradiction in Hegel's view: as a romantic art, it must be concerned with the inner life of the spirit, dealing with grief, sin, and death, as well as love and the deepest human emotions. Yet the permanence of the sculpted form requires a fusion of the external shape with the inner life, such that the latter is accorded a state of permanence that the subjectivity of emotions simply does not have. Thus Christian art lacks the unity of the classical because the development of the inner life of the spirit that is due to the Christian faith leaves its external form "alone in its own particular character without forcing its fusion with the inner and spiritual life, as the ideal of sculpture requires" (*VÄ* 2, 458; *A* 2, 788). Deep emotions such as grief, agony, and love simply cannot find adequate portrayal in the sculpted form; they are more easily depicted in painting. To be sure, sculpture is found in Catholic churches depicting events in the life of Christ, but Hegel, in spite of his praise for a work in Brugge, Belgium, attributed to Michelangelo, does not find Christian sculpture generally able to measure up to the demands of the profundity of spirit matched by the "plastic principle of the Greeks" (*VÄ* 2, 460; *A* 2, 790). According to Hegel, the art simply can not realize the Christian ideal of spiritual depth reconciled with the repose intrinsically demanded by the material of the permanent, sculpted form. One wonders if this is not more a priori deduction than empirical observation.

By this argument, Hegel places the entire history of Christian sculpture into a kind of historical backwater. Even the physical placement of sculpted figures of Christ and the saints within churches is to him relegation to the periphery: rather than occupying the central place in a temple, as did the figures of the Greek gods, these figures are simply adornments of architecture, placed in niches or as bas-reliefs, where they are perceived more as decoration than as objects of devotion (*VÄ* 2, 459; *A* 2, 789). Thus the role and placement of sculpture changed in the Christian era because of the change in the romantic art form's inner principle. Hegel's sudden introduction of classical sculpture into the midst of the Christian era, therefore, raises questions. For while it is certainly true that historically the classical Ideal was maintained from the Renaissance through to the nineteenth century, it must be regarded as an artificial revival according to Hegel's understanding of the history of the Spirit. This, however, ought instead to compel a reexamination of some of Hegel's arguments.

Certainly Hegel can be challenged on each of these arguments regarding sculpture in the romantic era. First, the notion that the subjectivity of emotions resists the permanence of the sculpted form is suspect now for different reasons: Michelangelo's *Pietà* in the Florence Cathedral shows Joseph of Arimathea intently looking on the body of Christ with an expression of both devotion and pity. Surely this is an example of effective sculpture on a Christian subject by an acknowledged master, and equally surely it is hardly unique in effectively conveying emotion frozen in stone. Second, Hegel's assumption that sculpted forms are placed solely around the periphery of Christian churches and are therefore not objects of devotion can also be challenged, for there are sculpted figures placed behind the high altars of churches. To be sure, placing sculptures at the altar is less frequent than the use of paintings, and Hegel may not have known any examples at all. But the issue here is not what Hegel knew, but the truth of his contention; that there are sculpted figures behind the high altars of churches should not be surprising. Nevertheless, it is true that the figures themselves are not objects of devotion, for they are only representations. Christ's real presence, according to Roman Catholic teaching, is in the Eucharistic elements, which are present on the altar itself and are the true objects of devotion.

Hegel also concedes that sculpture in his own era, classical in inspiration, placed figures in locations other than houses of worship: he gives as examples the allegorical figure of Victory on the Brandenburg Gate (executed in 1793) and the figure of Apollo in his chariot on top of the Berlin Opera (*VÄ* 2, 435–36; *A* 2, 770). Classical sculpture, even in the Christian era, therefore has a public role to play in displaying the truth of the Ideal as objective to the population. If Hegel's position regarding the inadequacy of romantic sculpture were true, however, then the public function of sculpture in the Christian world would be cast into doubt. For if the romantic Ideal could not be realized adequately in a publicly displayed form, then civil society would have no model for the Christian Ideal of character in the solid realm of stone or bronze. There would be no permanent marker depicting the union of the divine and the human in Jesus Christ, or the triumph of the saints in their suffering, or the victory of heroes who, in imitating the saints, helped to found a society or to rescue a state from threat of annihilation. There could only be the monument of the church itself, or the temporal, public rituals of opera and drama, but not a visual display around which a community could organize itself. Hegel's criticism of Christian sculpture misses the mark entirely.

One is tempted to say that his is a very Protestant view: the suspicion of religious art looms large here in Hegel's treatment of Christian sculpture. But the role of sculpture need not be artificially restricted to either the classical era or a religious function. For Hegel's central thesis regarding the development of the romantic form of art is its progressive inclusion and ennoblement of the secular as the field of realization of the divine. Thus romantic sculpture ought to be able to show Christ and the saints, if not in their agony, at least in the Ideal of a spiritual perfection. And the secular heroes, political and military, who have guided a society to its present moment ought certainly to be portrayable with a classical repose. In this sense, then, Hegel's aesthetic of sculpture can certainly be extended and corrected. Perhaps most important, however, is a recognition that the sculpted form can indeed show human emotion convincingly, and moreover, portray even the deepest feelings as universal in their occurrence and scope. In short, one could indeed construct an aesthetic of sculpture as the representation of the romantic Ideal in Hegelian terms by denying the tangential thesis that the permanence of stone requires the classical Ideal. That is, one can recognize the achievements of the art in the

Christian era as legitimate examples of a new style derived from a new Ideal. Even such an approach, however, cannot justify the modernist development of abstract sculpted forms, for sculpture demands a spiritual content that is intelligible. That aspect of Hegel's aesthetic of the art follows clearly from the concept of art, and is defensible even today.

Hegel's Account of Painting as a Romantic Art

As he does for sculpture, Hegel makes beauty the central aim of painting. As we have seen, artistic beauty is the mutual adequacy of form and content; it is the necessary aim of art, which has the purpose of unveiling the truth in sensuous form. That is, the shape must be adequate to its task of revealing truth, and so art must seek to be beautiful if it is to be the intelligible representation of truth. But Hegel finds painting a quintessentially romantic art form. It is not only that little of classical drawing or painting survived from Antiquity, so that the art appears to have its history almost entirely within Christian times. More fundamentally, painting's essence, as Hegel understood it, depended on content that could be developed only in a Christian context, with its emphasis on both bliss and grief in their spiritual depth (*VÄ* 3, 20–21; *A* 2, 799–800). Thus the truth of art in the Christian era is the Christian Ideal, found preeminently in the lives of Christ and the saints, and more broadly in the ideals of love and bliss as qualities of character in which love is essentially the sacrifice of personality. Thus, religious art is "the reconciliation of the individual heart with God" in a love that produces peace and bliss in spite of sacrifice and suffering (*VÄ* 3, 41–43; *A* 2, 816–18). Here Hegel makes the romantic Ideal explicitly the foundation of the art of painting.

The difference from the classical ideal is crucial: the agony and loss of sacrifice are not eschewed in favor of an undisturbed repose; instead, the peace and eternal beatitude of the Christian are present together with the agony willingly suffered for the sake of God. Because both are present, the character of the individual is developed much more deeply than in the classical Ideal, for the individual has had to accept both the demands of God and the suffering entailed in this world in order to win eternal peace and bliss. Individuality, therefore, is complex for the Christian: it unites worldly woe and heavenly hope, just as Christ united human with divine nature. In this manner, the saint imitates Christ, and Christian art, in depicting the saint, also participates in the imitation or representation of the truth of the Christian faith. But this means the primacy of place goes to the representation of individuality, which requires an emphasis on narrative wherein personality is made manifest, and on symbolism and allegory as the means of conveying truth. The artist's depiction of action is the vital element because only action explains feeling by making its motive recognizable (*VÄ* 3, 88–89; *A* 2, 854).

According to Hegel, painting is more adequate than sculpture for this task because its medium is more capable of nuance and its means of expression more suited to the complexity of Christian subject matter. Yet Hegel also finds that Christianity validates the world as such, not regarding it simply as a vale of tears or an occasion of woe but beautiful because it was made by God and valid because the Christian life is lived in the world. Hence, secular subjects also have their legitimate place in the representation of Christian truth, indeed even without any implicit references to religious perspectives. Thus, landscape represents "the free life of nature," corresponding to our nature as living beings, and also evokes the moods of nature, providing analogues of emotional states: Hegel invokes "their calm serenity, their fragrant peace, their freshness in spring and deadness in winter, their morning wakening and their evening repose. . . ." The human significance of these aspects of the natural context of life means that landscape painting ought always to strive for a sense of spiritual sympathy with nature, rather than a mere depiction of a scene (*VÄ* 3, 60–61; *A* 2, 831–32). Still life and genre painting (the latter the depiction of everyday life) are subject to the same requirement: they ought always to evoke a spiritual sympathy or the dignity of ordinary activities. Hegel justifies the latter in terms of the artist representing the common life of the nation (*VÄ* 1, 222–23; *A* 1, 169) and calls still life "a triumph of art over the transitory" (*VÄ* 2, 227; *A* 1, 599). Dutch dominance in landscape painting grew out of pride in winning independence from Spain and reclaiming their land from the sea. The Dutch glorified the prosaic subjects of everyday life because of their Protestant view of life. It appears, therefore, that nothing touching humanity is outside the domain of representation in the art of painting.

Yet here is precisely where Hegel's aesthetic of painting challenges the tradition of aesthetic reflection. The romantic Ideal is one of character rather than simply a state of being. Consisting in a joy taken in submission to grief and suffering, it points beyond the simple universality of bliss in the classical Ideal to the unique experience of individuals: for submission, grief, and suffering are inevitably individual experiences, even when collectively shared. The demands of God, the blows of fate, the sorrows of life—all these are uniquely felt by each person who lives through them, even though everyone certainly suffers them in some form. Thus, how a person meets them is a matter of individual character; joy, bliss, and rapture are not procured lightheartedly, but often only tragically. The courage required is always the courage of an individual and the crucial narrative is how such courage is found and developed as a part of one's character. Hence, Hegel claims that the kind of beauty appropriate to the romantic Ideal is "characteristic" beauty, which he specifically contrasts with the classical doctrine of "ideal beauty."

Ideal beauty is the representation of the classical Ideal of physical and mental perfection found preeminently in sculpture, whereas characteristic beauty depends on "the mental and physical particularity of personality" (*VÄ* 3, 100; *A* 2, 863). In depictions of the disciples, saints, and "the sages of antiquity," the beauty of these characters consists in "the power and constancy of courage, faith, and action," so that these emerge not as simply "ideal divinities, but entirely human ideals, not simply men as they should be, but ideal men as they actually" lived and existed (*VÄ* 3, 102; *A* 2, 865). In contrast to sculpture, which could borrow the doctrine of ideal beauty, painting is fundamentally a depiction of such depth of character that it could not be assimilated to such a doctrine. In saying this, Hegel appears to repudiate a large part of the aesthetics of painting since the Renaissance.

The classical Ideal we have already seen Hegel endorse for sculpture is closely related to the concept of "ideal beauty," which was an essential supplement to the concept of art as an imitation of nature. Indeed, Hegel explicitly requires ideal beauty for the art of sculpture, although not for painting (*VÄ* 3, 101; *A* 2, 864). Winckelmann, however, articulates the concept of ideal beauty for both sculpture and painting in his 1755 treatise. In describing art as "the imitation of the beauty of nature," he saw only two possibilities: either the artist imitates only a single object, producing simply a portrait of it, or one "gathers observations of various individual objects and makes of them a whole."[6] The latter leads to "general beauty and to ideal images of it": this was the approach of the ancient Greeks, he believed, and the reason that Winckelmann urged his contemporaries to imitate the ancient Greek effort, rather than the direct imitation of nature. To produce something more beautiful than the model in nature was the true goal of art; in this, the artist had to be guided by divine inspiration to see and to produce "ideal beauty."[7] In articulating this doctrine, Winckelmann's classicism informed an entire generation's return to Greek, rather than Roman, sources for their ideas. Nevertheless, this concept of ideal beauty was part of a longer tradition than would be apparent from an examination of Winckelmann's Greek inspired neoclassicism. That tradition was one that made ideal beauty the foundation of painting as well as sculpture.

For Alberti, already in the fifteenth century, the demands of beauty set limits on what an artist could depict. "So let us always take from Nature whatever we are about to paint, and let us always choose those things that are most beautiful and worthy."[8] For not everything in nature is beautiful; some things should not be painted. Moreover, sometimes beauty is "not to be discovered in one body alone," but must be sought by combining whatever feature of beauty is most praiseworthy in each of several models, "because the merits of beauty are dispersed here and there in many. . . . Therefore excellent parts should all be selected from the most beautiful bodies, and every effort should be made to perceive, understand, and express beauty."[9] Thus the artist is to improve on Nature, rendering his painting more beautiful than reality actually is. This is the doctrine of ideal beauty put into practice.

With this historical background, it is easy to understand the concept of an ideal beauty to be imitated by the artist, whether sculptor or painter. The sculptor should seek the ideal, forming a beauty that ought to exist rather than merely imitating what was already existent in Nature. Sir Joshua Reynolds provides a corroborating doctrine from the perspective of a respected painter in the eighteenth century. Holding that the artist should seek to improve humanity "by the grandeur of his ideas," he found the means of doing so "in correcting the blemishes and defects of natural things" and in making "an abstract idea of their forms more perfect than any one original." This was the "idea of the perfect state of nature, which the Artist called the Ideal Beauty," the guiding principle of genius.[10] This doctrine survived into the nineteenth century and Victor Cousin, in particular, repeated it.[11] It is this concept of ideal beauty against which Hegel argues in his *Aesthetics* as being largely inapplicable to painting.

Yet Winckelmann's treatment of the neoclassical doctrine of ideal beauty shows that it functions as the way of legitimating both the subject matter and the form in painting. For the composition of a painting, like that of a sculpture, cannot be divorced from the subject represented. Hence, Hegel's critique of the concept of ideal beauty as applied to the art of painting is aimed more at the formal aspect: the notion of taking a part from one body and another part from another in order to idealize the subject is, in his view, inappropriate to romantic art, which recognizes the intrinsic dignity of each individual. What Hegel rejected was the concept of perfect repose for romantic subjects that neoclassicists such as Winckelmann superimposed on the concept of beauty. But just for this reason, the Ideal tends to fade from Hegel's account of painting as a romantic art. Instead, there is "characteristic beauty," which does not suggest the bliss of even the romantic Ideal achieved in the midst of suffering. The result is that the success of Hegel's aesthetic of painting is in more serious doubt than his aesthetic of sculpture. Not only are there entire subjects common to the history of painting that do not have much connection with characteristic beauty, but it appears Hegel has abandoned the tradition he seeks to explain in denying the applicability of ideal beauty to painting. Therefore, it is necessary to seek a deeper understanding of both traditional art theory and Hegel's aesthetic of painting to see to what extent Hegel is able to explain the subject matter represented by the art, and what such subject matter implies for painting's artistic configuration.

The Aesthetics of Painting and the Tradition of Representation

As Hegel recognizes, the art of painting emerged into its own with the Renaissance masters. No longer simply an adjunct to religious worship, it developed a full range of subject matter represented, together with new techniques for that representation—most notably, linear perspective. The heart of the aesthetic of painting inherited from the Renaissance was the conviction that narrative subjects were the highest in importance, and that the aim of the narrative was what was both moral and aesthetic. But this is a post-Kantian division of the categories; for Renaissance theorists, the distinction was less between moral content and aesthetic form than between the whole and the parts of the composition; the purpose of representing Ideal beauty informed both.

Leon Battista Alberti's treatise, *On Painting* (1435), offers one of the most influential examples of the Renaissance aesthetic, as well as the earliest. It opens with instruction in linear perspective, advances to evidence for the dignity of the art, and concludes with how things are seen. Thus, Alberti's treatise appears to depend simply on the new technical discovery of linear perspective, which he and Brunelleschi had developed. This appears further confirmed in the third part of the treatise in which Alberti discusses first the drawing of the outline of objects in the framework provided by linear perspective, which he calls "circumscription." The second component of the art of seeing is composition, the placement of the people in a narrative painting, or "historia." The third is the "reception of light," including use of light and dark, and the harmony and variety of colors. Aesthetics are almost subsumed under technical advice.

In contrast, Hegel discusses the aspect of linear perspective under the heading of the sensuous material of painting. In his view, painting requires linear perspective in order to present its appropriate romantic subject matter. But because the painted surface is flat, a painting "must proceed to a mode of presentation which has to make apparent to us the distance between objects in all three spatial dimensions." It does not suffice for the art to present merely symbols or icons, after the manner of Byzantine painting, but rather must place the subject matter "before our eyes in its manifold movement, and to bring figures into a varied connection with their external natural landscape, or with buildings, the rooms they are in" (*VÄ* 3, 67; *A* 2, 837). Thus, Hegel explains the necessity of perspective in terms of a deficiency with respect to the reality sculpture portrays: painting can, and therefore must, represent only the appearance of reality.

This brief explanation contains within it the crucial insight: the subject matter of romantic painting displays movement. This is because romantic painting is essentially a narrative art. Thus, it is the quality of the narrative which demands the development of perspective. The two go hand in hand: historically, they developed simultaneously in the Renaissance, and this is why Alberti begins his treatise with a discussion of the technical aspect of drawing in linear perspective before proceeding to a discussion of the aesthetics of painting in which he emphasized the supreme importance of the historia, or narrative. Hence, romantic art, which represents above all the inner character in conflict with, and in response to the world, must, if it is to be true to its concept, represent character in narrative. It is possible for an icon to stand for a well-known story—as in Byzantine iconography—but the art of painting develops itself to its fullest potential only in narrative painting. As Hegel puts it, painting "only begins on its proper task when it departs from the relationless independence of its figures and from lack of definiteness in the situation, in order to be able to enter the living movement of human circumstances, passions, conflicts, and actions . . . " (*VÄ* 3, 89; *A* 2, 854). That is to say: painting's proper task is the representation of personality in confrontation with the world. Its beauty is "characteristic beauty."

Hegel's point illuminates Alberti's praise of the "historia," or narrative, as constituting true greatness in the art, and intimately linked with its beauty: "As the most important part of the painter's work is the 'historia,' in which there should be every abundance and beauty of things, we should take care to learn to paint well. . . . "[12] But the historia has parts: bodies and their members, and the members have surfaces, which the painter paints. Beauty arises from the composition of surfaces; it consists in the "elegant harmony and grace of bodies" (*concinnitas*).[13] Thus the narrative purpose of painting must aim at beauty in the composition, demanding variety of bodies and colors, dignity and modesty of depiction, depiction of emotion to arouse the sympathy of the viewer, and harmony and grace in the physical motions represented.[14] Beauty in the composition entails both the formal elements of harmony and grace and the ethical elements of dignity and modesty in appearance. But the effect of the art must be ethical as well, for the sympathy Alberti requires is to mourn with those who mourn, to grieve with those who grieve, and to "laugh with those who laugh."[15] The artist must aim to interest and please his public and he must go beyond the merely interesting to the ethical. This is why the narrative aspect is so important: only a narrative has the capacity to arouse sympathy by depicting a definite object of emotion. Beauty is an integral part of such a narrative's representation.

Subsequent theorists developed many of the same points, employing the Platonic concept of beauty to integrate the conceptual purpose and ethical nature of painting with aesthetic issues of composition. In the sixteenth century, Giovanni Paolo Lomazzo relied on the Neo-Platonic writings of Marsilio Ficino to make the same point, explicitly invoking the Platonic idea in connection with beauty. In *The Idea of the Temple of Painting* (1590), he quotes Ficino's definition of beauty:

> First, we must realize that beauty is nothing else than a certain living and spiritual grace which through divine ray infuses itself first into the angels . . . [and becomes the Platonic] exemplars and ideas. Beauty then

> passes into souls, where the figures are called reasons and thoughts, and finally into matter, where it creates images and forms. There beauty gives pleasure to all by means of reason and sight. . . .[16]

The latter is of greatest importance for the aesthetic of painting, for the beauty of forms in matter is the beauty of bodies. But here the beauty of the body has a definition similar to that in Alberti: it is "nothing else than a certain action, liveliness, and grace," in which the Platonic idea shines through the matter prepared for it by the formal elements of "order, mode, and species," or arrangement, quantity, and lines and colors.[17] This Neo-Platonic formulation was crucial for the neoclassical tradition in the Baroque. Again, the result was to emphasize the transcendent nature of the beauty sought by the painter: the beauty of grace is an ineffable radiance from the realm of the divine.[18] The great French painter, Nicholas Poussin, relied heavily on Lomazzo for his own formulation of the theory of painting while emphasizing the importance of great narrative subjects.[19] Eventually, the role of beauty subsumed the narrative content as well as the manner of representation.[20] Thus the concept of beauty, in which the beauty of the subject matter represented infuses the forms on the canvas, is of crucial importance to the practice of painting in the great tradition coming out of the Renaissance.

We see, therefore, that Hegel's Idea of beauty, in embracing both intelligible content and artistic configuration, is faithful to the tradition of theoretical reflection on the art of painting. Hegel's explanation provides powerful justification for regarding the traditional aesthetic as more persuasive than the contemporary emphasis on abstract form and the artist's intentionality. Hegel provides good reason to regard painting as necessarily representational in order to provide perceptible content; abstraction does not answer to the need for art that has as its aim the representation of the Ideal of bliss achieved through reconciliation to the divine. Nor will doctrines of merely emotional expression or materiality suffice to define the aims of the art, for emotions embodied in a painting are subordinate to the narrative represented, and the materials employed—whether oil or watercolor, for example—are simply means to an end. But the necessity of a narrative does establish criteria for the sensuous means of representation, in particular, the necessity of linear perspective. It was the development of this technical feat that allowed painting to assume such importance during the Renaissance, that indeed allowed narrative subjects to predominate over icon-like portraits.

Such a narrative purpose, however, is not the same as storytelling in literature. For painting represents only a crucial moment of an action, freezing it in time and allowing the viewer to ponder the ramifications of the action and the emotions of the characters portrayed. Indeed, Hegel emphasizes that the difference between art and reality lies in the contemplative way in which the viewer is invited to respond. If seeing is liberated from all practical considerations, then art can elevate ordinary subjects to a level worthy of contemplation. Subjects become ends in themselves so that even the everyday world becomes a subject worthy of painting. As a consequence of this elevation, the romantic Ideal evidences a disintegration in Hegel's account of the history of romantic art. The legitimacy of subject matter other than narrative, therefore, remains a problem for both Hegel and the tradition, for it is not clear that landscape, still life, or genre studies are best analyzed in terms of either the romantic Ideal or the Platonic Idea of beauty as including narrative. This points to the dilemma raised by Hegel's historicist understanding of the development of art and the types of subjects represented in painting through its history.

The Problem of Historicism in Romantic Painting

Hegel's account of the art of painting recognizes the uniqueness of its development since the Renaissance, so that for whatever difficulties his aesthetic poses for a proper appreciation of earlier art, he succeeds in explaining the rise of an art that was always understood to be fundamentally narrative in intent. Yet it would not do to minimize the difficulties this generalization poses even for romantic painting since the Renaissance: for there were other subjects, such as landscape, still life, genre studies, and portraiture. If these are to be understood as attaining any validity, the emphasis on narrative must be modified. Moreover, even Hegel's concept of the characteristic beauty of the individual personality does not account for landscape and still life, and perhaps only marginally for genre studies. Finally, the historical development of these other kinds of subject matter poses the same difficulty for painting already seen in romantic art in general: the Ideal is seen to disappear progressively. Thus, the complexity of the historical world threatens to undermine Hegel's aesthetic of painting. At its heart lies the problem of secularity within the context of historicism.

The emergence of secular subjects was a historical development of the seventeenth century. Since the romantic Ideal is preeminently religious, it is no surprise that the role and content of painting was often religious in the early Renaissance period. Only later, as a product of the Renaissance, did secular subjects emerge: initially, mythological subjects drawn from classical sources (which Hegel does not discuss) then landscape, first as background then in its own right beginning in the early seventeenth century in Belgium and flourishing in the Netherlands by the end of that century. Still life and genre studies also emerged at the same time. The importance of the secular only increased in the eighteenth and nineteenth centuries; thus any philosophical account of the diversity of types of painting must explain the appropriateness of these subjects or provide a reason for their rejection. Otherwise, Hegel's claim for the centrality of the Ideal, even in secular art, is inevitably empty.

Hegel's account of the history of painting emphasizes the increasing secularity of subject matter from the high Renaissance forward. In the early Renaissance, "sanctity approached reality," in that sacred subjects were represented in contemporary, increasingly realistic settings. In the later Renaissance, however, "painting proceeded more and more to associate life in the external world with religious subjects," sanctifying the secular (*VÄ* 3, 120; *A* 2, 879). Hence the development of landscape, views of cities, and portraiture—even in religious art. Hegel attributes this development to the new spirit of Italian cities, in which self-reliance, industriousness, freedom, courage and patriotism, and enjoyment of civic life constituted the virtues celebrated in painting, together with specifically religious themes. The new importance of civil society in the sixteenth century led to a new respect for secularity in general.

The painters of the northern Renaissance, however, developed their art in ways which emphasized the secular world all the more. For Flemish, Dutch, and German painters, there was no longer "an exclusive inner preoccupation with the interests of faith and the salvation of the soul," but also an interest in showing how individuals are troubled by affairs of this world and how they have acquired "mundane virtues, fidelity, steadfastness, integrity, chivalrous tenacity, and civil efficiency" (*VÄ* 3, 124; *A* 2, 882). Consequently, northern European painting lacked "the beauty of form and freedom of soul" found in Italian painting, depicting instead inner torment and the ugliness of the world, especially in images of the Passion of Christ. Thus, the northern Renaissance—also associated with a revival of civil society—produced a much wider range of subject matter than the Italian Renaissance, and in doing so often appeared to forsake the goal of beauty in painting altogether.

Here it is important to recognize a point that Hegel fails to make explicit. In listing the "mundane virtues" depicted in northern Renaissance painting, he identifies fidelity, chivalrous tenacity, integrity, and the like; but these are precisely the ideals of character associated with the development of the Christian Ideal he discusses earlier in the *Aesthetics*: honor, fidelity, and chivalrous duty. Although the field of action depicted by northern Renaissance painters is more explicitly and more frequently secular than in Italian Renaissance painting, nevertheless the same development of a civic consciousness forms the subject of the art, and the virtues portrayed within the secular realm are the qualities of character which the Christian faith produces when the field of action is secular rather than religious. Thus, the religious foundation of northern Renaissance art remains a central, if not explicit element, and the concept of characteristic beauty retains its ethical dimension.

Hegel perceived, however, that art in his own day lacked this religious foundation. He also perceived this was a historical development of the northern Renaissance, which retained an implicitly religious foundation, but which led progressively to the elimination of it and therefore to a much greater variety of subjects and styles of treatment. His explanation was the success of the Reformation, which removed the typical artistic expressions of piety in the churches. Hence, the new piety took the form of finding "joy in the world as such," including natural objects, domestic life, national celebrations, and country life. These are celebrated in Dutch art in particular because the Dutch, having won political independence from Spain and religious independence from Rome, attained a condition of bourgeois comfort through their characteristically pious, unassuming self-respect (*VÄ* 3, 127–29; *A* 2, 885–86). The Dutch "wishes now in painting too to delight in this existence which is as powerful as just, satisfying, and comfortable; in its pictures it wishes to enjoy once again in every possible situation the neatness of its cities, houses, and furnishings, as well as its domestic peace, its wealth," and its brilliance of culture. Hence, the Dutch cultivated above all landscape, genre studies of everyday and family life, and still life painting, all with a dignified cheerfulness and naivety (*VÄ* 3, 129–30; *A* 2, 887). Hegel finds this an essentially comic vision—although it may be difficult to reconcile that assessment with its religious origins in the Calvinist Netherlands. Because they are secular subjects, however, the religious origins recede into the background and eventually disappear altogether. By the nineteenth century, landscape was indeed the most popular subject.

A different way of stating these developments would be as follows: if the classical Ideal demanded sculpture as the most suitable mode of realization, and the romantic Ideal the art of painting, then it is nonetheless true that the classical Ideal fails to exhibit a true history in Hegel's account, while the romantic mode, being thoroughly historicized, fails to exhibit any stability of an Ideal. Whether the romantic art form is capable of sustaining any analysis based on an inner principle may indeed be doubted. Hegel's aesthetic of painting thus reintroduces all the problems of his historicist view of the arts. It is tempting to say that the history of painting, as well as the other arts, in the twentieth century only confirms the weakness of searching for an inner explanatory principle of history. Pure historicism is likely to appear far more convincing, leaving the aesthetics of painting in need of some other explanatory principle. Yet attention to the problems posed by some contemporary aesthetics of painting argues for the need for such an explanatory principle. The emphasis in the traditional theory of painting on the importance of narrative may yet prove a needed corrective to the problems posed by a merely historicist acceptance of whatever has been created.

In light of the overwhelming weight attached to high-minded narrative art in the theoretical tradition on which Hegel's aesthetic implicitly depends, the problem of the multiplicity of subject matter in the art of painting again demands attention. Whereas that tradition dismisses all subjects not centered on the human figure, Hegel strains his argument in order to vindicate the historical development of types of subject matter not easily accommodated to his system. For genre scenes of everyday life, pure landscape without human figures, and still life appear to be trivializations of painting, especially inasmuch as the latter two types depart entirely from a study in narrative or character. Hegel himself also points to the development of a transition from subjects of piety "to the portrayal of torments and the ugliness of the world generally" in the work of north German masters, who often represent scenes from Christ's Passion with a depiction of malignity and barbarity—although Dürer preserved the representation of "inner nobility" (*VÄ* 3, 126–27; *A* 2, 883–84). Hegel emphasizes the early nature of these developments: it was the Renaissance itself which discovered many of these at the same time the Italians were painting scenes of harmoniousness and reverential piety. Thus, Hegel explains these anomalies in terms of their different national origins, and in particular, as a result of the Reformation. Nevertheless, whether realism was a creation of the northern Renaissance or the product of the Reformation, Hegel argues that it is possible to find a "taking of joy" in the natural world or a cheerfulness in genre scenes; he also points to a religious symbolism in still life painting.

Yet it is clear that many of the results of realism bothered Hegel. He could praise the Dutch masters, and say, "In their paintings we can study and get to know men and human nature," but in the very next sentence lament that in his own day, portraits and historical paintings, despite all realism, show that the artist did not know human nature (*VÄ* 3, 131; *A* 2, 887). Such realism was lacking in characteristic beauty.

Hegel's earlier remarks on the contemplative way of seeing which painting both cultivates and requires point to a solution to the difficulties his aesthetic of representation raises. For if the purpose of painting is to make the subjects represented ends unto themselves, so that the viewer is invited to contemplate a reality devoid of practical considerations, then the development of secular subjects is easy to explain and the emergence and popularity of nonnarrative subjects such as still life and landscape can be legitimated. It is only necessary that subjects be taken from real life and subjected to the criterion of beauty. It is not necessary to invoke the development of the Ideal into a post-Reformation secular consciousness in order to justify the emergence of landscape painting. Nevertheless, an artistic culture (such as exists today), in which only landscape survives as the typical representational art form, might well be suspected of lacking somewhat in seriousness. Nonnarrative subjects have their place in Hegel's account, as they did historically, but only in the larger context of an artistic practice of painting that allowed the full expression of the Ideal in historical subjects, religious narratives, and ancient mythology. Certainly these dominated the art of painting from the Renaissance through to the nineteenth-century academic tradition.

Hence, it would be well to ask if Hegel's core position regarding the romantic Ideal does not offer insight into both the predominant tradition of narrative art since the Renaissance as well as the strange world of artistic culture in the twentieth century. For historicism's account of the increasing secularization of painting and the increasing popularity of landscape and other subject matter far removed from the romantic Ideal need not be taken as an altogether faithful development of the romantic Ideal, even in their celebration of the beauty and dignity of the world. While the goodness of the world as God's creation is fundamental to Christian teaching, the romantic Ideal as Hegel conceives it requires above all a representation of the beauty of character; this in turn demands a fundamentally narrative context. Moreover, with regard to developments in painting since the twentieth century, historicism need not be taken as justifying their development any more than it did for Hegel, who was critical of many developments in the arts of his own day. Thus, as high culture painting is exclusively abstract in nature, and popular culture painting exclusively nonnarrative though representational, the nature of the art appears riven between two equally unsatisfactory positions. Both render the subject depicted as of little or no importance and have the inevitable tendency to trivialize the art. Equally for sculpture: the rise of abstract sculpture and the decline in the representation of significant religious figures or historical political heroes render that art trivial as well. Without significant intellectual content, the significance of art inevitably tends to disappear.

Only a concept of the Ideal, in which beauty is the adequacy of the form to the intelligible content, will succeed in justifying the representational arts to public attention. This Hegel's aesthetic provides: the ideals of religious belief, historical events, heroism, and the value of family and civic life afford a content that is at once universal and capable of infinite particularization. The representational arts have the obligation to set before us what we essentially are—that is, the end to which we ought to aspire—by showing what is the object of faith, what is best in the history of human achievement, and what is worth remembering in the characters of our families and our cities. The concept of the Ideal was once vital to the articulation of such purposes in both painting and sculpture; without it, the visual arts pale into insignificance and desuetude. Hegel's aesthetic, therefore, deserves to be taken seriously as a vindication of a substantive intellectual content in these arts, and of their relevance to a world in which a shared civic life and shared beliefs have their proper value.

Chapter 5

The Sounds of the Ideal

If sculpture and painting maintain a close link to classical and romantic Ideals, respectively, music presents a much more ambiguous, if not puzzling, case in Hegel's aesthetics. Like painting, music is considered a romantic art, one that, like painting, came into its own only in the Renaissance. Yet the connection with the Ideal is not at all obvious at first glance. Moreover, whereas painting exhibits a richly developed history in Hegel's account, music appears not to have the same historical development. Thus the art of music appears much less nuanced than painting. This is somewhat surprising, given the importance attached to this art by Hegel's contemporaries, for the early nineteenth century was precisely the time when the operatic canon was transformed by Weber and Rossini, and the symphonic canon was defined as beginning with the works of Haydn, Mozart, and Beethoven. But if Hegel's aesthetic is to account for the nature of all the arts, then it behooves us to examine his discussion of music in more detail. Perhaps there is more of a connection with the Ideal than appears at first glance, and more awareness of the historical development of the art that has proven so crucial to the success of music from the so-called Classical and Romantic periods. If so, then Hegel's musical aesthetic must be taken far more seriously than it has been.

As in the case of the other individual arts, Hegel's treatment of music has received comparatively little attention. It has generally been regarded as not very satisfactory, a condition shared by other idealist philosophies of music.[1] Yet Hegel was more qualified than most philosophers of his day to discuss music. It is known that he sang in a choral group; he attended operas by Gluck, Mozart, Rossini, and Weber; and he heard performances of symphonies and string quartets by Haydn and Mozart.[2] Nevertheless, his remarks on music have been dismissed as the product of someone who knew very little about music and who had little sympathy for the newer genres and styles of music.

The important question, however, is whether or not Hegel's aesthetic of music makes sense musically and if it is philosophically coherent. If so, then his arguments would be of more significance than has been recognized. In fact, they reveal the principles and aims of the art of music as it was practiced in his day, and as it continued to be understood by many critics in the nineteenth century. Hegel's aesthetic poses a challenge, however, to the prevailing ahistorical ways of understanding music in the twentieth century, in which music becomes defined in terms of sound, the least common denominator accommodating both tonal tradition and the practices of modernism. Precisely because Hegel provides a philosophical argument justifying specific musical practices of the tradition dating back to the Renaissance, it cannot anticipate the developments of twentieth-century modernism: the emergence of atonality, the prevalence of dissonance, the deemphasis and often complete disappearance of melody, and the development of aleatoric practices. It is not simply that Hegel occupies a limited historical place in musical aesthetics; rather, he provides a way of conceiving a critique of modernism that makes fundamental the question of what music is. Perhaps, indeed, such an implicit critique is one reason for the neglect of Hegel's idealist aesthetics generally.

An idealist aesthetic of music is not necessarily easy to sustain. Hegel's musical sense has often been questioned because his aesthetic defines art as the representation of a content, leading to a dilemma that is especially troublesome for instrumental music. On the one hand, a content is easy to specify in the case of vocal music, since the text gives what the music usually expresses. But in the case of instrumental music, a theory of music as the expression of a content may require a devaluation of instrumental music for its apparent lack of content.[3] On the other hand, such a theory appears to impose content on instrumental music that it simply does not have. As one commentator concludes, Hegel's view "represents a total misunderstanding of the nature of music, by demanding a 'content' or meaning which is not there."[4] And if instrumental music is "pure" music—music purely and simply, as Hanslick claims[5]—then to assume that vocal music expresses its text may be to misconstrue the nature of music in that case as well.

This critique of idealist musical aesthetics is rooted in formalism, a position completely at odds with the main traditions of musical interpretation and aesthetics in the eighteenth and nineteenth centuries, the very time that gave birth to the repertoire of orchestras and opera houses that remains standard today. These traditions insist on the expressive nature of music, giving music a content of affections, emotions, or character. The ascription of content to instrumental music lay at the heart of cultural expectations that helped shape the standard repertoire. Only the prevalence of formalist aesthetics in the twentieth century has obscured that fact and thereby made it difficult to understand the cultural significance of instrumental music. But Hegel shared this much in common with the musical tradition: he saw in music a representation of a subjective content that is given concrete form.

The Challenge of Hegel's Idealism

The coherence of Hegel's aesthetic of music may be questioned on the matter of the connection between his remarks about art in general and his treatment of music in particular. In spite of the fact that he begins by defining art as the representation of the Ideal, at first glance there is little connection between his analysis of music and the discussion of the Ideal. There is only one passage where he speaks of "ideal music," which he identifies as "the melodic expression of Palestrina, Durante, Lotti, Pergolesi, Gluck, Haydn, Mozart" (*VÄ* 3, 198; *A* 2, 939). Emotional restraint and "tranquillity of soul" are the qualities he prizes in these otherwise disparate composers, but there appears to be no factor other than personal taste involved in the selection of these composers from the Renaissance (Palestrina), Baroque (Durante, Lotti, and Pergolesi), and Classical eras (Gluck, Haydn, Mozart); in particular, there appears to be a reluctance to connect specific elements in their musical styles with the earlier grounding of the *Aesthetics* in the Ideal.[6] Some famous names are curiously missing: Corelli, Handel, and Bach, from the Baroque era that he seems to prefer together with the Classical era over his contemporaries. Beethoven presumably might have been too wild or too untranquil to suit Hegel (assuming he might have heard his music). Thus, while the connection between the Ideal as serenity or bliss and ideal music as emotionally restrained and tranquil is clear enough, the reliance on personal taste and impressionistic claims about styles would seem to weaken his argument. But since Hegel's claim, that philosophy has something to say about what art is, and since art is a contingent product of human consciousness, a retreat to merely personal taste would be nothing less than a tacit confession that the contingencies of artistic creation and taste overrule any purely philosophical deduction. Such a contradiction in the enterprise of the *Aesthetics* would be astonishing. There is good reason, therefore, to reexamine Hegel's aesthetic of music in light of his larger argument, for the question of the ideal in music must be related to the Ideal as Hegel defines it.

Hegel considers music one of the romantic arts: that is, it manifests the principles of the specifically Christian or romantic Ideal. Certainly the historical musical styles Hegel has identified as illustrating ideal music took shape within the context of Christian culture, and the Western musical tradition can be traced no further back in time than the Middle Ages. Moreover, many of the composers he names as "ideal" are famous for their religious music. The purity of Palestrina's counterpoint is exemplary of the Catholic Counter-Reformation and the model for all composers through Beethoven for learning the art of counterpoint. But the Christian religion, having both raised the individual to a new status of infinite worth in the sight of God and given recognition to man's need for reconciliation to God, has implications for art. For, as we have seen, love became the Ideal of art in the Christian era. It produced a conception of spiritual beauty and submission to God which yielded "a joy in submission, a bliss in grief and rapture in suffering, even a delight in agony." Hegel notes that these qualities are found in the (Catholic) religious music of Italy (*VÄ* 1, 209; *A* 1, 158). He sees them as determinative for all music that befits the Christian era.

The result is an approach to music that is predisposed to seek qualities other than what twentieth-century formalist aesthetics has found valuable. Hegel regards sacred music as the expression of the religious feelings of the Church,[7] and takes the dramatic nature of opera seriously; the virtues of love, friendship, and honor are determinative for the pure and noble quality of the passions expressed in the music of Gluck and Mozart (*VÄ* 3, 207–8; *A* 2, 946–47). Analogously, then, instrumental music is easily perceived as the expression of feeling as well.[8] But the ascription of a subjective content to music is not merely an assumption based upon a "logocentrism" peculiar to Hegel, for it is man as a rational being who necessarily seeks a conceptual understanding of all acts and all relationships with things.[9] Thus Hegel offers a philosophical argument: the dimension of time is the only dimension in which music exists as it is performed. It therefore lacks the quality of physical objectivity that the formative arts possess and the conceptual objectivity that literature can possess. It is instead the pure art of "subjective inwardness" (*VÄ* 3, 133; *A* 2, 889). The very nature of sound enables it to become "a mode of expression adequate to the inner life," and because it lacks objects, "on this account what alone is fitted for expression is the object-free inner life, abstract subjectivity as such" (*VÄ* 3, 135; *A* 2, 891). But the inner life "has as its first differentiation the one that music is connected with, namely feeling" (*VÄ* 3, 150; *A* 2, 902). Certainly there is more to music than simply the expression of feeling, but that is its foundation.

Therefore, for this approach to yield a useful and coherent aesthetic of music, Hegel must explain the following:

- what specific forms music requires in order to be an art of expression;
- the specific means by which music can be expressive of feeling; and
- the connection between the musical expression of feeling and the Ideal.

If Hegel is successful, the result will vindicate the relevance of the traditional category of beauty to the understanding of music.

The Expressive Forms of Music

Today, the possibility of defining the formal requirements of any art is generally held to be impossible. The diversity of styles within the twentieth century alone seems to argue against such an undertaking, so that it often appears safest to define an art by the medium it employs rather than by its form or purpose. Hence, music becomes an art of sounds in textbook definitions and allows no discrimination between sounds that are music and those that are not. Since some composers refuse to make such a distinction, this state of affairs has the appearance of being necessitated by historical developments. In fact, however, such an approach is profoundly ahistorical, for it ignores the traditions by which music was cultivated and understood for many centuries. It imposes on music from all times the definitional criteria of the present, as if the imperious demand to accommodate the radically new sounds created by avant-garde composers must also require altering historical aesthetic understanding. But the modernist avant-garde aesthetic is nothing less than a rupture with the past that cannot be glossed over by any ideology of historical necessity.[10] The most that can be said is that the definition of music differs in the twentieth-century avant-garde from that of earlier centuries; it remains an open question whether such a difference is philosophically justifiable. We can say, however, that the definition of music in terms of sound alone contains no clue as to the value or significance of the art. It is as philosophically empty as it is historically unjustifiable.

Thus when Hegel takes the trouble to define the basic material of which music is composed, he is not engaged in an idle exercise. Music requires tones, not merely sounds, and tones have definite pitches with definite timbres and definite durations. This is not simply a matter of tradition or convention; he argues that it must necessarily be so, for music is "not to be purely a natural shriek of feeling but the developed and artistic expression of it" (*VÄ* 3, 159; *A* 2, 910). Unless feeling is transformed into a specific form, it cannot be said to be art. This insistence on form as the defining characteristic of artistic representation is vital lest the notion of musical expression be misunderstood, for only the form of language or music separates the universality of ideas from mere interjections (*VÄ* 3, 151; *A* 2, 903). The definition of the material of music follows, then, from the definition of music as an art of expression. But the insistence on the material as having a specific artistic form is vital: tones are the form that is necessary to the particular content of music.

Nevertheless, considered merely by themselves, tones are not sufficient to constitute a work of musical art. They must be ordered in relationships that possess perceptible coherence—temporally, harmonically, and melodically. The temporal coherence of music is guaranteed by regular patterns of accented and unaccented beats, just as in poetic meters; they are the ordering of the passing of time, which would otherwise be indeterminate and incomprehensible. The regular repetition of accents, like that of columns in classical architecture, creates a uniformity "in which self-consciousness finds itself again as a unity..." (*VÄ* 3, 166; *A* 2, 915); the unity of musical meter corresponds to the fundamental unity of the self in time and indeed helps to raise the unity of the self to self-consciousness. Again, this argument deserves attention in light of the twentieth century's rejection of metrical order in architecture, poetry, and music. The constantly shifting meters of Stravinsky's *Rite of Spring* established a precedent for much of music in the past century; even the retention of a minimal melodic interest was vitiated by metrical incoherence. But if the arts present a world that is free of order, then the world is not only incomprehensible, but alien and hostile, a place in which no one can feel at home.[11] Hegel's argument is therefore a profound insight, an explanation of why there is a tradition of metrical order in so many arts, as well as an explanation of the powerful appeal of well-ordered music. Of course, a simple beat in itself is of no artistic value; rather, the meter enables the music to possess rhythmic variety that is comprehensible precisely because it takes place within a framework of order (*VÄ* 3, 170; *A* 2, 918). Thus meter is only the foundation of musical coherence.

The harmonic coherence of music has always been more central to discussions of musical theory and aesthetics. Hegel repeats the traditional understanding that the relationship between two tones is governed by numerical ratios, and that some intervals necessarily sound better than others because they have simpler proportions. Hence, an octave (the simplest perfect consonance), has the ratio of 2:1, whereas the major second, a dissonance, has the ratio of 9:8. The perception of consonance and dissonance is fundamental to both the ordering of tones in the diatonic scale and the expressive character of those tones in relation to the tonic. The scale provides the underlying tonal unity in a piece of music; some tones "harmonize directly with the keynote" (the tonic), while others, which are active, require resolution because they are dissonant with the tonic triad (*VÄ* 3, 179; *A* 2, 925).[12] Thus, distinguishing between consonance and dissonance is a necessary condition for maintaining tonal unity in music, and that unity is essential for tonal coherence.

In the twentieth century, every attempt has been made to deny the necessity of tonality as the foundation of musical coherence and to assert that the pervasive use of dissonance has no effect on the perception of coherence.[13] Such claims have produced music audiences do not want to hear, and they are surely false.[14] What Hegel provides is a way of understanding why: coherence is not only a property imposed on a musical work by a composer through the relatedness of motives, themes, or a series of intervallic relationships. Rather, it is a quality that must be acknowledged as inhering in the tonal materials themselves. This helps shape what the composer may do in a musical work. The unity of tonality is not merely a natural phenomenon, although it certainly is that, but more crucially the logically necessary condition of tonal coherence. Similarly, the tonal simplicity of consonance is naturally perceptible and must introduce an implicit order that is the foundation of any higher order of coherence. Without consonance as the norm and a tonic as the goal of all harmonic motion, music would be lacking in the order and unity essential to any art.[15] What Hegel explains is why tonal unity is necessary. This also explains (long before the emergence of the modernist avant-garde), why atonal music cannot be considered art by any definition that requires coherence. His aesthetic has an even greater relevance to our present aesthetic dilemmas than it had to the art of music in Hegel's own day.

Harmonic order, however, like metrical order, is still not sufficient to define the art of music. It is melody that is the essence of music, the primary carrier of expression and the principal focus of a listener's attention. It is the freest element in music, yet it is bound to the laws of harmony and meter, and it must possess its own particular coherence: "Accordingly, melody is the infinite determinability and possibility of the advance of the notes, but it must be so regulated that what we apprehend is always an inherently total and perfect whole" (*VÄ* 3, 189; *A* 2, 933). Thus, Hegel argues that melody is vital to music, and melodic coherence is a necessary formal requirement. In saying this, he does not differ from the prevailing understanding of music in the eighteenth and nineteenth centuries; even Hanslick argued for the primacy of melody and the necessity of "organic, rational coherence."[16]

Unlike the formalist Hanslick, however, Hegel saw in melody "the poetic element in music, the language of the soul, which pours out into the notes the inner joy and sorrow of the heart, and in this outpouring mitigates and rises above the natural force of feeling by turning the inner life's present transports into an apprehension of itself. . . ." Thus music is by no means simply the tonal art of the expression of feeling. It is a means of self-apprehension and cathartic liberation "from the pressures of joys and sorrows" (*VÄ* 3, 185; *A* 2,

929–30). This is an extremely important point. For now, it is sufficient to note that the expressive nature of music requires melodic coherence: only by having a definite beginning, middle, and end "does melody correspond to that free self-subsistence of subjective life which it is its task to express" (*VÄ* 3, 190; *A* 2, 933). Once again, Hegel's arguments call into question the twentieth century's repudiation of melody along with other forms of order and expressiveness.

The Means of Musical Expression

Nevertheless, if claims for music's expressive power are to be vindicated, it must be through some generally recognized system of signification. Particular feelings that music can express include "all nuances of cheerfulness and serenity, the sallies, moods, and jubilations of the soul, the degrees of anxiety, misery, mourning, lament, sorrow, grief, longing, etc., and lastly, of awe, worship, love, etc." (*VÄ* 3, 150; *A* 2, 903). Given the specificity of these nuances, it would take a fairly well-developed language of musical signs to convey these to listeners, who would have to be well-trained enough both to perceive them and to recognize their meanings. It is with good reason that a substantial portion of Hegel's discussion is devoted to elucidating the means of musical expression. It is an integral part of any aesthetic of expression.

The tonal material of which music is composed constitutes the most codifiable element for a language of expression. The sense that dissonance is "opposition" and consonance is "harmony" is easily made into a metaphor of tension and repose of the soul. When Hegel gives as an example the use of sevenths and ninths to express grief (*VÄ* 3, 183; *A* 2, 928), he is describing the musical tradition since the late Renaissance, which was rooted in this kind of natural metaphor of dissonance to express pain. The most influential musical theorist of the eighteenth century, Jean-Philippe Rameau, specified how dissonant chords were expressive of tenderness, lamentation, suffering, and despair.[17] Thus Hegel was musically knowledgeable enough to make his philosophy of music consistent with the prevailing theory of music.

The other expressive capacities of the diatonic scale within the context of tonality are the differences between the major and minor modes and the pitch of the tonic itself. He compares modern keys with ancient Greek modes—a traditional exercise—and thereby justifies the expressive nature of key by analogy with the expressive nature of the modes described by Plato, Aristotle, and others. Hegel does not elaborate on the expressive nature of keys except to claim that "they have a specific character which corresponds again on its side to a particular mode of feeling, e.g., to sorrow, joy, grief, incitation to courage, etc." (*VÄ* 3, 180; *A* 2, 926). Again, this is a summary account of an elaborate theory concerning keys and their meanings. That major keys generally correspond to happiness and courage, and minor keys to sorrow and passion, was widely recognized since the Renaissance and is one of the fundamental elements in musical expression. But by the time Hegel delivered his lectures, a much more detailed treatment of key levels and their expressive characters had been published: that of C. F. D. Schubart, in 1806.[18] It is often dismissed by music historians as a fanciful invention, but it was widely disseminated in the nineteenth century and became extremely influential, especially in Germany. Clearly Hegel had something of the sort in mind. Thus the expressive character of tonal relationships was justified by both natural phenomena and cultural traditions of signification; music had at its disposal all the means necessary to be an art of the expression of feeling.

The important point here, however, is that all of these means of expression are rooted in the ordering of the tonal materials which gives music its formal coherence. Without such ordering, there could be no expression of nuances of feeling. The tones of the diatonic scale are ordered around the tonic in a hierarchical relationship based upon consonance and dissonance, and the use of dissonance is ordered by "the necessity for a resolution of the discords and a return to the triad," which gives satisfaction both "to the ear and the heart" (*VÄ* 3, 184; *A* 2, 928). The chords employed as vertical combinations of tones are further ordered in the system of tonality as it developed since the Renaissance by a sense of what is called "functionality." That is, certain chords should follow others, so that the harmony always has a sense of direction leading away from and back to the tonic (*VÄ* 3, 184; *A* 2, 929). So, too, with key levels: modulation leads away from and back to the tonic in a way that is perceptible and which allows key levels to be used expressively. Thus, Hegel was aware of the basic elements of music theory even if he was not exactly well-versed in the subject; and he was aware of the traditional interpretations of expressive metaphors. The significant argument lies in connecting the principles of music theory with a genuinely philosophical understanding of musical expression.

The Expression of the Ideal

Having shown the possibility of music expressing a content of feeling, it remains for Hegel to show that it actually does so in the principal genres, and thus in what sense such musical expression is an art representing the Ideal. In other words, it remains to consider music in a more specific way: how the tonal material is shaped into actual works, and what aesthetic purposes those works serve. The difficulties were clear enough to him at the outset of his discussion of music, for music has its own laws and easily "acquires an especially architectonic character" that may cease to be expressive (*VÄ* 3, 139; *A* 2, 894). If that happens, however, "music remains empty and meaningless, and because the one chief thing in all art, namely spiritual content and expression, is missing from it, it is not yet strictly to be called art" (*VÄ* 3, 148–49; *A* 2, 902). This is a risk in both vocal and instrumental music. Especially in vocal music (although these remarks would apply equally to the program music which became fashionable after 1830), "music must not sink to such servitude that, in order to reproduce the words of the libretto in their really entire character, it forgets the free flow of its own movements . . . " (*VÄ* 3, 195; *A* 2, 937). That is, when music attempts to express character and emotion too literally, it ceases to have any distinctively musical beauty in its structure, harmony, or melody (*VÄ* 3, 208–9; *A* 2, 947–48). The task the composer faces is to balance expression with musical beauty and development. But there is a genuinely philosophical problem concealed here as well: how to understand music as a unity of form and content having an aesthetic rather than a merely affective significance.

Instrumental music unavoidably presents further problems. When it has expressive content, it is often, as Hegel admits, "a rather vague one" (*VÄ* 3, 217; *A* 2, 954). More generally, however, the composer "clothes a mood in the form of a musical theme which he then elaborates further . . . and his immersion in the topic becomes not the formation of something external but rather the retreat into the inner life's own freedom, a self-enjoyment, and . . . even an assurance that as artist he is free from subject matter altogether" (*VÄ* 3, 141; *A* 2, 895). This appears to vitiate the entire thesis regarding the expressive nature of music in the interest of accounting for the clear necessity of musical development, which in any case does not seem to be strictly required by any expressive content. But the purity of instrumental music, if it is regarded as having no expressive content, would then imply that music per se is not primarily an expressive art.

Hegel, however, avoids this formalist conclusion by insisting instead on a resolution of the dichotomy of form and content. The creation of beauty as a pure and self-subsisting perfection makes it "a liberation of the soul," which music carries "to the most extreme heights" (*VÄ* 3, 141; *A* 2, 896). This theme of liberation from finitude is repeated frequently throughout the chapter on music; Hegel uses it to account for the importance of development and elaboration to musical art (*VÄ* 3, 143; *A* 2, 897), and for the freedom of melody which transcends the element of necessity embodied in harmonic laws (*VÄ* 3, 190; *A* 2, 933). Even more fundamentally, it accounts for why the affective content of music is idealized in tones rather than in being expressed by natural interjections: "Music must, on the contrary, bring feelings into specific tone-relationships, deprive the natural expression of its wildness and crude deliverance, and mitigate it" (*VÄ* 3, 151; *A* 2, 903). In this way, musical expression is an artistic liberation.

Thus a sense of freedom is common to both the expression of an affective content and the development and elaboration of themes as they are formed into musical structures. It is not a matter of arbitrariness or capriciousness; it requires laws of structure and harmony (*VÄ* 3, 186–87; *A* 2, 930–31). Freedom in this sense is a matter of deep rationality, one of the essential characteristics of human nature. But art provides the sensuous knowledge of freedom in this sense of rationality. In music, such freedom is perceived in the mitigation of feelings in tonal relationships, melody, and development and elaboration in the context of musical structure. This is why Hegel says that music is a means of self-approbation and liberation from the force of emotions. It is the essential self of freedom and rationality which is apprehended as a "subjective inwardness." Thus is the apparent dichotomy between form and content resolved into a higher unity.

This understanding of the art of music accounts for the significance of musical form as well as the value of expressing an affective content. But not all feelings are worth expressing in music or any other art:

> But as a fine art it at once acquires, from the spirit's point of view, a summons to bridle the emotions themselves as well as their expression, so that there is no being carried away into a bacchanalian rage or whirling tumult of passions, or a resting in the distraction of despair, but on the contrary an abiding peace and freedom in the outpouring of emotion whether in jubilant delight or the deepest grief. (*VÄ* 3, 198; *A* 2, 939)

That is, the very concept of art as the representation in sensuous form of what we truly ought to be restricts the emotional expression appropriate to music as an art. The soul ought not be enslaved to wayward passions, but should be free and self-possessed. Thus when Hegel cites in the same passage the truly ideal music as that of Palestrina, Pergolesi, Gluck, Haydn, and Mozart, he is not simply giving a list of his personal favorites among composers. Rather, this passage is precisely the connection with the Ideal, for the Ideal is characterized as sensuous blessedness, "a ring of bliss" (*VÄ* 1, 207; *A* 1, 157).

The romantic Ideal, however, is not the static tranquillity of ancient classicism: it is a dynamic resolution of conflict. What music expresses is not simply serenity, but rather the reconciliation of opposing emotions, the finding of bliss even in the midst of grief. This is why music is fundamentally a romantic art. The aspect of reconciliation is emphasized in the remainder of the passage describing ideal music:

> Tranquillity of soul is never missing in the compositions of these masters; grief is expressed there too, but it is assuaged at once; the clear rhythm inhibits extremes; everything is kept firmly together in a restrained form so that jubilation does not degenerate into a repulsive uproar, and even a lament gives us the most blissful tranquillity. (*VÄ* 3, 198; *A* 2, 939)

Beauty and feeling are both required in the art of music, for the art consists not just in the expression of feeling, but more essentially in the restraint and ordering of feeling for a higher purpose. The ordering of tones into musical forms is at the same time an ordering of the emotional life.

The simultaneous apprehension of beauty and expression is easiest in vocal music that specifies the foundation of what the music expresses. But Hegel argues that the way is now open for the proper understanding of instrumental music as the purest representation of the ordering of subjective inwardness:

> Now if this subjective experience is to gain its full due in music likewise, then music must free itself from a given text and draw entirely out of itself its content, the progress and manner of expression, the unity and unfolding

> of its work, the development of a principal thought, the episodic intercalation and ramification of others, and so forth: and in doing all this it must limit itself to purely musical means, because the meaning of the whole is not expressed in words. (*VÄ* 3, 214; *A* 2, 952)

The emphasis here on unity, structure, and principles of musical development clearly recognizes the legitimacy of instrumental music and the formal principles vital to it. But it is only the understanding of such music in the context of broader aesthetic principles that enables the aesthetic significance of instrumental music to be ascertained. Even more clearly than in vocal music, its structure becomes a metaphor for the ordering of the soul, and the freedom of development becomes an expression of the soul's inner freedom (*VÄ* 3, 218; *A* 2, 955). Therefore, beauty in music is inherently expressive of the romantic Ideal.

We can make this point concrete by considering the essential principles of sonata form, which was fundamental to instrumental music in the Classical and Romantic periods. From the opening of a sonata form movement in the tonic key, the thematic complexity of the movement emerges parallel to the tonal departure from the tonic—to the dominant in the case of a major key, and usually to the relative major in a minor key. The development section takes the listener through a succession of keys, often far removed from the tonic, before returning to the tonic at the recapitulation, which (aside from brief departures) remains in the tonic. Thus Hegel's requirement of resolution is found to hold true not only at the level of localized dissonances resolving to consonance, but also at the largest scale of musical form. This resolution of key level enables music to be not just expressive, but narrative in the sense of a metaphor of temporal ordering toward wholeness and tranquillity as the Ideal.[19] Certainly later nineteenth-century composers felt free to impose a poetic narrative on essentially sonata form movements, as in the tone poems of Franz Liszt and Richard Strauss, or even the programmatic *Symphonie Fantastique* of Hector Berlioz. Thus, to extend a point already seen in the visual arts, music may also be considered a representational art, even when there is no explicit program. The potential of sonata form to serve as a metaphor of the ordering of the soul is sufficient to guarantee a narrative of the temporal development of the wholeness of the soul.

Thus Hegel recognizes that a composer may not have any specific expressive content in mind when he writes an instrumental work; in no way does Hegel demand a meaning to the music which is not there already. Of course, the composer can "put into his work a specific meaning, a content consisting of ideas and feelings . . . but, conversely, he can also not trouble himself with any such content and make the principal thing the purely musical structure of his work and the ingenuity of such architecture." Then, however, there is a risk of creating music that sounds empty: "Music is therefore more profound when the composer gives the same attention even in instrumental music to both sides, to the expression of a content (true, a rather vague one) and to the musical structure . . ." (*VÄ* 3, 217; *A* 2, 954). This is Hegel's way of explaining the difference between music that seems profound and music that seems to have "nothing to say."[20] Inasmuch as the question of what makes some musical works profound and other works not is still a mystery for analytic philosophy, Hegel's requirement of both expressive and structural detail bears remembering.

In fact, much instrumental music has an expressive content: certainly in the nineteenth century, emotional content was commonplace, but even in the Classical period, the gestures of symphonic music must be understood as arising from operatic music, and as carrying the same potential for expressing meaning.[21] It is the twentieth century which has forgotten that vocal music was once much more important than purely instrumental music and that it furnished the context for the comprehension of the latter. After all, it is usually possible to say what the general character of a piece or a theme is; indeed, musicians rely on just such notions of character to guide their performances. Often composers provide indications of character in their markings in the score—as when an "*Allegro*" is modified by "*giocoso*," that is, "joyful." But even when the composer has not supplied such a character marking in the score, a theme's possession of character is understood by a musician as being the essence of the music: notes without character do indeed sound "empty."[22] Hegel's position on instrumental music, then, corresponds to the way in which composers themselves characterize music in the markings they provide, to the way musicians interpret the music in performing it, and to the way most people respond to music. Hegel's aesthetic, therefore, is musically credible for instrumental as well as for vocal music.

It is clear, then, that Hegel's aesthetic of music makes sense, both musically and philosophically. It is philosophically coherent, for it is able to locate the musical consequences of the Ideal of human nature as free and rational. It is musically coherent because it offers an interpretation of music as the expression of subjective inwardness consistent with the traditions which formed the foundations of musical composition from the Renaissance through the nineteenth century. In particular, Hegel is able to explain:

- the justification of music's tonal and rhythmic ordering as a necessary condition of its being an art;
- the specific means of musical expression of feeling and their origin in the ordering of the tonal materials; and
- the aesthetic significance of music as a metaphor of ordered feeling and inner freedom.

For Hegel, art is the form of the sensuous intuition of the truth; music, then, is the tonal representation of the truth about human nature and the Ideal of human character. Its beauty lies in its being adequate to its purpose and content.

This leads to one final consideration: Hegel's true relation to his own age and to our understanding of the course of musical history since the emergence of Romanticism. His silence with respect to Beethoven and his criticism of Carl Maria von Weber have often been noted, although it is not entirely certain that he had heard the music of Beethoven.[23] His criticism of Weber, however, is not a wholesale condemnation, only a criticism of the melodramatic, unmelodic music of the Wolf's Glen scene in *Der Freischütz*, where the expression of unrestrained grief overwhelms the musical aspect proper to opera (*VÄ* 1, 210; *A* 1, 159). Moreover, Hegel generally praised the music of Rossini, so that his treatment of contemporary developments is certainly not one of automatic rejection. But representing passion without tranquillity became the hallmark of the emotional realism of both Verdi and Wagner, for instance, in the years after Hegel's death. Hegel saw this emerging trend not simply as an artistic crisis, but as a symptom of the weakening of the beliefs that had formed the center of Western civilization. The Ideal had been specifically Christian in its romantic historical form; now there was no longer any dominating subject matter to which artists, writers, or composers perceived any allegiance (*VÄ* 2, 235; *A* 1, 605). Hegel attempted to understand this as a historically necessary development, freeing art to depict "the depths and heights of the human heart as such, mankind in its joys and sorrows, its strivings, deeds, and fates"

(*VÄ* 2, 237–38; *A* 1, 607). But there is no question that he saw it—accurately—as a loss of true transcendence.

For the twentieth century, Hegel's outlook has often seemed prophetic.[24] For the rise of the musical avant-garde—of first atonal Expressionism, then Serialism, and finally even more radical styles of electronic and aleatoric music—is precisely a rejection of the Ideal of tranquillity, order, and beauty in both human nature and art. This, however, appears to pose a stumbling block to any philosophical deduction of the nature of art and music: how could an aesthetic legitimately criticize historical developments? Yet how, if it cannot, could the most contradictory styles be accommodated under one aesthetic? The truth is rather the reverse: it should be Hegel who appears as a challenge to the self-understanding of the musical art of twentieth-century modernism. If we do not accept the rationality of human being, then civilization becomes impossible; but if human nature is rational, there can be no purpose to the intrinsic incoherence of atonal, aleatoric, and unmelodic music, such as has dominated the art music of the twentieth century. The avant-garde, therefore, cannot be assimilated to the musical traditions of our civilization, and it cannot be understood as a historically inevitable development out of those traditions. It is nothing less than a rupture with everything that has gone before, the significance of which a proper understanding of traditional aesthetics helps us comprehend. Whereas music was once held to be the tonal expression of the Ideal of human nature, twentieth-century modernists have lost their belief in such an ideal.

Thus Hegel's philosophy of music both challenges prevailing ahistorical ways of understanding the art of music today and clarifies the radical rupture with the past that has characterized so much of musical history since the early years of the twentieth century. His aesthetic of music deserves to be taken seriously as a historical document of the understanding of the musical traditions of our civilization and also as a philosophical argument pertinent to the understanding of the history of Western musical culture. Any adequate philosophy of a contingent artistic tradition must attempt to do both.

Chapter 6

The Ethical Function of Poetry

The critical interpretation of literature today is beset by many problems. Chief among them is the politicization of interpretive stances arising from postmodernist perspectives: the tendency to reduce all writing to issues of race, class, and gender, whether those concerns were foremost for earlier authors or not.[1] Yet even among more sober and thoughtful accounts of literary aesthetics, serious questions arise: now that our civilization does not possess a uniform structure of basic religious and moral beliefs, is it necessary for a reader to accept the belief structure on which a work of literature is based? The earlier formalist New Criticism held that such acceptance is not essential to the enjoyment of a work, but Malcolm Budd, for example, argues that since the value of a poem does not reduce it to the thought it expresses, but is rather a matter of the experience of a particular linguistic construction expressing a particular thought or feeling, a reader's failure to share the belief structure or moral perspective of a poem must affect the evaluation of the poem.[2] Other literary critics are more forthright in placing moral values as central to literature: John Gardner, in particular, defends what he calls the "traditional view" that "art is moral: it seeks to improve life, not debase it."[3] Against both the formalists and postmodernists, such an argument is indeed important. It also echoes the main concerns of Hegel's aesthetics of poetry, which reflected the traditional view.

The discussion of poetry is the longest of the sections in Hegel's consideration of the individual arts. It is the most straightforward:

granted the definition of art as the sensuous representation of the truth, truth expressed in language always seems to have the character of art. Yet such a broad conception of literature would not qualify as poetic, and Hegel himself recognizes this, for in that case, philosophy, history, and other prose would have to count as poetry. For Hegel, the art of poetry embraced all forms of literary art, including epic, lyric, and dramatic poetry, but also, marginally, the novel. Thus prose fiction, whether found in drama or in the novel, is in effect considered a species of poetry; this was the result of the traditional restriction of literary art to the poetic. Poetry, however, has always denoted something higher than mere prose. In both the seriousness of its ideas and the elevation of its language, it has exhibited that mutual adequacy of form and content that Hegel made the very definition of art.

In terms of its content, Hegel argues that the proper subject matter lies in inner ideas, not in abstraction, such as philosophy discusses them, but rather in their particular details. The content of any art must have a purely contemplative purpose, so that it forms "an inherently independent and closed world" (*VÄ* 3, 231; *A* 2, 965). Thus, poetry lifts the spirit above the realm of the finite into the purely spiritual, and accordingly it seeks poetic ideas, rather than using merely prosaic ideas (*VÄ* 3, 236; *A* 2, 969). It is for this reason that poetry is distinguished in the form of its language by elevated expression, rather than everyday speech. The use of poetic meters, figures of speech, and often rhyme sets off the art from the realm of the prosaic and the form of prose.

Nevertheless, Hegel's discussion of poetry is not without idiosyncrasies and puzzling aspects. First, there is no explicit mention of the Ideal—even less implicitly than in the case of music. This means that for the art considered the most intellectual, having the clearest content, there is a remarkable absence of the very category that was so important to Hegel's concept of art in general. Instead, what takes its place is the concept of the ethical life, although this is now to be understood in Hegelian rather than Aristotelian terms. Second, Hegel discusses poetry according to its genres, the three principle divisions being epic, lyric, and dramatic. Within each, there is a treatment of the history of the genre, but there are problems in the relation of history to the genres. Hegel's ordering principle is dialectical, rather than historical: lyric is the opposite of the epic, in that lyric is subjective, whereas epic is objective. The resolution of this opposition in the form of their synthesis is the drama. But only drama is actually concerned with character; even so, it—like epic and lyric poetry—lacks a connection to the Ideal. Thus, the history of poetry as a whole is replaced by the history of each genre, and the art of poetry suffers from a want of conceptual unity beyond that supplied by the sensuous and formal elements of elevated language and poetic meters.

The Epic and the Ethical

Hegel's concept of an epic is of a poem in which there is a representation of a national spirit of a particular people at an early and definitive stage of its historical development. But such a poem does not have as its definitive stage a people's emergence or situation; rather, it is in conflict, and specifically in war, that the epic finds its ground. The epic is the story of the heroes of a people, but also the story of their activity in war that involves their entire nation (*VÄ* 3, 349; *A*a, 1059). Homer's *Iliad* is the best illustration: it is the story of the Trojan War, in which Achilles and Agamemnon and many other heroes of ancient Greece battle against Hektor, Paris, and the rest of the Trojan host. Other societies also have their epics: the Icelandic sagas, the Spanish Cid, and the English Milton, the last whose rendition of the battle between God and Satan takes on epic proportions. Thus, Hegel recognizes the universality of the epic form, while accounting for the uniqueness of particular epics to their societies. The ancient Greek epic, however, remains normative.

Nevertheless, even a casual reading of the *Iliad* raises questions regarding Hegel's conception of the epic. For the *Iliad* is not a poem celebrating the founding heroes of Greek city states in their war against Troy. Indeed, the Greeks do not win the war and conquer Troy in the course of the poem; it will be left to the cunning of delivering the army inside the walls to bring about the fall of Troy. But this outcome is not related in the *Iliad* at all. The *Iliad* is primarily a record of all the battles that took place between the time of the quarrel of Achilles and Agamemnon and their reconciliation. Its vivid description of all the gruesome ways in which men die in battle occupies the greatest number of lines, as if death were its focus and the heroes its victims.

Yet the focus on death provides Homer with countless occasions to remark on the bravery of men in facing it. Hegel recognizes this aspect of the epic, correctly understanding such bravery as not being "a moral conviction adopted by the will itself," but rather as a "natural side of the spirit character" (*VÄ* 3, 350, my translation). That is, bravery is more a matter of temperament than will; although Menelaos may urge his men to overcome their fear and face single combat with Hektor, Menelaos himself is willing to fight Hektor out of his own courageous self-confidence.[4] It is not a matter of choosing for him; the duel simply must be fought, because the Greek sense of honor in going to war demands it. It is a quality of character demanded by the situation rather than commanded by a sense of moral obligation.

The epic hero, then, stands in a peculiar relation to the action. He is not like a dramatic hero, whom we see in all his individuality of personality. Rather, Hegel insists that the epic hero's character concentrates within himself all the traits of national character, so that as he fights for the national enterprise, the nation is concentrated in him. His individuality of action is interwoven in the larger conflict, "bringing into view every aspect of national character" (*VÄ* 3, 354; *A* 2, 1063). The epic is neither world history, nor private biography; it is a unique fusion of the world historical narrative with the story of the hero. Nevertheless, the hero is not merely a representative man: as in the *Cid*, he also exhibits the ethical relations of "son, hero, lover, spouse, householder, father," subject, friend, and enemy (*VÄ* 3, 359; *A* 2, 1067–68). Here we see Hegel's concept of the ethical in terms of the customary obligations arising from the particular relations of the individual to others; this is the standard translation of the German *Sittlichkeit*.[5] It is a definition of the ethical in terms of the individual's fulfillment of specific, given roles. Hence, the hero is seen as a concrete individual and, at the same time, the embodiment of all the ethical relations in the society he defends. This makes the epic an eminently ethical genre of poetry. It gives the reader (or hearer) a perspective on the defining relations of ethical life in the society of the heroic age.

Several difficulties present themselves, however, in Hegel's account of the epic. The *Iliad* poses a problem for Hegel's account of the epic as the record of the actions of the founding heroes of a society in their battle against a mortal enemy. For the poem is cast in the beginning as the story of the conflict between Achilles and Agamemnon in the context of the war against Troy, yet it does not focus on that conflict as its principal object of attention. Rather, the personal conflict is more an explanation for why Greek efforts, after nine long years, had proven so ineffectual against the Trojan defenders. Thus, the personal dispute between Achilles and Agamemnon emerges as the source of Greek weakness, until, after the death of Patroklos, Achilles decides to reenter the battle.

Moreover, especially considering the *Iliad*, it appears that Hegel may be stretching a point to make the epic more than it is. For we do not see the entire spectrum of ethical relations among the heroes: they are far from their spouses and households, more concerned with capturing concubines than remembering their wives. Although Hegel insists that Achilles is not to be judged by ordinary moral standards (*VÄ* 3, 360; *A* 2, 1068), nonetheless, it remains true that the relations of the hero as friend or enemy are more important than any other. The epic is not a representation of the totality of ethical relations even in heroic society. Also, it does not rely on the classical Ideal of serenity for the essential character of its heroes.

What appears indisputable in Hegel's account of the nature of the epic is his emphasis on the circumstances instead of the heroes as really determinative of the epic action: what the hero "achieves passes before us just as what happens from without does, so that his deed must prove to be conditioned and brought about just as much by his entanglement in external circumstances" (*VÄ* 3, 363; *A* 2, 1070). The epic hero does not act freely; he is part of the larger nation's purpose. Hence, "necessity lies at the heart of events and happenings." This is presented most often (and certainly in the *Iliad*) as a matter of fate, and fate is determined by the gods, who have their own purposes in supporting either Greece or Troy. The gods maintain control over human events and determine their outcome; all men can do is submit. Indeed, mourning is the predominant mood of the true epic, for most of the heroes will fall victim to fate, to the wrath of the gods, and therefore to the blows inflicted by the enemy (*VÄ* 3, 364; *A* 2, 1071). The deaths of Hektor and Achilles are the necessary tragic outcome of the battle of Troy, and all the other gory deaths described by Homer are only so much the more tragedy heaped onto a world of suffering. Life appears tenuous, of little count, in spite of the imperative of winning the war and preserving honor.

Hegel's account of epic poetry, therefore, appears defensible in its broad outlines, although subject to revision in the purpose of the epic and the incompleteness of the ethical relations informing it. It is useful, however, to compare Hegel's concept of the epic to Aristotle's account in the *Poetics*, for Aristotle stood closer to a firsthand knowledge of the religious and ethical assumptions out of which the

Homeric epic originated. Significantly, epic poetry was considered more elevated than dramatic poetry in ancient Athens: the theater was the vulgar institution in ancient Greece. Aristotle disagreed with this judgment, arguing that tragedy in particular was more vivid, compact, and unified[6]—an assessment with which Hegel would agree. But otherwise, Aristotle found epic and tragic poetry to have many of the same characteristics. In particular, there were two types of epic: that of character, and that of suffering (*Poetics* 1459b). The *Odyssey* was the principal example of the former, the *Iliad* the principal illustration of the latter. That is, the *Odyssey* was designed to emphasize more the individuality of its hero, Odysseus, in the context of his voyage and tribulations, while the *Iliad* emphasizes more the suffering of all the heroes among the combatants engaged at Troy. The *Iliad* confirms Hegel's account of the primacy of fate and the atmosphere of mourning in the epic genre. It remains true, however, that Hegel's description of the entire genre depends on a selective reading of just one example.

Aristotle's account of the chronological priority but poetic inferiority of the epic makes it a first stage in the emergence of a body of poetic literature. With this, Hegel agrees: the epic, although essentially classical in spirit, can arise only after a people has awakened, but before law has become codified (*VÄ* 3, 332; *A* 2, 1045). It precedes the more fully developed classical spirit of ancient tragedy, for example, and inevitably falls short in more modern times because the treatment of an epic subject becomes too abstract and fanciful: "For an epic lives and is always new only if it continuously presents primitive life and work in a primitive way" (*VÄ* 3, 372; *A* 2, 1077). Thus, there is only a limited history of epic poetry: after ancient Greece, there is the paler, more artificial imitation in Virgil's *Aeneid*. To be sure, there are many various medieval epics—Dante's *Divine Comedy*, the *Cid*, the *Nibelungenlied*, the *Song of Roland*, and tales of King Arthur's court—and modern imitations of Virgil such as Tasso's *Jerusalem Delivered*. There are also the Reformation epics, Milton's *Paradise Lost*, and Klopstock's *Messiah*. Yet Hegel finds these medieval and romantic epics inferior to the classical: like the art of sculpture, epic is quintessentially Greek, he argues, because of its objectivity in both form and content (*VÄ* 3, 394; *A* 2, 1093–94). The romantic era, founded on the individuality brought about by Christianity, cannot produce this kind of objective poetry of heroes and their suffering in battle. Hence, the epic is dead in the modern world.

Hegel further extends the argument against the possibility of the epic in the modern world. He argues that modern society itself is inimical to the cultivation of epic poetry for a variety of reasons. Epic originates after a people has awakened to its consciousness of being a people, but before religious dogma, and moral or civil law have become codified. That is, the heroic individual does exactly what he feels like doing without the restraint of law; what he feels is precisely the same as the people as a whole. This is the sense in which the epic hero can function as the representative figure of his people. When the individual and the nation become separated, then there arises the need for law, but also the possibility of conflicts between the individual and the law, or between the various requirements of the ethical life itself. This is the condition for the rise of drama (*VÄ* 3, 332; *A* 2, 1046). Viewed in one respect, the epic is the product of the wholeness of the individual and society; what follows is decay. Viewed in another way, however, the epic is the genre of poetry corresponding to and expressing the relations of precivilized society. In either event, it cannot be the poetry of the modern, civilized world, with its legal codes and defined religious dogma. There is no room for an autonomous epic hero in a prosaic legal order.

Hegel cites another reason for the impossibility of epic poetry in the modern world: while there are founding events in the lives of nations analogous to the determinative events in ancient epic, they are too recent. Specifically, the French Revolution was simply too fresh in people's memories to be made into the subject of a properly epic treatment, even if other conditions allowed it (*VÄ* 3, 414–15; *A* 2, 1109–10). Although it would be only a few decades until Charles Dickens would render the horrors of the French Revolution into the background for *A Tale of Two Cities* (if we may consider a prose novel a modern substitute for epic poetry), Hegel's point was valid at the time he was lecturing. The one thing most people wanted was a return to peace, a forgetting of the bloodshed and terror. After all, we now know that at least four centuries separated the Trojan War from the writing of the Homeric accounts; if during these centuries substantial parts of the poems were recited orally, nevertheless, the commission of these memories to writing was undertaken only at a safe distance when it was possible to look back upon the events and make sense of them as ordained by the will of the gods. But the fact that Dickens embodied the Terror of the French Revolution in prose, rather than in poetry, appears to confirm Hegel's perception that true epic poetry is impossible in the modern world.

Moreover, although the need for epic heroes did in fact continue to inspire poetry based upon older epic tales, they were often idyllic and lyrical rather than truly epic. A prime example from later in the nineteenth century is the *Idylls of the King*, by Alfred, Lord Tennyson, which offers at least a reference to the world of the Arthurian romance as the romantic equivalent to the Greek epic. In that sense, the nineteenth century was not as bereft of heroic models as Hegel feared. What might be said of the twentieth century, however, is another matter. Heroism does indeed appear dead, a matter of no interest to the broader population, and Hegel's words of doom regarding the epic in the modern world appear as a portent and prophecy of a world exhausted from the horrific violence of total war.

The Subjectivity of the Lyric Genres

As we have seen, Hegel considers lyric poetry to be the subjective antithesis to the objectivity of the epic. If the lyric is subjective, its Concept must be subjective expression itself. This is bound to appear trivial, as long as the need of the poet to express himself is considered in isolation. But Hegel understands that the value of lyric poetry is indeed minimal if it is merely cathartic or therapeutic—exactly the position of the modern doctrine of poetic expression. He insists instead that lyric expressions must possess "a universal validity" as "meditations for which the poet invents or finds the adequate and lively expression." That is, the feelings expressed must be understood as common to humanity, and the poet's task is less one of creativity in terms of the substance of what is expressed than one of discovering the adequate means of expression in terms of phrasing, form, and figures of speech. Poetry delivers the heart—the reader's heart as well as the poet's—from "the blind dominion of passion" arising from not being able to express the feelings, but it also "makes of it an object purified from all accidental moods, an object in which the inner life, liberated and with its self-consciousness satisfied, reverts freely at the same time into itself and is at home with itself" (*VÄ* 3, 417; *A* 2, 1112). That is, lyric poetry (and this applies to song as well) both achieves the self-perception of passion and the purification of passion from the accidental. The result is the cultivation of inner freedom, the very essence of the subjective as the goal of life. Thus the Ideal of repose is implicit in lyric poetry, but Hegel, surprisingly, does not make it explicit, and it is achieved in the poet and reader, not represented in the poem. The result further weakens the ties of poetry to the broader concerns of his aesthetics.

Hegel recognizes that there are many different subjects and forms of lyric poetry; there is no authoritative standard or example, as there is for the epic in the work of Homer. Among the subjects of the lyric, there are those which are universal in themselves, including faith, ideas, religious and philosophical knowledge; those which are the reflective union of the universal and the particular, such as elegies; and many kinds of poems which offer reflections on commonplace or even trivial objects of significant feeling (*VÄ* 3, 420; *A* 2, 1114). Among the forms of lyric poetry, there are ballads, romances, poems written for particular occasions but still full of high-minded reflections, and love poems; other kinds of lyric poetry include hymns and psalms, odes, and the various species of songs such as folksongs, sonnets, sestinas, and more philosophical lyrics (*VÄ* 3, 424, 452–60; *A* 2, 1117–18, 1140–46). These classifications, however, do not establish much about the general character of the lyric, and Hegel's entire treatment of this branch of poetry remains curiously weak. Even his treatment of the lyric's history is astonishingly brief, given the outpouring of lyric poetry that had begun with Schiller and Goethe and continued into the early years of the nineteenth century: he discusses Greek and Roman lyric poetry briefly, then the romantic in an almost superficial glance at the entire history of the lyrical genres. He distinguishes the post-Reformation period from the medieval; Klopstock, Schiller, and Goethe are the preeminent poets of the Protestant period, and they receive clear approbation from Hegel (*VÄ* 3, 473–74; *A* 2, 1156–57). If the lyric is so important, and if it occupies such a crucial conceptual place as the alternative to the epic, then should not more be said? Has Hegel done justice to this branch of the highest art form?

Certainly more could be said than simply to give a list of the various forms and kinds of lyric poetry. If lyric poetry is a determinate expression of feeling or passion, then it follows that the body of lyric poetry for each nation and each language is the expression of that people's way of feeling. Indeed, the inherited body of lyric poetry, constantly added to, is the accumulated yet ever changing determination of the ways in which passions are perceived, and, among the higher kinds of poetic expression of ideas, the way in which ideas are rendered into language. Lyric poetry, therefore, forms the conception of feeling in order to give higher expression to otherwise inarticulate, or poorly articulated, joys, sorrows, longings, and other sentiments. Its role exceeds even that of music in this regard, for music by itself—in its instrumental genres—is conceptual only implicitly, and hence inarticulate unless it is joined to poetry in song. But then music acquires its expressive power precisely from the determinate passions expressed first in words, and only renders the feelings intelligible because the listener has already learned how to feel passions from the point of reference in the poetic language. Truly, therefore, we learn to feel by reading and listening to lyric poetry, and we learn to attach significance to our feelings from the ideas to which they are poetically joined. This is the genius of the lyric.

The lyric, therefore, appears quintessentially "modern," in Hegel's sense of post-Reformation times. Developing in vernacular languages as a consequence of the Renaissance, it typically addresses subjects of love and death in fixed forms such as the sonnet. The seventeenth century, particularly in Britain, added metaphysical and theological subjects to the concerns of lyric poetry. As the rigidity of lyric forms was relaxed in the nineteenth century, the lyric blossomed into its own and found among educated readers everywhere an eager and expanding audience. But this development requires an explanation, which Hegel does not give because he does not give serious consideration to this history. If the principle of the lyric is subjectivity, it is understandable that it would flourish as never before in the period when subjectivity and inwardness came into their own: that is, in the romantic, or Christian period. Yet the lyric flourished only with the Renaissance and its historical outgrowths, the Reformation and the Counter-Reformation. For the principle of both Protestantism and Tridentine Catholicism was an emphasis on the interiority of faith. If the Protestants discovered this, nonetheless, the Catholic Church understood clearly that a return to the principle of inner faith, together with moral works, was essential to salvation. Thus, the interiorizing of faith led to an emphasis on the interiority of the passions in general, and eventually to the flourishing of the most interior of poetic genres, the lyric forms.

Nevertheless, if we look to the history of lyric poetry during Hegel's lifetime and after his death, we find that the nineteenth century frequently produced lamentations more than the confident expressions of faith that had been the staple of seventeenth-century poetry. To take English poetry as a case in point: Wordsworth worried in "The World Is Too Much With Us" that the materialism of modern society was eclipsing the sense of spiritual presence that had animated both Classical and Christian culture; later Matthew Arnold lamented the loss of faith in the modern world in his famous "Dover Beach." Coleridge was haunted by the permanent loss of repose in his tale of the mariner who cursed an innocent natural creature; and Keats yearned for the lost world of classical Greek beauty in his "Ode on a Grecian Urn." Shelley, in a metaphor of nature standing for the human spirit, longed for the rebirth of the world in the "Ode to the West Wind." But although the quest for a spiritual unity with Nature informed much of Romantic poetry, the separation from love was perhaps the most frequent lament in nineteenth-century poetry—in both England and Germany. This means that it was the absence of the deepest human relationships and the sense of the loss of God's presence which were most important. The character of the modern lyric in the nineteenth century was the longing for the lost unity of love and faith.

Lyric poetry's historical emergence, therefore, became a dialectical necessity, although not as Hegel located it in opposition to the epic. Hegel understands that lyric poetry flourishes when feeling and the moral will become separated, which can happen only after the individual and the nation become disentangled. But the latter is the condition for the rise of drama, which indeed flourished from the late Renaissance through the eighteenth century. But the lyric also flourished from the late Renaissance through the nineteenth century in most European nations, so that lyric poetry would seem to arise in association with drama, and to survive as the last historical stage in the evolution of poetry. The historical progression of poetic genres would therefore appear to be rather epic—dramatic—lyric. Viewed in this light, the lyric genres are the product of decay, a loss of the unity Hegel posits for the drama. What drama held together, lyric poetry preserved one-sidedly.

Thus, Hegel's observation that the creation of new epics is impossible in the modern world finds its corollary in the flourishing of lyrical poetry, wherein the wholeness absent in the epic expression is the object of yearning for the lyric. Lyric is indeed the opposite of the epic, but it is the historical endpoint of poetical development rather than the intermediary between epic and drama. Or rather, since the

Idea is the union of the Concept and actuality, the completion of the state in the modern era is not only the achievement of the Idea in the political realm, but also the occasion for the diminution of the worth of the individual in action, as Hegel realized. Hence, the more intimate dimensions of the ethical life suffer. But this means that the fulfillment of one dimension of what Hegel considers the ethical life (the state) is simultaneously the decay of its foundation in integrative relationships among individuals. Thus, there is inevitably a profound sense of alienation in modern society. It could be said, although Hegel does not, that lyric poetry remembers the Ideal of bliss and longs for it even as its realization is lost.

The Tragic Nature of the Ethical in Ancient Civilization

Hegel describes drama conceptually as the synthesis of the epic and the lyrical in poetry. It is the poetry of a fully developed society, with the city as its locus of existence. The category of drama is in turn divided into two main genres: tragedy and comedy. Although Hegel discusses both tragedy and comedy, tragedy clearly receives the most attention. Nor should this be surprising, for tragedy has always been held as the highest dramatic genre. If Hegel's treatment of comedy is much less complete and convincing, therefore, it is of little importance to his overall argument concerning the nature and purposes of drama: tragedy is the exemplar of the dramatic form. Indeed, Hegel's position is that the genre reveals precisely the inevitably tragic nature of the ethical life in the fully developed city. As in Hegel's treatment of the epic, the role of the ethical life appears to displace completely the concept of the Ideal as the guiding principle of the genre.

The essence of drama is the collision of opposed circumstances, passions, and characters. But drama only arises in the civilized state because ends are individualized; the action depends on the will of individuals, who are the cause of everything. Hegel holds this much in common with any theory of drama that recognizes the contribution of the individual characters to the plot. Hegel goes on to recognize the origin of the opposition of ends in the diversity of ends possible in the civilized state and their origin in the plurality of divine powers exemplified in Greek polytheism: "the all pervasive cause is therefore indeed the eternal powers, i.e., what is essentially moral, the gods of our actual life, in short what is divine and true. . . . " They are "the substance and aim of human individuality..." (*VÄ* 3, 480; *A* 2, 1162). Thus, there can be conflict among what the gods require, such that a conflict can arise between what the family requires and what the state requires. As in the case of the epic, Hegel here takes ancient classical drama as paradigmatic. Ancient tragedy represented to the citizens of the *polis* their own understanding of the nature of the moral and ethical life and the possibility of conflicts within it.

Ancient tragedy embodied this ethical function because the gods themselves represented the different forces essential to the ethical life of the *polis*. Hegel's rehearsal of the various constituents of the conflicts central to Greek tragedy reveals the relation of the gods to daily life: "family love between husband and wife, parents and children, brothers and sisters; political life also, the patriotism of the citizens, the will of the ruler; and religion existent...as an active grasp and furtherance of actual interest and circumstances" (*VÄ* 3, 521; *A* 2, 1194). That is, the gods were held to be intimately involved in what Hegel calls the ethical life of family and the state. But this ethical order is the result of the inherent differentiation of powers in the civilized state; they necessarily come into conflict in such a way that they both justify each character's action and impute a guilt to it at the same time (*VÄ* 3, 523–24; *A* 2, 1195–96). The collision of one-sided interests brings about the tragic downfall, which is both the means of reconciling opposed yet fully justified ends, and the means of divine justice bringing the guilt of one-sidedness to an end. This doctrine of the tragic collision of the differentiated components of the ethical life is the heart of Hegel's concept of tragedy.[7] The crucial question is whether it does justice to the self-understanding and practice of ancient Greek tragedy.

As the beginning of an answer to this question, Aristotle's definition of tragedy and its elaboration in the *Poetics* should be taken seriously:

> Tragedy, then, is the imitation of a good action, which is complete and of a certain length, by means of language made pleasing for each part separately; it relies in its various elements not on narrative but on acting; through pity and fear it achieves the purgation (catharsis) of such emotions. (*Poetics* 1449b)

He immediately explains that "language made pleasing" means that language has poetic meter and musical melody, sometimes one alone or both together. What is striking here is the emphasis on tragedy being the representation of a good action; he insists on the goodness of character and the rightness of moral choice elsewhere as governing the aims of characterization.[8] Therefore, the ethical function of tragedy is paramount.

Aristotle, however, notoriously leaves the concept of catharsis unexplained. Most commentators focus on bringing to the surface deep emotions of pity and fear, while Aristotle's brief remarks indicate that catharsis may have been largely a matter of having tragic poetry sung. Perhaps the most controversial theory is that of Else, who regards catharsis as created by the resolution of the action itself in Greek tragedy; others cite especially choral lamentations that frequently closed the works of Aeschylus.[9] Aristotle lays such emphasis on catharsis as the essential completion of the tragic effect, in part surely because it brings his emphasis on tragedy as the imitation of a "good action" to a logical close. But this only adds to the mystery, for a fall into misfortune can hardly be described as a morally good action in all cases. If we regard Oedipus' relentless investigation into the cause of the plague or the courage of Antigone in resisting Creon's decree as good actions, then the end of Oedipus' quest in his remorseful self-blinding, and Antigone's resistance in her death, hardly seem good or cathartic. Even if in these examples there is a sense of the action having come to a logical and inevitable conclusion, then there are more disturbing examples extant. The murderous revenge of Clytemnestra, the madness of Orestes and Elektra, and the futile enmity of Eteocles and Polyneices are subjects treated in multiple instances by Aeschylus, Sophocles, and Euripides. There is little sense of relief in the ultimate restoration of justice and moral order as a result of the characters' actions. If there is indeed a purgation of pity and fear, a better explanation should be found.

Here, Hegel's explanation appears as a persuasive alternative to the emphasis on goodness of character and action arising out of Aristotle's virtue-centered ethics. Because Hegel regards each principal character in a tragedy as the embodiment of only one dimension of the ethical life, he finds that the tragic hero must be both ethically justified in one respect, and not necessaily justified in others. But this paradox is just what gives rise to pity and fear. "What a man has really to fear is . . . the might of the ethical order which is one determinant of his own free reason and is at the same time that eternal and inviolable something which he summons up against himself if once he turns against it." Similarly, "True pity . . . is sympathy at the same time with the sufferer's moral justification, with the affirmative aspect, the substantive thing that must be present in him" (*VÄ* 3, 525; *A* 2, 1198).

Thus, tragedy arouses both pity and fear because at the same time that the tragic hero has a moral justification, he also lacks justification in other respects: he cannot embody the totality of the ethical life. Pity and fear are the necessary effects of the tragic character being both innocent and guilty, the tragic action being both legitimate and blameworthy. Thus, as in Aristotle's account, pity and fear are appropriate responses to tragic drama.

This is quite different from Aristotle's paradoxical union of guilt and innocence in the concept of *hamartia*, or the tragic flaw. For Aristotle, the tragic plot must be one in which someone falls into relatively undeserved misfortune. It would be merely shocking to witness a good person falling from prosperity into misfortune, morally offensive to see a wicked person rise from adversity to prosperity, and merely satisfying to see the wicked brought to justice. Hence, the tragic character must lie in a mean between these extremes, someone "who is neither outstanding in virtue and righteousness," who does not fall "through wickedness and vice," but "through some flaw," in the sense of an intellectual error or moral weakness (*Poetics* 1453a). As he explains further (citing Oedipus as one example), tragic action may consist in the commission of a great crime arising from an error rather than from intentional wrongdoing. Such a crime entails guilt, yet it is a misfortune that is not deserved. In this way, Aristotle, too, maintains a doctrine of paradoxical guilt and innocence, but Aristotle does not insist on a conflict between ethical powers.

The resolution of the tragic conflict reestablishes justice, although not in a simple, moralistic sense. Hegel sees tragic reconciliation restoring the harmony of the ethical powers. The one-sidedness of the tragic character must be destroyed and the strife of the ethical powers purified. This may come about in several ways. In *Antigone*, Hegel sees Creon as "punished by the voluntary deaths of his son and his wife," whereas in the *Eumenides*, the gods themselves are reconciled by the final trial of Orestes in the Athenian court. In contrast, *Oedipus at Colonus* shows the inner transfiguration of Oedipus as he overcomes the curse of Laius at last. There is an ultimate purification "into the unity and harmony of the entire ethical order itself" (*VÄ* 3, 549–52; *A* 2, 1217–20). These remarks are persuasive, for they are borne out by the comments of the characters themselves. For example, Creon himself recognizes his crimes as "so senseless, so insane," having lost a son to his own self-confessed stupidity.[10] The final chorus confirms what he has learned: "The mighty words of the proud are paid in full/ with mighty blows of fate, and at long last/ those blows will teach us wisdom."[11] Similarly, the *Eumenides* of Aeschylus ends, after the acquittal of Orestes by the closest of all possible votes, with the alternation of Athena and the Furies rejoicing at the just outcome of the vote and the bestowal of the blessings of justice on Athens.[12] And finally, although Oedipus continues to recognize the unholiness in his crimes, he insists at length, toward the end of his life, on their being "all against my will!"[13] He has the courage to denounce Polyneices when his son asks his blessing, and then he courageously and willingly goes to his death in the Furies' grove. These tragedies, then, end with a sense of justice and reconciliation in which Aristotle's concept of catharsis can be understood as the effect of the characters' own reconciliation with justice. Thus Hegel claims: "Therefore the drama . . . must display to us the vital working of the necessity which, itself self-reposing, resolves every conflict and contradiction" (*VÄ* 3, 480; *A* 2, 1163). This is the merest suggestion of the Ideal in Hegel's discussion of classical tragedy.

Nevertheless, although Hegel's explanation of catharsis appears more persuasive than Aristotle's, the question remains as to whether or not his understanding of the tragic collision is borne out by the ancient practice that is his model. Both Aristotle and Hegel cultivate a sense of the paradoxical guilt and innocence in the tragic character, but for Aristotle the paradox arises from the lack of intention in great crime, whereas for Hegel it arises from a partially justifiable one-sidedness. These contrasting explanations are grounded in different characteristic examples: for Aristotle, it is *Oedipus the King*; while for Hegel, it is *Antigone*.[14] But the choice of the illustration may well have the effect of coloring the entire conception of the tragic character and action, for *Oedipus* supports Aristotle but not Hegel, and *Antigone* supports Hegel but not Aristotle. It is possible that neither one is entirely suited to confer an explanation of ancient Greek tragedy in general, for their explanations of tragedy are rooted in their underlying conceptions of ethics and the ethical order rather than in ancient practice as a totality. Specifically, Aristotle offers an account of the ethical life in terms of virtues, whereas Hegel discusses the ethical life in terms of the duties owed to particular entities such as the family and the state. In that case, while no theory of tragedy can overcome the limitations of its own moral and ethical perspective, it is possible to ask a more limited question: do the most famous examples of Greek tragedy confirm one or the other theory?

In this regard, Hegel's account of the tragic collision is suspect. Holding that the collision is always of equally justified powers, Hegel claims, "In Greek tragedy. . . , the occasion for collisions is produced by the moral justification of a specific act, and not at all by an evil will, a crime, or infamy, or by mere misfortune, blindness, and the like." Especially, there is no mere "thirst for power, lust, honour or other passions" (*VÄ* 3, 543; *A* 2, 1212). Yet, to use Hegel's own favorite example, *Antigone*, we have already seen that Creon refers to his actions as "crimes." Moreover, Hegel offers contradictory accounts of tragedy: first he says that they are "just as much innocent as guilty"—a statement consistent with Aristotle—but then he claims they cannot be guilty because they do not choose among alternative courses of action (*VÄ* 3, 545; *A* 2, 1214). Yet Oedipus himself refers to his murder of Laius and his marriage to his mother as crimes for which he is guilty. These recognitions remain valid even if we understand that Creon meant to uphold the sanctity of the *polis*, and Oedipus intended no crime. The issue is deeper, however, than their intentions, for both men are ruled at crucial times by blind passions, which tempt them to abuse their power.

Careful attention to Hegel's model for tragedy, Sophocles' *Antigone*, reveals the clear evidence of passion. Hegel sees the issue as the claims of the state versus the claims of family, or as he explains it in terms of the duties owed the gods: "Antigone honours the bond of kinship, the gods of the underworld, while Creon honours Zeus alone, the dominating power over public life and social welfare" (*VÄ* 3, 544; *A* 2, 1213). These are certainly not the terms in which Antigone sees the conflict, however: "It wasn't Zeus, not in the least,/ who made this proclamation—not to me./ Nor did that Justice, dwelling with the gods beneath the earth, ordain such laws for men." Here is the origin of Hegel's perception of the conflict between the god of the sky and the gods of the underworld, but Antigone denies Creon's edict came from either. "Nor did I think your edict had such force/ that you, a mere mortal, could override the gods,/ the great unwritten, unshakable traditions."[15] The issue, therefore, is not one god against another, but the attempt of a ruler to overrule divine law altogether.[16] In a later formulation, it could be regarded as the issue of the relation between human law and divine law.

Yet even this is too complimentary to Creon: for what he issues is an edict that, by overriding divine law, fails to acquire legitimacy. His treatment of any opposition to his will displays a degree of anger greater even than that of Oedipus; he abuses Antigone, his own son Haemon, and Tiresias. In a telling exchange, he asks Haemon, "Am I to rule this land for others—or myself?"[17] He will not be told by the citizens how to rule Thebes. But this identifies what any Athenian audience would have recognized as tyranny: the wish to rule for his own benefit rather than for the welfare of his subjects.[18] There is indeed a political issue here, but it is not the claims of the family against those of the state. Rather, it is tyranny against legitimacy, arising from the moral corruption of passion against the claims of reason. In the largest sense, Creon's passion is his tragic flaw, the source of his crimes, and the origin of his tyranny. In denying the centrality of the passions to ancient Greek tragedy, Hegel misrepresents the nature of the tragic conflict and mistakes the nature of the tragic character.

If we turn to Oedipus, we find a similar character study of passion at the heart of his tragedy. Hegel considers Oedipus an example of a second type of conflict, between a wide-awake consciousness and unconscious obedience to fate (*VÄ* 3, 545; *A* 2, 1214). Yet the matter is not that simple. Oedipus proclaims his own intelligence with arrogance—"With no help from the birds," that is, from the divine oracle—in mocking the prophet Tiresias, and acting in arrogance in threatening Creon.[19] While it is possible to understand these instances as natural anger in the face of a quest for truth that points uncomfortably close to home, Oedipus also gives a picture of himself in relating what happened when he killed the stranger who turns out to have been Laius, his father: he admits to striking the driver "in anger" and then paying the old man back "with interest."[20] Although seeking the welfare of his city with noble zeal, he is a man given to a hot temper and an arrogance that ridicules the power of the gods. Thus, if Oedipus is at once an example of the collision between the fate ordained him by Apollo and his own noble intentions to avoid it, it is equally true that his nobility of character is fatally compromised by his passions. Fate and passion are simultaneous explanations of the tragedy of Oedipus. Perhaps, indeed, passion becomes the explanation of fate in this second great exemplar of ancient Greek tragedy.

Hegel is correct, however, to insist on the centrality of the various components of the ethical life to Greek tragedy. The individual is never isolated from either family or the state. Both are determinants of a person's obligations, which, if broken, define the extent of a person's crime. But the tragic character's passions are the immediate source of those crimes. The difficult aspect of Greek tragedy is precisely that we are called upon to have pity for fundamentally flawed individuals. This is possible because they are shown as both noble and flawed, admirable and blameworthy, and cognizant of some obligations but astonishingly blind toward others. This paradoxical quality is closer to Aristotle's understanding than Hegel's. Yet, as Hegel understands, the nature of tragic justice is crucial to the tragic effect. Justice must be a reconciliation of the collision or conflict in such a way that the tragic hero himself is purified. It is crucial that Oedipus and Creon recognize their crimes for what they are; this is their purification and their catharsis. Their catharsis, in turn, becomes the foundation for the audience's catharsis of pity and fear, emotions arising from the simultaneous innocence and guilt of the tragic character. In the final conciliation of justice, these paradoxical contradictories are cancelled. Such is the glory of ancient tragedy.

The Dilemma of Tragedy in Christian Culture

If ancient tragedy depends on the ethical relation of the individual to both the family and the state, tragedy in the romantic art form, in which assumptions about human nature are provided by the Christian conception of the inherent dignity and autonomy of the individual, must exhibit substantial differences, and may possess great difficulties. Hegel, like many in the nineteenth century, perceived that the contemporary condition of drama was not altogether well. But even achievements in the theater at the height of the Renaissance, when the revival of classical culture was the foundation for the renewal of the arts, exhibited the problems inherent in the Christian conception of the individual cast into the genre of tragedy inherited from the classical world. Hegel recognized these difficulties in ways that prove instructive for the possibility of the genre in the modern world.

As we have seen, the ethical life provided the crucial dimension of the obligations defining the individual in the classical world. In Hegel's eyes, the components of the ethical life, "country, family, crown, and empire," are still found in romantic drama, but only as the "specific ground on which the individual stands with his subjective character." They are the context of his conflicts, but not "the proper ultimate object of his willing and acting" (*VÄ* 3, 537; *A* 2, 1207). What really matters is the passions of the individual. Hegel illustrates his point by referring to Goethe's *Faust* (Part I), Schiller's *Wallenstein*, and Shakespeare's *Hamlet*. In *Faust*, there is "the tragic quest for harmony between the Absolute in its essence and appearance and the individual's knowledge and will." In *Wallenstein*, the "unity and peace of Germany" is the laudable goal of the general, but he is guilty of revolt against the authority of the Emperor; and in *Hamlet*, only Hamlet's personal character is of real interest, as we see he is "not made for this kind of energetic activity." He perishes, not out of an ethically justified revenge, but merely owing to his own hesitation and external complications (*VÄ* 3, 557–59; *A* 2, 1224–26). External circumstances appear wholly accidental, so that these tragedies do not depend on the ethical forces of the situation. If there is justice, it has an accidental character, or a merely retributive character. It lacks the quality of necessity found in the eternally fated nature of justice in classical tragedy (*VÄ* 3, 565; *A* 2, 1230). The tragic effect, therefore, is utterly different.

Nevertheless, Hegel's brief remarks on the specific examples he discusses indicate a need for reconsidering the nature of romantic tragedy. His understanding of *Faust*, *Wallenstein*, and *Hamlet* is straightforward, but these are precisely the kinds of plays which require sensitivity to the nuances of character if sense is to be made of the emphasis on the individual which lies at the heart of romantic tragedy. For all three examples, the crucial point is indeed character, in the sense of the motives for the choices to be made. As Hegel notes, these choices are not made primarily as expressions of the determinate obligations of kinship, country, or God, but rather as either the expression of obligation toward abstract justice or, more frequently, of passion that corrupts the will and erodes the sense of ethical obligation.[21] It is individual choice rather than the individual's suffering that is the focus of romantic tragedy. *Hamlet, Faust*, and *Wallenstein* illustrate this amply, but in ways Hegel misses altogether.

Hamlet's task is to establish with complete certitude that the justice demanded of him by the ghost of his father is true justice: he must establish the necessity of punishment administered without benefit of a trial. Far from being a weakness of character, as Hegel, among many interpreters, claims, this is evidence of the religious sensibility of Christian civilization. His famous monologue makes this clear: "Whether 'tis nobler in the mind to suffer/ The slings and arrows of outrageous fortune,/ Or to take arms against a sea of troubles,/ And by opposing end them."[22] But the possibility of ending "[t]he oppressor's wrong, the proud man's contumely" through an avenging death is not as simple as it appears when considered in itself. For who would bear any burdens, "But that the dread of something after death,/ The undiscover'd country from whose bourn/ No traveller returns, puzzles the will/ And makes us rather bear those ills we have/ Than fly to others that we know not of?/ Thus conscience does make cowards of us all. . . ."[23] Hamlet's character is not that of a fatally weak will but rather of an admirably scrupulous one. When Hamlet finally kills the usurping King, it is because he has all the evidence of treachery he needs: the Queen has drunk the poison intended for Hamlet, and Laertes has been felled by the poisoned sword intended for Hamlet's murder. Hamlet takes the poisoned cup for himself only then, precisely because—in Hegel's words—he has been "forced in the process to violate the ethical order" (*VÄ* 3, 559; *A* 2, 1225). Even if Hegel is right to see that the play is not simply about "an ethically justified revenge," he nevertheless misses the centrality of Hamlet's conscience to the action of the play. The individual's responsibility to the principles of justice lie at the heart of Christian morality.

Similarly for *Faust* (which Hegel would have known only in earlier versions of the present Part I): the crucial point of the play is Faust's motivation to seek experience beyond what knowledge could give him, having already despaired of the knowledge of philosophy, law, medicine, and theology. He turns first to the spirit of the whole in the Sign of the Macrocosm, and then to the creative Demiurge, the Earth Spirit, in an attempt to grasp what is beyond human knowledge.[24] Hegel implies that this is the Absolute, but it is much less than the Absolute as Hegel conceived it, a point that is confirmed by the entry of Mephistopheles as the response to Faust's quest for illegitimate knowledge. When Faust wagers for his soul, he seeks what he has never experienced: sensuality, enjoyment, hate, distress, and pain. The highest and the deepest, agony and bliss, are to Faust the objects of desire.[25] But this is precisely to seek the life of passion as a substitute for the life of knowledge, so that the remorseless seduction of Gretchen follows from his abandonment of rational knowledge and moral scruples. Hegel's reading of *Faust*, as the quest for harmony between the Absolute and the individual's knowledge and will, appears woefully inadequate as a reading of Goethe's intent in Part I. The character of Faust is crucial to the unfolding of the tragedy.

Finally, Schiller's portrayal of *Wallenstein* in the midst of the Thirty Years War is considerably more complex than Hegel allows. Hegel sees the primacy of character rather than the obligations to the Emperor as the focus of interest, but it is too simple to say that Wallenstein, the Duke of Friedland, is motivated principally by a desire for peace, pursued at the price of treason. He is motivated more by his own ambition and ambition for his family: "The Empire shall revere me as its saviour;/ Myself conducting as befits a Prince/ Of Empire, I shall take any place among them."[26] Moreover, he hopes for his daughter, Thekla, to be graced with a "queenly diadem."[27] But he is also bitter at his earlier treatment by the Emperor, when at Regensburg he was deposed from the Imperial command.[28] Thus, his ostensible motives—peace for the Empire and pity for the sufferings of his countrymen, with a generous admixture of pride and a sense that fate has chosen him[29]—are lies to conceal, perhaps indeed from himself, the true passions that move his heart. Max Piccolomini accuses him justly, then, in saying, "You blindly trample/ The lives of all about you in the dust; The god you serve is not a god of mercy."[30] Wallenstein's betrayal of the Emperor is not an accident offsetting an otherwise admirable motive for peace, but rather the inevitable expression of the pride and lust for power that have been Wallenstein's motivation from the beginning. Schiller is perhaps the closest of all romantic dramatists to recapturing the spirit of classical tragedy, seeing the conflict between the tragically flawed hero's passion and his ethical obligations to the Emperor. Hegel's one-sided reading of Wallenstein as a seeker after peace misses the exploration of the corruption of character by passion, in spite of his general point that the passions are the focus of romantic tragedy. Wallenstein's lack of mercy is the betrayal of the highest expression of Christian morality and his lack of loyalty is the expression of his consuming pride. As Hegel recognizes, guilty passion is central to romantic tragedy.

Romantic tragedy, then, emerges from these three examples as a much more complex phenomenon than classical tragedy. The tragic figure's character is explored more deeply, as we would expect, given the emphasis in Christianity on the importance of one's inner motivation. Yet no attempt is made to find a ruling paradigm for the tragic hero. He may be thoroughly guilty, as is Wallenstein; or he may be an essentially noble figure, as is Hamlet; or he may be deeply ambiguous, as is Faust in Goethe's presentation. Hence the dilemma of romantic tragedy: in its emphasis on the tragic hero's character, the ideal of nobility of character becomes so attenuated it ceases to inform the drama.

Conclusion

Tragedy is the product of seeing life as ruled by paradoxes; both necessity and freedom, and fate and choice determine the tragic individual's dilemma. Tragedy sees life as complex, in which an individual may be both guilty and innocent, both corrupted by passion and cognizant of ethical ties to family, state, and the divine. Hegel recognizes the ethical dimensions of tragedy for the classical world but misses the extent to which, in both classical and romantic forms, there is conflict between the passions, the demands of ethical ties, and simple humanity. Because the Christian world emphasizes the guilt of individuals to a much greater extent than the classical, true tragedy becomes difficult in the Christian era; the element of fate is eliminated, and reduces the sense of paradox in choices freely made. Thus, it should be no surprise that the history of the tragic theater should be written in terms of the flourishing of a tragic vision in only brief periods for each society: Elizabethan England, neo-classical France, and the Germany of Schiller and Goethe. If Hegel preferred the new dramatic form of the *drame* as a fusion of tragedy and comedy, a blend of the former's seriousness with the latter's happy ending (*VÄ* 3, 567; *A* 2, 1232), then this confirms the difficulty of the tragic vision outside the classical world's integrative ethical ties and its overriding sense of fate.

Moreover, Hegel could not have entirely predicted the great era of the novel that lay ahead in the nineteenth century. To be sure, the novel is prose work, but it was to reach epic proportions in both length and complexity by the mid-nineteenth century. His familiarity with this genre would have been restricted to the novels of Goethe and Rousseau, whose works lay as much emphasis on sentiment as on character; the development of the novel as an essay on character and the perception of virtue was primarily a nineteenth-century process. In Austen, Balzac, Dickens, Trollope, and Tolstoy, there would be the union of the personal with the social dimensions of morality and corruption such as is found in true epics, but with the difference that the heroes are not founders of a people, but simply representative types. Thus, the romantic novel in the modern period makes the character of individuals the principal point of interest, as a way of understanding the nature of the entire social fabric in which they live. Anthony Trollope illustrates the point: in *The Eustace Diamonds*, he remarks on the flawed characters that are his heroes, who possess, in effect, tragic flaws, even when the novel moves in an essentially comic resolution of the plot. His heroes are neither faultless nor villains, but they are true to life. His aim, like all teachers, is to make them—and the reader—better "not by one spring heavenwards to perfection . . . but by slow climbing. . . . " In other words, there is a ladder reaching toward perfection, and the purpose of the novel is to lead us upward toward the perception and practice of virtue.[31]

Thus Hegel is correct in claiming that the modern world can no longer produce a classical epic. But then, the modern world is not the classical: the interior world of virtue and feeling is indeed the proper focus of romantic art. It appears, then, that the prosaic modern world both begets and deserves a prose genre of literature that belies Hegel's pessimism regarding the state of poetry. Once again, Hegel's account of the history of poetic genres would have to be modified to reflect the rise of these prose epics. What is most serious for Hegel's aesthetics as a whole, however, is the sudden absence of the Ideal from the account of poetry, traditionally the highest-ranked art. If a case can be made that the purgation of pity and fear in tragedy depends on a reconciliation of characters with justice, then that implicitly constitutes an ideal of repose. And if we allow that lyric poetry frequently expresses a longing for the Ideal, then nevertheless, it is true that Hegel himself does not mention it. Instead, he makes the ethical life—the relations of the individual to family, civil society, and the state—central to both epic and to tragedy. But what Hegel calls "the ethical life" is therefore specifically not the Ideal as a quality of character. Thus, while the ethical function is more specifically vindicated for poetry than it is for the other arts we have examined, it is at the price of a severance of poetry from the general aesthetic of the Ideal that Hegel took such pains to develop as a context for the understanding of the individual arts. This means that it will become necessary to reconsider the general criteria of aesthetics in light of these puzzles raised by Hegel's treatment of the individual arts.

Chapter 7

Beauty and Ornament in Architectural Styles

Having examined Hegel's treatment of the representational visual arts, music, and poetry, we are now in a position to understand in what sense Hegel could view architecture as the foundational art that reveals the essence of what art is. This task is not rendered easy by the diversity of accounts Hegel has already offered for the other arts: from an initial position in which art is cast as the representation of the Ideal, we have seen that the Ideal becomes progressively obscured in Hegel's account of the more spiritual and intellectual arts of music and poetry. Indeed, in poetry the Ideal is completely replaced by an emphasis on the ethical life in Hegel's sense of the determinate duties arising from one's social roles. Finding the Ideal in architecture would seem difficult enough, and Hegel does not even attempt to base his aesthetic of architecture on the Ideal. But discerning the ethical life appears at first glance even further removed from this most nonrepresentational art. How architecture reveals the essence of art in itself, when the other arts do not appear motivated by the same conceptual representation, is surely mysterious.

There are further difficulties within Hegel's presentation of architecture. Architecture, in Hegel's view of artistic and historical development, is preeminently a symbolic art form, not a classical one. That is, it is most paradigmatically art when it is an expression of a universal, such as a unifying religious idea, rather than a means to an external end, such as a dwelling or place of worship (*VÄ* 2, 276–78; *A* 638–40). This opposition between symbol and function in architecture is fundamental for Hegel, as he takes symbolism to be an intrinsic representation of meaning, in contrast to a merely extrinsic end that a building might serve and yet not represent. Moreover, although all architecture may have symbolic elements, Hegel claims it is the architecture of early civilizations that manifests this aim most clearly. In Babylonian towers, Egyptian obelisks, and temple complexes, any functional end appears strictly secondary in importance to the symbolism of the planets in the seven stories of a tower, the rays of the sun in an obelisk, or the calendric cycles in the configuration of pillars in a temple complex. Thus, preclassical civilizations appear to have erected their most ambitious and significant structures precisely as symbolic expressions of the cosmic order.

Yet according to Hegel, architecture achieved perfection only in the classical era. But classical architecture itself is problematic for Hegel, for he sees it as owing its essence to the particular religious and political conditions of ancient Greece, so that its Roman achievements are of little consequence, and the revival of classical style beginning in the Renaissance appears as an anachronism. Yet the classical style of architecture was the dominant style of Western architecture for nearly two and a half millennia. In spite of the rise of the Gothic in the High Middle Ages and its revival in the nineteenth century, the vocabulary and syntax of classicism stood out as the authoritative language of architectural practice until the emergence of modernist styles in the twentieth century. It was a practice defined by both a tradition of building using inherited ornaments in a system of proportion and balance and a tradition of theoretical reflection, which articulated the principles underlying the habits of building. Today, however, the style appears outmoded, its legitimacy vanished; it is merely historical, lacking the capacity to speak to the modern world. In these circumstances, aesthetic understanding of the once normative foundations of the style becomes all the more imperative. Modernist architecture's denial of ornament has left the art without a clear sense of direction and has produced a built environment devoid of charm.

Instead of the classical style, the architecture Hegel considers paradigmatic for the romantic Christian era is Gothic. Arising in the High Middle Ages, the Gothic was initially a purely religious style, but soon was adapted to other kinds of building as well. Nevertheless, Hegel considers all architecture to be fundamentally religious in origin and significance, so that the question of other usages of any style becomes strictly secondary. Thus, passing over the Renaissance repudiation of the Gothic in favor of classical models, Hegel attaches great significance to the revival of the Gothic in his own lifetime (*VÄ* 2, 330; *A* 2, 684). In effect, he sees it as both the highest expression of the Christian faith of the Middle Ages and the most suitable style for his contemporary society. Yet even the nineteenth-century revival of the Gothic cannot be said to have displaced the authority of classicism as the stylistic norm; neo-classicism remained the model for most secular architecture in Europe and for nondomestic architecture in America. Historical developments, therefore, do not necessarily confirm Hegel's presentation of art history. While his view of the primacy of the Gothic is certainly possible for a critic to maintain, it is rather more astonishing to see it in a philosophical account of the art, especially one that seeks to explain the historical dimension of that art in a philosophical way. In particular, any argument for the worth of architecture in general must recognize the actual universality of the classical style.

To be fair to Hegel, philosophical reflection on such a contingent historical practice as architecture is fraught with difficulties. For understanding artistic styles in relation to the universals of aesthetic ideals risks either speaking so generally as to eliminate the specific elements defining styles, or denying the possibility of universality altogether, thus seeing artistic traditions as merely historical accidents justified by temporally defined aesthetic aims. It is the great merit of Hegel's philosophy of the arts that he attempts to do justice to the historical contingency of styles in the context of the universality of aesthetic principles. His understanding of classical and Gothic architecture, therefore, is of great importance to the question of the intrinsic legitimacy of these styles.

Difficulties in Hegel's Aesthetic of Classical Architecture

Classical architecture is problematic for Hegel. The reasons are deeper, however, than simply the dismissal of all but the achievements of the ancient world. The quintessential classical art form for Hegel is sculpture, for it joins spiritual meaning with sensuous representation in aesthetic independence; this he sees as defined historically by Greek classicism (*VÄ* 2, 372–74; *A* 2, 718–20). Classical architecture, therefore, appears caught in his aesthetic between a symbolic artistic end that is degraded in the classical world, and a classical aesthetic purpose realized best in another art. Yet classical forms had been ascendent since the Renaissance, so that it can hardly be argued that it is of so little significance in itself. Thus, in spite of Hegel's restriction of classical architecture to the practice of ancient Greece, it demands attention as a tradition of practice having continuity from ancient times to the nineteenth century.

At the level of aesthetic principles, moreover, Hegel's treatment of classical architecture proves troubling in a more genuinely philosophical sense. The concept of beauty, in particular, was central to traditional theories of classical architecture. Vitruvius had insisted that all public and private buildings should be built for "durability, convenience, and beauty [*venustas*]."[1] Leon Battista Alberti, the great Renaissance classicist, concurred, on the grounds that "graceful and pleasant appearance, so it is thought, derives from beauty and ornament [*pulchritudo et ornamentum*] alone. . . ."[2] Finally, the influential Andrea Palladio began his treatise on architecture by repeating the Vitruvian triad, arguing that beauty [*belleza*] was essential to the perfection of a building.[3] Thus, architecture in the classical style had a long history of association with the idea of beauty. Indeed, no other concept seems so well suited to capturing the essence of the style.

Given the length and unity of the theoretical tradition, it is no surprise that Hegel also sought to explain the nature of classical architecture in terms of beauty: "it comprises a perfect totality in itself which makes its one purpose shine clearly through all its forms, and in the music of its proportions reshapes the purely useful into beauty [*Schönheit*]" (*VÄ* 2, 303; *A* 2, 660). This is a crucial reminder of what is easy to overlook in Hegel's *Aesthetics*: that he made the concept of beauty the generating principle of his entire aesthetic theory. For Hegel, it will be recalled, the beauty of art resided in the mutual adequacy of the Idea as individual reality and its configuration in sensuous reality (*VÄ* 1, 104–5; *A* 1, 73–74). Hence his claim that art has as its vocation to reveal the truth in sensuous form, and that this vocation is realized in the Ideal of serenity and bliss. The problem is to understand how such a concept of intelligible beauty can provide a meaningful account of the visual beauty of architecture.

The importance of architecture for Hegel, however, is indicated by his remark that this art stands at the beginning of the historical development of art in general, precisely because it embodies the essence of art:

> What we have to do is to establish the beginning of art by so deriving it from the Concept or essential nature of art itself that we can see that the first task of art consists in giving shape to what is objective in itself, i.e., the physical world of nature, the external environment of the spirit. . . . The art on which this task is imposed is . . . architecture. . . . (*VÄ* 2, 267; *A* 2, 631)

Here, in spite of the earlier position that art is the sensuous appearance of the truth, in which the intellectual content is well developed and suited to the material form, Hegel says that architecture has its first task in giving physical form to nature simply as the environment for the human spirit, rather than in representing an intellectual content. As an explanation of why architecture reveals the essence of art, this solution appears to trivialize the Concept of art. As a solution to the problem of the relation of visual charm to intelligible beauty, this move is even more troubling. The role of intelligible truth is at risk of being lost from the essence of art.

The problem of intelligible beauty in architecture, therefore, constitutes the principal difficulty in Hegel's account of the art. For it is not clear that there is a truth presented in architectural forms at all. Hegel regards even the intelligible element of a building's purpose as altogether extrinsic to the art of architecture:

> For its vocation lies precisely in fashioning external nature as an enclosure shaped into beauty by art out of the resources of the spirit itself. . . . Its meaning this enclosure does not carry in itself but finds in something else, in man and his needs and aims in family life, the state, religion, etc., and therefore the independence of the buildings is sacrificed. (*VÄ* 2, 270; *A* 2, 633)

He repeats this point specifically for classical architecture, claiming that it "divests architecture of its independence and degrades it" to provide a setting for spiritual meanings realized by other means (*VÄ* 2, 271; *A* 2, 634). Even romantic architecture, arising in a monotheistic culture, appears to him to allow the independence of the style to transcend the spiritual purpose of the buildings, so that the purpose does not determine the character of the whole (*VÄ* 2, 330–31; *A* 2, 684). It is little wonder that commentators have found Hegel's account of the individual arts, and of architecture especially, confused and inadequately developed.[4] If the idea of a spiritual meaning or purpose of a building remains extrinsic to the architecture of the building, then the concept of intelligible beauty appears to make little sense for the art.

Thus, Hegel's aesthetic of classical architecture presents two difficulties at precisely the points where his philosophical approach demands rigorous solutions. The first, at the historical level, takes the classical style as preeminently Greek; Roman developments are limited to the additions of the arch and the vault to the already existing repertoire of columns and entablatures. As a result, the Renaissance appears as an afterthought, while the Baroque—surely the most impressive classicist style in German history—is barely mentioned at all (*VÄ* 2, 327–30; *A* 2, 680–83). But if instead we see the Renaissance revival of classicism as a third period of Christian architecture, following the Romanesque and the Gothic, then the capacity of the style to be adapted to Christian culture focuses attention on the elements of the entire tradition rather than simply on the original Greek usage. But it is the task of classical architectural theory to explain and justify the elements of the style, so that the works of Vitruvius and his Renaissance interpreters, Alberti and Palladio, for example, become relevant to understanding the development and continuity of the classical tradition. This points to the second difficulty for Hegel. At the philosophical level, architecture in general and the classical style in particular appear artistically deficient because any intellectual meaning the art or style has will be extrinsic to the building itself. Attention to the theoretical writings of the classical tradition reveal the extent to which this position is justified or not.

Hegel, however, does not place his aesthetic of classical architecture within the context of the theoretical tradition. In his defense, good reasons can be adduced for such an omission. Hegel relied on Aloys Ludwig Hirt's *Geschichte der Baukunst bei den Alten* (1821–27) for his knowledge of Vitruvius and ancient practice; Alberti's treatise was not translated into German until 1912, and Palladio was of only modest influence in Germany in the century preceding Hegel.[5] Nevertheless, placing Hegel within a tradition of theorizing about architecture from Vitruvius through Palladio is important for understanding the relation of his philosophy of the art to the larger classical tradition and the possible solutions to the difficulties his aesthetic of classical architecture poses. The context of the classical theoretical tradition is especially important for understanding Hegel's solutions to the philosophical difficulties raised by that tradition.

For the modern world, the principal difficulties are precisely the emphasis on the necessity of beauty and the legitimacy of ornament. The temptation in post-Kantian aesthetics is always to make the essence of beauty a matter of pure form, and therefore to see decoration as external, possessing no compelling reason for being.[6] Ornamentation then ceases to be integral to the practice of architecture, and the concept of beauty ceases to be the ruling principle in aesthetic theory. But an examination of the leading theorists of classical architecture will show that they made a building's function integral to the art, providing an intrinsic idea which was represented in every aspect of the building's design, including its ornamentation. Moreover, the relation of a building's function to the elements of visual beauty required such beauty if architecture in the classical tradition was to be the sensuous representation of functional meanings. Thus, Hegel's concept of beautiful art as the sensuous representation of truth can be vindicated from the theoretical tradition of classical architecture through a revision of his account of architectural significance. His aesthetic of classical architecture emerges, then, as a persuasive critique of modern skepticism concerning the necessity of ornamentation and its relevance to the beauty of a building.

To insist that Hegel's aesthetic of architecture should not be read in isolation from the theoretical sources which articulated the classical tradition is to claim that philosophy participates in that tradition as a reflective understanding of its aesthetic issues. Instead, Hegel's work invites a reading in isolation, because he does not refer directly to historical sources, and because his aesthetic occupies a central place in his own integrated philosophical system. Yet, for Hegel the philosophical problems of art arose at the intersection of aesthetic, religious, and ethical principles with historical styles; for the modern world, in contrast, the fundamental problem is the validity of any particular historical style. The theoretical context, therefore, becomes vital both for making sense of Hegel's philosophical concerns and for addressing modern uncertainties. It is imperative, then, to consider the issues raised by the history of classical architectural theory, the most important of which are the roles of ornamentation and meaning in visual beauty.

Aesthetic Issues in the Tradition of Classical Architectural Theory

The most easily identified elements of visual beauty in classical architecture belong precisely to the category of ornament: the columns, entablatures, and other decorative aspects, which the sympathetic modern viewer is apt to take as beauty per se. How ornament might be justified, however, is the crucial philosophical problem, especially after nearly a century in which the legitimacy of ornamentation has been under attack by modernism. In the theoretical tradition of classicism, however, beauty was generally held to consist in harmony of proportions articulated and complemented by appropriate ornamentation. The concept of beauty was therefore complex and nuanced, one in which ornament played a crucial but not exclusive role. Vitruvius defined beauty (*venustas*: loveliness, charm, attractiveness) as existing "when the appearance of the work is pleasing and in good taste, and when its members are in due proportion according to correct principles of symmetry."[7] By "symmetry" he meant a proper agreement in the relations among the parts of a building, essentially what might be called the rhythmic pattern determined by a specific metric unit.[8] Establishing such agreement required constructing columns and other components according to proportions laid down later in the treatise. In turn, these proportions depended both on the kind of column employed and on the kind of temple or other building. Thus, propriety (*decor*) became the fundamental principle of both symmetry and good taste: as "that perfection of style which comes when a work is authoritatively constructed on approved principles," it forms the core of the Vitruvian concept of beauty.[9] Perfection of style could be defined by clear principles.

Ornamentation was governed by thoroughly contingent traditions of propriety: the Doric column was to be used in temples of masculine gods; the Ionic for those of Juno, Diana, and Bacchus; and the Corinthian for the delicate feminine goddesses such as Venus, Flora, and Proserpine. There is no need for philosophical justification here: the character of the columns sufficed as a metaphor for the character of the gods through the resemblance in their proportions and the gracefulness of their capitals. In addition, Vitruvius recognized propriety in the ornamentation of private dwellings, reflecting the social status and political role of the owner.[10] Hence, for the authoritative source from antiquity, beauty consisted in correct proportions and the proper ornamentation suited to the type and function of a building. Beauty was required, and a building's function was expressed in its visual appearance.

In the Renaissance, however, Alberti explicitly separated the concepts of beauty and ornament, although he found both necessary for pleasing appearance. He defined them as follows:

> Beauty is that reasoned harmony of all the parts within a body, so that nothing may be added, taken away, or altered, but for the worse. . . . If this is conceded, ornament may be defined as a form of auxiliary light and complement to beauty.[11]

Writing in a deliberately classical Latin, Alberti uses *pulchritudo* here instead of Vitruvius's *venustas*, suggesting excellence rather than attractiveness; *pulchritudo* has a broader meaning, touching on the moral quality of nobility (like the Greek *tò kalón*), and opposed to the aesthetic charm of *venustas*. Hence, it must name a quality inherent in a building, discernible throughout every part. In contrast, Alberti finds ornament an extrinsic addition to the fundamental design of a work. But this must not be misunderstood. Alberti insisted that harmonious proportions were crucial to beauty as nobility, and, like Vitruvius, described the correct proportions for columns, entablatures, and their component parts in minute detail. Thus ornament itself was also governed by the criterion of beauty.

Although it may seem as though ornament risks becoming unnecessary in Alberti's dichotomy, he explicitly denies this, "for the art of building is composed of very many parts, each one . . . demanding to be ennobled by much varied ornament." What dictates both the requirements of ornamentation and the harmony of parts proportionate to one another is *concinnitas*, "in which beauty shines full face." Once again, Alberti employs a term from classical Latin, meaning "elegance and harmony of style." This, then, is the essence of beauty, "the main object of the art of building, and the source of her dignity, charm, authority, and worth."[12] Therefore, like Vitruvius, Alberti makes beauty the central concept for architecture, and ornament necessary for visual charm.

If ornament is important, then, it is the column which is the principal ornament, having both grace and dignity.[13] These, however, are precisely the qualities associated with beauty, so that ornament is not a separate concept for Alberti. Moreover, in considering why a temple ought to be "so beautiful that nothing more decorous could ever be devised," he remarks that "ornament will give it dignity."[14] Ornament, therefore, is essential to the beauty which encourages piety toward God. Hence:

> In view of all this, surely it is our duty to strive with all enthusiasm, application, and diligence to make what we build as ornate as possible, especially those buildings which everyone would want to be dignified. Within this group lie public works, and in particular sacred ones: since no man would allow them to be naked of ornament.[15]

Both ornament and harmonious proportions, therefore, were essential to the beauty and dignity of a building. What is significant here is the emergence of a justification of ornamentation explicitly in terms of beauty and dignity. Thus beauty becomes the central concept for classicism.

Propriety, or *decorum*, however, was no less important for Alberti than for Vitruvius. After a discussion of ornament in general, Alberti proceeds to a discussion of ornament in sacred buildings, followed by public secular buildings, and concluding with private dwellings. He repeats the associations given by Vitruvius concerning the characters of columns and the ancient temples of the gods, affirming their capacity to evoke similar associations in a quite different cultural context.[16] He expects the highest degree of ornamentation in sacred architecture, and only slightly less in public secular buildings. Private dwellings should not be excessively ornamented, yet a moderate amount is appropriate, for "we decorate our property as much to distinguish family and country as for any personal display. . . ."[17] Such decoration is a virtue of the good citizen, not a vice of ostentation. Thus, there were principles of propriety for Alberti, as for Vitruvius; propriety was implicitly the foundation of visual beauty. As for Vitruvius, a building's function was a crucial determinant of its actual appearance. Beauty was the greatest where ornamentation was the highest as a condition of the building's expression of its purpose. This principle becomes even more central for later Renaissance theorists.

Palladio, the last and greatest of the Renaissance theorists, achieved his reputation in large part because of the clarity with which he presented the propriety of the orders in his *Four Books of Architecture*. Book I discusses the five orders as the most considerable part of the ornamentation of a building, specifying the proportions of the columns, entablatures, and intercolumniations. The remainder of the treatise is devoted to the different types of buildings: Book II to private dwellings, Book III to public buildings, and Book IV to temples and churches. In this exclusive concentration on a building's purpose and the attendant propriety of its ornament, Palladio differs from both Vitruvius and Alberti: for they devoted substantial portions of their treatises to practical questions of building materials, siting, and methods of construction. The difference reflects the change in the role of the architect during the sixteenth century, but it also serves to focus attention on the primary role of functional propriety in ornamentation. The selection of ornament to create the beauty of a building becomes the central concern of the architect.

Like Vitruvius and Alberti, Palladio defines beauty as resulting from the agreement of the parts among themselves and with the whole,[18] and this leads to a consideration of the proportions most pleasing for all the parts of a building. Yet, in spite of this association of beauty with proportion, Palladio's emphasis in discussing beauty falls equally on the ornamentation. This shift from Alberti's distinction between beauty and ornament reflects a shift in Renaissance architectural practice to a greater complexity of detail in general, visible in Palladio's own work.[19] Thus, at the beginning of Book IV, Palladio offers a justification of both ornament and harmonious proportion in churches. The argument turns on the nature of the goodness of God's creation, in contrast to Alberti's simple ascription of dignity to the ornamenting of temples:

> And indeed, if we consider this beautiful machine of the world, with how many wonderful ornaments it is filled, and how the heavens, by their continual revolutions, change the seasons according as nature requires, and their motion preserves itself by the sweetest harmony of the moderate; we cannot doubt, but that the little temples we make, ought to resemble this very great one, which, by his [God's] immense goodness, was perfectly completed with one word of his; or imagine that we are not obliged to make in them all the ornaments we possibly can, and build them in such a manner, and with such proportions that all the parts together may convey a sweet harmony to the eyes of the beholders, and that each of them separately may serve agreeably to the use for which it shall be required.[20]

Here both ornament and proportion are explicitly required, in order that a temple or church might reflect the beauty of the world as God's creation. The ancient doctrine of cosmic harmony is only one part of this beauty of the world; the other part, equally important, is the plenitude of ornament, the variety and complexity of being which constitutes the world. This is a much deeper argument than Alberti gave in defense of the ornamentation of sacred buildings. But in this integration of ornament into beauty, Palladio anticipates the direction Baroque architecture would take.

For the principal theorists in the classical tradition, therefore, the concept of beauty was crucial to both the description of a building and the justification of architecture as an art. For all the theorists, the concept of beauty entailed a harmony of proportions, but ornament also played a substantial role. For Vitruvius, ornament was part of the larger concept of propriety, whereby a building reflected its function according to traditional principles of good taste. For Alberti, ornament was the complement of beauty in a building's pleasing appearance; whereas for Palladio, ornament was an essential component of the concept of beauty along with harmonious proportions. For all the theorists, ornamentation was especially linked to the principle of propriety or *decorum*, the greatest amount of ornamentation being required in sacred architecture, a slightly lesser amount in public secular buildings, and a moderate amount befitting the private dwellings of people of significant social status. But although both Alberti and Palladio repeated the Vitruvian canon identifying the Greek orders with specific classical gods, they did not provide explicit rules for Christian churches.[21] In practice, however, the Corinthian and Composite orders came to dominate sacred architecture in the Renaissance, leaving the Tuscan, Doric, and Ionic for secular buildings.[22] Through the customs governing propriety, the orders reflected the social function and status of a building, making the principal ornament the chief bearer of meaning. In this way, the idea of a building's purpose became the foundation of its visual beauty.

In spite of the justifications offered for ornamentation by the principal theorists, however, they stop short of a genuinely philosophical explanation of the necessity of beauty. Hegel calls beauty the combination of metaphysical universality with the determinateness of particularity (*VÄ* 1, 39; *A* 1, 22), so that beauty is required to the extent that universals are justified. But the theory of classical architecture rarely attains universality. The concept of beauty is never justified by reference to either first principles or a tradition of philosophical explanation. It could have been: the role of harmonious proportions in beauty was traditional and can be traced back to Plato's account in the *Timaeus* (35–36), where he defends the goodness of order and describes its mathematical foundation.[23] So, too, Palladio's justification of ornament and proportion in temples, as reflecting the harmony of the cosmos in the changing of the seasons, echoes a similar passage in the *Timaeus* (37), where Plato speaks of the demiurge's ordering of the heavens to create the cyclic units of time: days, months, and years. Such order constitutes the goodness of the cosmos. For a civilization steeped in the learning of antiquity, such references would have been largely unnecessary; the concept of beauty could be taken for granted as implying the content given it by the tradition of philosophical reflection. The task of theory, then, was to articulate general principles and to supply models of specific forms in the orders and their employment in larger designs. For practicing architects working within a tradition, theory need not aspire to philosophical explanation.

Nevertheless, the theoretical accounts considered above do raise philosophical questions. First, it is evident that the concept of visual beauty is not restricted, except for Alberti, to the idea of harmonious proportions, and even for him, beauty (as *pulchritudo*) requires the complement of ornament. But the entailment of ornamentation in beauty, or in conjunction with beauty, requires more justification than simply precedent or tradition. This Hegel provides in his aesthetic of architecture. Second, even the traditional principles of propriety call for a more explicit justification than the theorists usually give; Palladio's justification of beauty in sacred architecture as a reflection of the beauty of God's creation is a beginning. The beauty of secular architecture, however, requires a similarly cogent explanation. That is to say: what is required is a justification of ornamentation in itself. Again, Hegel provides just such an explanation. Although Hegel's philosophy of classical architecture is not without its difficulties, it addresses important questions arising in the tradition of classical architectural theory.

Hegel on the Aesthetic Necessity of Ornamentation

As we have seen, Hegel regarded beauty as the aim of architecture. Nevertheless, his sense of what constitutes visual beauty departs considerably from the emphasis on rational proportions found in Vitruvius, Alberti, and Palladio. Although he briefly remarks that classical architecture "in the music of its proportions reshapes the purely useful into beauty," he argues that the relations between walls, columns, and beams "cannot be reduced to settlement by numerical proportions with perfect precision" (*VÄ* 2, 303, 306; *A* 2, 660, 663). Instead the eurhythmy was secret in classical times, more a matter of a sense of balance than a rigid code. Now it is true that classical practice was more flexible than the Vitruvian code of proportions recognized; Hegel is historically accurate in this observation.[24] Yet the abandonment of the theoretical insistence on visual beauty defined by such a code is a significant move in its own right; it leaves the concept of beauty to be defined by other elements of architectural style. Inescapably, detail and ornament emerge as what really matter in visual beauty, as Hegel acknowledges for villas and secular public buildings in particular (*VÄ* 2, 305; *A* 2, 602).[25] In ancient Greek architecture, however, he does recognize that the ornamentation was essential for breaking up wall surfaces so that the proportions would be visible (*VÄ* 2, 319; *A* 2, 674). This, however, was not so much a justification of ornament, but only one visual effect of ornamentation. The justification of the essential kinds of ornament in classical architecture—columns, capitals, entablatures, and pedimented roofs—required another kind of argument.

In common with the theoretical tradition, Hegel saw "the column as the fundamental element in the purposiveness of architecture and its beauty" (*VÄ* 2, 310; *A* 2, 666). Hence, it was no merely extrinsic ornament, but an element having a clear purpose of its own in any context where freedom from utilitarian demands allowed architecture to develop its potential. In Hegel's view, such was the temple in ancient times (*VÄ* 2, 305; *A* 2, 662). Holding that the "column has no other purpose but to be a support," he deduces its upper and lower moldings from this end: the use of a pedestal and a capital arises in order to link the column with the ground and with the load it carries. Such architectural terminations serve the same function as illustrated letters in medieval manuscripts; the decoration articulates the form (*VÄ* 2, 310–11; *A* 2, 666–68). Since the importance of moldings and terminations has received renewed attention recently, Hegel's argument attains greater significance than it otherwise might.[26] After nearly a century, in which such detail has been dismissed as unnecessary, an argument for its aesthetic necessity is all the more pertinent. What may have seemed a trivial point in Hegel's day in fact provides the justification for the principle of providing moldings in ornamentation in general.

Nevertheless, Hegel's argument may appear to reduce the function of the column to a minimally interesting level, since he holds that it is used simply to support a load. Yet here the significant load must be specified: "What the columns carry is the entablature laid above them" (*VÄ* 2, 313; *A* 2, 669). It is the appearance of load-bearing that matters rather than the actual load. But this appearance must give rise to moldings in the entablature itself: the architrave and the cornice constitute the appropriate terminations, and the frieze—at least in the Doric order—displays its function of allowing the ends of the roof beams to rest on the main beams. Thus arise, according to the traditional explanation, the triglyphs and metopes of the Doric order.

Here, Hegel takes the story of the origin of a specific decoration to serve as the explanation of the function of the frieze in general. Moreover, he goes farther in applying the law of appearance of load-bearing to justify pedimented roofs supported by the entablature. For the roof "must no longer support a load but only be supported, and this character of not supporting must be visible on itself, i.e., it must be so constructed that it cannot now support anything and must therefore terminate at an angle . . ." (*VÄ* 2, 314; *A* 2, 670–71). A horizontal roof, in contrast, might still bear a load; it does not mark the completion of a whole. Thus Hegel is able to offer a powerful aesthetic argument in defense of the most characteristic elements of classical architecture. This defense of ornament in terms of the appearance of load-bearing will not account for the details of the orders, but it does offer an argument against the scourge of plain walls and flat roofs, which have been the hallmarks of twentieth-century modernism. The intelligibility of form is a necessary condition of beauty.

Two final arguments strengthen the case for the use of columns and the maintenance of a system of proportions based upon them. The first is that the Greeks took the height of their buildings from a man's height. Hegel is vague on this, but the point is clear: the buildings were not more than one story high. Thus the human scale of the height kept the buildings horizontal. The second point is that this horizontality was articulated by columns, which helped make the proportions of the building visible. As Hegel notes:

> Wholly simple lines and big surfaces, for example, appear in this undivided simplicity not so big as when some variety or interruption is introduced into them, with the result that the eye is only then presented with a more specific proportion. (*VÄ* 2, 319; *A* 2, 674)

What is presented here as the contribution of Greek architecture is in fact a general truth: an architecture on a human scale must be predominantly horizontal, and it must be articulated by vertical elements which have at least the appearance of a visible structural function. Hegel presents, therefore, a philosophical defense of the continuing relevance of classical architectural style. This is what the modern world desperately needs, and what Renaissance theorists never undertook, largely because they were concerned with the reconstruction of the iconography of classicism. Hegel provides many of the crucial arguments.

Hegel's aesthetic of classical architecture is a genuinely philosophical understanding of the style. The aesthetic necessity of columns, terminations and moldings, pedimented roofs, and building proportions kept to a human scale is justified on the grounds of the intelligibility of form. Yet such intelligibility is only a necessary condition of beauty; on Hegel's understanding of beauty, it cannot be a sufficient condition. For Hegel, beauty in any art depends on an intellectual content, for art is the sensuous appearance of truth. But the mere appearance of load bearing is certainly not the truth cast in stone: it establishes only the general form of the ornamentation. The specific forms of ornamentation—the orders of columns and their corresponding entablatures—come closer to having intellectual content because of their historical origins and their traditional associations with particular divinities in the ancient world (*VÄ* 2, 321–29; *A* 2, 676–80). But these are highly contingent details, which, although reiterated by Renaissance theorists, do not appear to be susceptible to a genuinely philosophical justification. As a result, it is difficult to see how architecture reveals the essence of art as Hegel claims. Artistic beauty, in Hegel's view, requires both truth and artistic configuration: classical architecture ought to present the most perfect unity of these two elements of beauty. Thus, the question remains: does Hegel's aesthetic of architecture rest on a concept of beauty at all? Is there a truth manifested sensuously in the proportions and ornamentation of classical architecture? More specifically, is there a classical Ideal represented in this style of the art?

The Ethical Function of Classical Architecture

For Hegel, art is the representation of the Idea of beauty or the Ideal; for this reason, he defends the classical form of art in ancient Greece as the perfect union of form and spiritual content (*VÄ* 1, 389–91; *A* 1, 299–301). But the spiritual content of the classical Ideal is given by the "nobility and loftiness of spirit" which the gods themselves manifest in Greek sculpture as "infinite security and peace, untroubled bliss and untrammelled freedom" (*VÄ* 2, 81–84; *A* 1, 481–83). Neither materiality nor anthropomorphic form are impediments to divinity: Greek classicism, in Hegel's view, reconciled the divine and the human, although at the price of not recognizing the dimension of humanity that is capable of transgression against both the ethical life and the Absolute (*VÄ* 2, 24–25; *A* 1, 436). Thus, the Idea of the beautiful, recalling the concept of *tò kalón* in the ancient Greek sense, was a perfect spiritual tranquillity and a perfectly harmonious form reflecting this tranquillity. This was the Ideal of classicism expressed most characteristically in the art of sculpture. For only the three-dimensional sculpted figure can represent the spiritual nobility of the gods in human form. This is why Hegel regards classical architecture as a "degradation" of the art, because in contrast to the independent symbolic form of towers and obelisks, works which have no external utility, the classical Greek temple was only an inorganic environment for the spiritual art of sculpture placed within it. Therefore, Hegel does not make classical architecture a representation of the classical Ideal.

It might be possible, however, to extend the concept of tranquillity from the humanized figures of the gods in Greek sculpture to architecture itself. The harmonious balance Vitruvius demands as an essential element of the beautiful is also the harmony Plato demanded of the soul: a well-ordered soul is the essence of virtue.[27] This is an ethical concept in the Greek, if not the Hegelian sense; but as a state of character, it is precisely what Hegel intends by the Ideal. The Ideal of the gods became the ideal for humanity to emulate. If architecture can create a similar sense of tranquillity, as the classical theorists imply, it too might reflect the classical worldview. Indeed, the emphasis on harmonious proportions in the theoretical tradition becomes intelligible only on this premise. Thus, although Hegel does not make this particular argument, it should be possible to see an extension of the concept of character from the human form to the architectural environment of a building. If so, the beauty of classical architecture should become the representation of the classical Ideal.

The classical Ideal itself sprang from the felicitous union of subjective freedom and the ethical life of the state in ancient Greece (*VÄ* 2, 25–26; *A* 1, 436–37). In the Hegelian sense, the ethical life entails the living out of customary obligations arising in the contexts of family, civil society, and the state (*GPR* §§150–52; *PR* 107–9). The union of freedom and the ethical life, then, was directly responsible for the beauty of Greek art; for the serene harmony of Greek ethical life was also reflected in the gods of their religion, the statuary of which were placed in the temples. This serenity should be reflected in all the arts cultivated in ancient Greece, however, not just in sculpture, although sculpted figures of the gods express it most clearly. Moreover, surely the argument for the origin of the classical Ideal in the ethical life can extend to republican Rome as well. Thus, the spirit of the classical world is perceivable as the foundation of the classical style of architecture; to see how requires attention both to the concept of propriety emphasized by all theorists in the classical tradition and the structure of the ethical life in Hegel's philosophy.

Hegel regards the vocation of architecture in general as fashioning external nature into an enclosure for the human spirit or divine images, so that architecture finds its meaning "in man and his needs and aims in family life, the state, religion, etc." (*VÄ* 2, 270; *A* 2, 633). Although he regards these sources of meaning as extrinsic to a building, nevertheless, they are recognizable as the aspects of the ethical and religious life. Family life and the state, in particular, comprise an abbreviated list of the components of the ethical life for Hegel. For classical architecture, he finds that a building's purpose "now becomes what rules, what dominates the entire work, and determines its fundamental shape, its skeleton as it were . . ." (*VÄ* 2, 304; *A* 2, 661). The greatest unity of purpose and form is found in the classical style. It is all the more mysterious, then, why he should regard architecture as degraded by its use for purposes of the human spirit independent of the purely artistic.

Close attention to the tradition of classical architectural theory, however, reveals a connection to the realm of the ethical life that Hegel misses the opportunity to construct. Hegel says that a building's purpose in the classical style determines its fundamental shape—but no more than that. The Vitruvian canon of propriety, however, assigned the Doric order to masculine deities, the Corinthian to delicate feminine goddesses, and the Ionic to divinities intermediate in character. This sense of associative meaning in the orders, repeated by Renaissance theorists even when irrelevant in any literal sense for Christian culture, is largely absent in Hegel's account. The only allusion to it is his repetition of the origin of the Corinthian order in the acanthus tree that grew on top of a girl's grave, the leaves surrounding the girl's basket of toys left there by her nurse (*VÄ* 2, 326; *A* 2, 680). Otherwise, Hegel simply describes the Doric as firm, solid, and masculine, and the Ionic and Corinthian as having more elegance and grace. The result is that the orders lose the capacity to communicate the meanings they possessed according to traditional theory. Moreover, by concentrating on ancient architecture as revealing the essence of the classical style, Hegel misses the richness of development and interpretation of the style since the Renaissance. In particular, the Renaissance practice of associating the hierarchy of the orders with both the distinction between secular and sacred and with the hierarchy of status is precluded. Hence, although he takes ornament to be the most substantial part of beauty in classical architecture, the possibility of connecting ornamentation to a building's purpose is lost. It need not be: whereas Hegel finds a building's purpose in classical architecture to be what "determines its fundamental shape" only, a revision of his aesthetic, recognizing the continuity of the theoretical tradition, would regard the orders as also properly reflecting a building's purpose. In the classical tradition, purpose suffuses ornament as well as shape.

Thus, the theoretical tradition becomes vital for completing the account of architecture on Hegelian principles. The three fundamental building types are private dwellings, public secular buildings, and sacred edifices. In Palladio, for example, these embrace villas and townhouses, public squares and basilicas of justice, and temples and churches, respectively. These correspond directly to the categories of family, civil society, and the state in Hegel's development of the ethical life, and to religion. Thus, the tradition of classical architectural theory from Vitruvius through Palladio provides a thorough vindication for regarding a building's purpose as the foundation of its intelligible beauty, and for conceiving the categories of purpose as answering to the deepest human needs for family, civic life, and religious worship. Hegel's dismissal of all but the temple is justified in one sense: sacred buildings have always been considered as having supreme importance. They reveal the essence of the art of architecture, narrowly defined. But the absence of a thorough consideration of Roman secular architecture, for example, or of subsequent theory and practice in secular categories, substantially weakens Hegel's ability to discover how the full complexity of the ethical and religious life might be represented in a variety of architectural forms.

The Problem of Romantic Architecture

The full development of the religious purpose of architecture emerges, however, only in Hegel's account of the Gothic; the classical temple appears reserved simply for standing or strolling about, rather than for assembly of a congregation in worship. The Gothic, on the other hand, reflects the Christian emphasis on worship in the inwardness of the heart, because its enclosure sets it completely apart from the world. The characteristic aspects of the Gothic form—the pointed arches, the seeking of height in the cathedrals, and the elimination of the difference between load and support—express a "free striving upwards," a sublime elevation above the finite world suggesting the Infinite (*VÄ* 2, 332–34; *A* 2, 685–87). If these aspects are characteristic of the Christian church in general, however, it is not the case that only the Gothic is capable of expressing them. Indeed, Hegel regards the Romanesque as the first stage of romantic architecture; but this stage was in fact dependent upon classical, not Gothic, models. Moreover, Hegel admits that his aim is only to account for the appropriateness of stylistic characteristics in his analysis of the Gothic; he does not assert actual intent on the part of the builders to create a style uniquely reflective of Christian theology (*VÄ* 2, 341; *A* 2, 692–93). Yet the Gothic style was in fact thoroughly informed by a theological intent, which is crucial to understanding its historical uniqueness.

The most important aspect of the Gothic was its aim of suffusing the interior of the church with light. This was for theological reasons: light was a metaphor of the divine, of God incarnate in His Son. The concept of light as a metaphor of the divine was founded on the Gospel of Saint John 1: 4: referring to the Word (Logos), "In him was life, and the life was the light of men." This is also captured in the Nicene Creed's second article, "God of God, light of light, very God of very God. . . . " This metaphor was vital to the replacement of wall area by windows.[28] Yet Hegel not only misses the aim of the Gothic to allow more light than Romanesque churches had, but asserts that the interiors are dark, rather than light (*VÄ* 2, 333; *A* 2, 686). Compared to later Baroque churches in particular, this is not altogether unfair, but the prominence of windows in the choirs of Gothic churches shows a concerted effort to allow light to shine on the most sacred space around the altar of the church.

The proportions of the Gothic edifice were also important to the originators of the style. Integer ratios of length and breadth were for architecture, as for music, the guarantee of consonance and harmony, and these can be found in the Gothic churches if sufficient attention is paid to them.[29] Again, Hegel misses this aspect of the Gothic style, arguing instead against the "mystical meaning" of proportions, thus leaving only the decoration as the constituent of beauty (*VÄ* 2, 339, 344; *A* 2, 691, 695). But the reason for the original emphasis on proportion was the same as for classical architecture: it is at the very core of the concept of beauty. For the Gothic, proportion and light were the two components of beauty.[30] The worship of God demanded just such visible beauty.

The matter of decoration is also of clear importance to Gothic churches. Hegel regards the decoration as only functional, splitting up the large surfaces of lengthy walls through a wealth of detail (*VÄ* 2, 344–46; *A*, 695–97). Certainly there was an ambivalence about ornament in the Gothic style: classical orders were often altered or abandoned, in order not to suggest any associations with pagan antiquity.[31] The walls were plain stone, in order not to suggest the worldliness of visual charm that would detract from the spiritual purpose of a place of worship; this was a legacy of the ascetic Cistercian monastic reforms out of which the Gothic emerged.[32] Yet there was equally a wealth of sculpture, especially on the exterior: the symbolism of the cathedral as an image of heaven was often inscribed in the very façade of the structure.[33] The gargoyles that are so well known as an apparently whimsical aspect of the Gothic were perhaps depictions of the terrors of hell that would befall those who remained outside the salvation offered within the sanctuary.[34] Thus Hegel's interpretation of the Gothic must be amended substantially: the decoration was not simply functional, but rather symbolic and explicitly theological and pedagogical. Again, although Hegel does not derive the Gothic style from the romantic Ideal, it is easy enough to make that argument. For if it encompasses both the vision of heaven and the threat of hell in its iconography, then bliss and woe dwell together, reconciled in the promise of salvation.

The same principles which informed the Gothic style, however, also came to inform the sacred architecture of the Renaissance and Baroque periods. The dome borrowed from Roman models expressed the perfection of God, so that the church was even more clearly a metaphor of the kingdom of heaven on earth.[35] The addition of the drum to the dome allowed light to penetrate the interior from above to an even greater degree than in the Gothic style; the pursuit of light was just as explicitly a motive of Baroque builders as in the earlier period.[36] Finally, the height of Baroque churches often overshadowed their horizontal dimensions (as in Mansart's church of Saint-Louis-des-Invalides, for example), so that they too expressed an elevation above the finite toward the Infinite. Finally, of course, decoration was extremely important to the Baroque style, but less for symbolic significance than as reflecting the propriety of honoring God with the finest human efforts at visual beauty. In these ways, the return to an architectural style rooted in the classical language transformed the characteristics of the classical temple to suit the needs of Christian worship, so that many of the same theological principles were expressed in both the Gothic and the Baroque. This means that the ways in which the classical language was employed are more important than the specific origins of the formal elements or building types. Although Hegel almost completely neglects the Renaissance revival of classicism, the ability of the classical language to reflect the religious needs of Christian worship completes the development of historical architectural styles in Hegel's philosophical system.

The ability of the language of ornamentation in architecture to express a building's function through a commonly accepted code of propriety provides an intrinsic ability to represent the truth of the ethical and religious life in the forms of private dwellings, secular public buildings, and classical temples or Christian churches. This intellectual content, moreover, provides precisely the foundation for the concept of beauty in the Hegelian sense. In saying that the beauty of art resides in the mutual adequacy of the absolute truth and its sensuous configuration, Hegel isolates two components, one intellectual and one material, that must conform to one another for the truth to be perceptible in sensuous form. This principle of conformity justifies the classical principle of propriety. But whereas classical theorists simply asserted what constituted beauty and propriety, Hegel provides a genuinely philosophical justification. It is only in his application of the concept of art to architecture that Hegel weakens the concept of beauty, losing the complexity of the truth that might be reflected in architecture as the unfolding of the ethical and religious life.[37] With our understanding of the categories of a building's purpose answering to Hegel's categories of the ethical and religious life, however, it is possible to see that architectural beauty can have an intellectual component, and that this should inform every aspect of a building's visual beauty.

Hegel's aesthetic of architecture, therefore, is worth taking seriously as an argument in defense of the particular styles that have dominated Western architecture. In an age which has sought to banish the traditional heritage, it is essential to recover both the necessity of ornamentation and an appreciation of the appropriateness of particular forms of ornament. Although modernist architects argue that beauty requires only the pure form of harmonious proportions, the banishment of ornament in the twentieth century has necessarily resulted in the elimination of beauty. Hegel's aesthetic explains why columns, entablatures, and pediments are essential types of ornament, and his philosophical respect for history provides the justification for preserving the particular ornaments of the classical and Gothic traditions as reflecting the dignity of the ethical and religious life. This is why Hegel is justified in placing architecture as the foundation of all the arts. To ornament the public space appropriately—that is, with *decorum*—is to affirm its dignity and our worth as human beings. This affirms the centrality of the *civitas*, whether the city of God or the city of man. Such was once the purpose of architecture as well as the other arts. But we need, then, to explore the coherence of Hegel's aesthetics of the Ideal and the ethical life.

Part III

The Foundations of Art

Chapter 8

Art and the Beauty of the Ethical Order

The examination of Hegel's treatment of the individual arts reveals a curious puzzle. In spite of his insistence in Parts 1 and 2 of the *Aesthetics* that art is the sensuous representation of the Ideal, his reliance on the Ideal is completely lacking in his treatment of architecture, only implicit in his treatment of poetry, and strikingly muted in his discussion of music. Instead of the Ideal, however, the arts of architecture and poetry rely heavily on what Hegel terms "the ethical life," which is the actual life of determinate duties defined by the specific social roles an individual occupies. A revision of Hegel's general aesthetic theory appears to be in order: it must address the relation of the ethical life to the Ideal, the latter being ultimately religious in origin.

Yet it is all the more imperative to examine the logic of Hegel's concepts of the ethical and religious life in order to explore their possible relevance to today's world. For as controversial as a deduction of artistic norms from a religiously grounded Ideal may be, the validity of the ethical life is even more dubious. The family appears in dissolution; civil society is reduced to the pursuit of economic gain, and attachment to one's country or state is defined minimally by legal obligations. Individualism has usurped community: that is the essence of modernity. The relevance of all these dimensions of the ethical life to art in the modern world is therefore not likely to be persuasive. Yet their validity would be the only possible ground of Hegel's argument for their role in the ethical nature of the arts, and it is by no means clear that radical individualism is satisfactory or sustainable in itself. Perhaps Hegel's insights are important not only for the arts, but for the question of the relation of the individual to the larger community.

Thus, a philosophical understanding of art must address the connection between aesthetics and the wider social world in which art finds its activity. But the modernist rupture in the arts both corresponds and contributes to a similar rupture in the role of art in forming the ethical life. For of at least as great a consequence as the stylistic divide between modernism and the classically inspired tradition has been the loss of the classical world's articulation of the role of art in both individual and social life. For evidence of this, we may take Aristotle and Heidegger as representative figures from the two historical worlds. We shall then be in a position to assess the significance of Hegel's conception of the ethical life for the arts and the extent to which it might remain pertinent to the modern world.

Civic Life and the Arts in the Classical Polis

Aristotle provides a succinct statement of the role of the arts in ancient Greek society in Book 8 of *The Politics*, where he discusses the content of a liberal education, that is, what is required for the education of a free citizen who is to be active in the political affairs of his city. He identifies the customary branches of education in his day: reading, writing, gymnastics, music, and sometimes drawing. Of these, the first two have obvious utility in the active political and economic life of the citizen, and Aristotle does not dwell on them or treat them as arts in our sense. But drawing and music are arts in the modern sense, and they are for nonutilitarian purposes. Since Aristotle rejects as a subject of education anything that makes a person a "mechanic," as well as anything that would risk becoming an occupation if carried too far, music and drawing are appropriate to study, but only to a certain extent; becoming a professional at them would be unbecoming to a citizen.[1] Although drawing has a utility of sorts, in forming a "correct judgement of the works of artists" (*Pol* 1338a18), it is clear that this presupposes a prior end in the enjoyment of such works; this is confirmed when Aristotle says that the value of drawing as a subject of education of men "is perhaps rather because it makes them judges of the beauty of the human form" (*Pol* 1338b1–2). Thus, appreciation of human beauty would appear to be the principal end of education in drawing, because it was the principal end of the art of drawing in ancient Greek society.

The value of learning music, however, receives far more attention, for not only is listening to music pleasant in itself; the art has a profound moral effect. "Rhythm and melody supply imitations of anger and gentleness, and also of courage and temperance, and of all the qualities contrary to these, and of the other qualities of character, which hardly fall short of the actual affections . . . " (*Pol* 1340a19–20). Here it is clear that not only does music arouse the passions (as is familiar from post-Renaissance musical theory), more to the point, music can strengthen or weaken the virtues of character, the habitual dispositions of the heart and soul. Music is the art with the strongest connection to morality and character; hence being trained in it sufficiently to judge rightly in what we hear, and to take delight in the proper rhythms and melodies will bear fruit in our ability to take delight "in good dispositions and noble actions" (*Pol* 1340a19). A similar, but weaker, case can be made for drawing, since "figures and colours are not imitations, but signs of character, indications which the body gives of states of feeling" (*Pol* 1340a34). The connection with ethics is slight in drawing, whereas it lies at the heart of music. For the ancient Greeks, music had a necessarily ethical effect and therefore an ethical purpose. This, of course, echoes his remarks in the *Poetics* concerning the ethical purpose of epic, tragic (and comic) poetry, of which music was considered a part. The arts in ancient Greece, then, always had a humanistic content and an ethical role in the society.

Nevertheless, Aristotle's way of characterizing the use of music (and presumably poetry in general) goes well beyond any didactic or purifying function. He remarks that music is used "for intellectual enjoyment in leisure," and considers music to be an "amusement" as well—"for the sake of relaxation" (*Pol* 1338a21, 1339b15). Such amusement, however, is an example of a good that is partially constitutive of the good life of the city, according to Aristotle. As he explains in Book 3 of the *Politics*, where he discusses the good of the state as depending upon but transcending the prevention of crime and the promotion of trade:

> These are conditions without which a state cannot exist; but all of them together do not constitute a state, which is a community of families and

> aggregations of families in well-being, for the sake of a perfect and self-sufficing life. . . . Hence there are in cities family connections, brotherhoods, common sacrifices, amusements which draw men together. (*Pol* 1280b32–40)

Here the role of amusement is included within a list of social institutions, from the family to private associations, religious observances and the like: we may infer that the performances of tragedy and comedy, as well as various kinds of musical events, are examples of the sorts of amusements crucial to the formation of the community in "a perfect and self-sufficing life." Such arts draw people together and create friendship, which is in turn crucial for community. Noble actions are the end to which men strive for the happiness of the community.

We can summarize the classical conception of the arts as being activities which draw people together in relaxation and amusement, but which nevertheless have serious ethical content and morally formative purpose. Leisure is not the supreme end, but is a relaxation from toil necessary to an individual citizen's health and well-being (*Pol* 1339b15–16) and required for the cultivation of the arts. When properly employed, leisure has a legitimate place in the lives of citizens, but it is not the supreme end for which life is lived. Thus the arts, in filling leisure and creating community, constitute one kind of good in a hierarchy of goods that go into creating the common good of the city.

The Modern Devaluation of Civic Life

In the modern period, however, we find a complete contrast in views: modernity seeks to exalt the arts to a plane untouched by moral effect or social function, while denying the contribution of the ethical or moral life to a common good. The modern point of view celebrates creative achievement in art while denying the arts a status as part of a common good. For this phenomenon, Martin Heidegger again serves as a particularly cogent witness, given his rejection of classical philosophy, and particularly his hostility to Aristotle.

Heidegger's *Being and Time* articulates the most important framework for the way human life is conceived in the twentieth century. The perception that life is not in itself meaningful is the significance of his analysis of the inauthentic life, in which entanglement in everyday affairs produces the loss of being at home in the world. What he calls "Idle talk and public interpretedness contained in it" constitute a loss of one's existence in "falling prey to groundlessness." It is "being-with-another," which is both tempting and alienating. This "entanglement" in the world produces a tranquillizing "busyness," in which one's "ownmost potentiality for being-in-the-world is concealed."[2] For that very reason, however, it is the alienation of one's authentic existence. Heidegger does not suggest this is somehow unique to the modern world; rather, he implies its inherence in life at any time. Nevertheless, his criticism of entanglement with the world is the hallmark of the twentieth century: it appears to analyze the peculiar historical condition of a bifurcated social and personal life. The social life of the community is denigrated, while the personal life of the individual is exalted by the quest for authenticity in the face of alienation. Thus we find rejection of both the claims of the community and the kind of toil for which relaxation in leisure would be a necessary antidote. Heidegger's alienation from ordinary life sets the stage for the enlarged but segregated claims for art as an end in itself.

We have already seen the consequences of Heidegger's existentialist philosophy for art. For either art will retreat into a purely subjective "truth" arising out of a solipsistic concern with the materiality of the artistic medium, as Heidegger's own aesthetic encouraged, or it will become politically radicalized, as Adorno prescribed. The aesthetic of materiality, like that of formalism, refuses to consider art as having moral or ethical purpose. But a poetic construction of truth as essentially subjective becomes a license for the Nietzschean artist-tyrant that is most dangerous. Even Heidegger's own remarks on the relation of architecture to the concept of "dwelling" must be understood as a retreat from the formerly predominant public nature of architecture into the domain of the private and personal.[3] For dwelling is precisely what an individual does in his own home; the public realm, then, retreats from view altogether. Thus Heidegger's concept of art denies the ethical and civic role that was so crucial to the classical conception of art. The public function of art in creating a community of ethical individuals ceases to exist.

If we are to choose between the classical and the modern points of view, there is little doubt the modern will seem more familiar and more comfortable. The messy world of shared common life is banished from sight, and the individual's autonomy is reflected in the artistic creation of a subjective truth. Nevertheless, there ought to be something unsettling and ultimately unsatisfying about such an account of the authenticity of human existence, for the banishment of the public realm means the elimination of both responsibilities to the larger community, and the negation of that community's obligations to individuals. In this, it is not irrelevant to remember the form Heidegger's own rejection of ordinary life took in joining and defending the Nazi Party.[4] Thus the relation between the individual and the community cannot be simply cut off from consideration. If it is denied, it will return with a vengeance that uproots the individual, not only denying the autonomy he seeks, but the very existence of persons as human beings. The civic life, therefore, cannot be eliminated as the context from reflections on either the individual's activities or the nature of truth: Heidegger's radical privatization of the "authentic" life must be rejected. But the sense that shared amusements such as the arts are part of the good life of the city, as in the classical *polis*, is largely missing from today's discourse. Instead, the arts are considered to be authentic self-expression and private entertainment, the indulgence of the autonomous individual rather than the reflection of the ethical life of the city. For a corrective to this impoverished view of life, it behooves us to return once again to Hegel and his discussion of the ethical life. Doing so will permit a deeper understanding of the necessity of the ethical role of art in the public realm.

The Idea and the Ethical Life in a Hegelian Theory of the Arts

Hegel's discussion of the ethical life in the *Philosophy of Right* has the appearance at first glance of a reasonably liberal reading of the Prussian state in his lifetime. He defends the traditional institutions of that society, especially the centrality of the family to the landed classes and the guilds in their role in the towns and Estates. But he conceives the towns as the locus of the origin of freedom, and presents the Estates in their legislative capacity as "a guarantee of the general welfare and public freedom" (*GPR* §301; *PR* 196). Although he defends the monarchy, he envisions a constitutional monarchy. Yet it is imperative to look beyond the details specific to his time and society to see what justification he presents for the ethical life so conceived. The legitimacy of the family, civil society, and state together comprise the justification of the ethical life of customary duties (*die Sittlichkeit*). Although each of these receives its due in the *Philosophy of Right*, the issue of the ethical life as a totality is larger than the sum of the parts. Its justification derives ultimately from the Concept of human life as freedom, in which the metaphysical freedom of the will grounds social and political freedom. But the realization of this Concept is the Idea:

> Ethical life is the Idea of freedom in that on the one hand it is the good become alive . . . while on the other hand self-consciousness has in the ethical realm its absolute foundation and the end which actuates its effort. (*GPR* §142; *PR* 105)

Thus the Idea of human freedom is the fundamental principle of both the ethical life and the arts. A closer investigation of the relation among these is essential for understanding the role of the ethical life in the arts for Hegel's aesthetic.

The Idea is the fundamental principle in Hegel's metaphysics as well as the starting point of his discussion of the content of art. As he explains it in *The Encyclopaedia Logic*: "The Idea is what is true in and for itself, the absolute unity of Concept and objectivity." That is, something is true when it is what it ought to be; hence the Idea is the totality of such truth: it is the knowledge of the whole. This involves understanding the world as created by God, and "in such a way that God has manifested himself to us in it." But it also involves understanding the world as governed by divine providence, so that it is "eternally led back to the unity from which it came forth . . . " (*Enz* 1, §213; *EL* 286–88). Thus, Hegel's Idea echoes the theological tradition of divine creation and providence, but adds the concept of divine immanence to that of transcendence. Hegel's Idea, however, is not simply static: it is "essentially process," a development from life to cognition to absolute Idea as self-conscious knowledge of the truth (*Enz* 1, §215; *EL* 290). But the crucial question is whether this furnishes an Idea cognizable as the content of the arts.

Hegel makes the move from the Idea to the Ideal as the content of art early in the *Aesthetics*. This reflects the narrowing of the truth found in art from who we are and what kind of world we live in, to the specifically moral truth about the reconciliation of duty and passion. Thus art becomes defined in terms of its moral vocation and an ethical content (in the Greek sense of character) concerned with the ultimate good of bliss, together with the traits of character such an ideal implies. But the analysis of the individual arts has had the result that architecture and poetry, in particular, appear devoid of relationship to the Ideal. Instead, they depend crucially on the concept of the ethical life of customary duties, which does not receive explicit formulation in the *Aesthetics*. This leaves the treatment of these arts as having the appearance of a rather ad hoc explanation of their content in terms of Hegel's philosophy, even though it accords well with the traditional practice of the arts. The problem, then, is accounting for the role of the ethical life in the arts both in a manner consistent with Hegel's approach to aesthetics, and in the hope of providing a cohesive explanation to ground a more generally persuasive aesthetic.

Hegel's development of the Idea in the *Philosophy of Mind, Part Three of the Encyclopaedia of the Philosophical Sciences*, articulates a much clearer picture than that provided in the *Aesthetics* of the relationship between the ethical life and the activities of art, religion, and philosophy. This has a direct bearing on the question of the relationship between the ethical life and the Ideal. After first considering the subjective mind (or psychology), Hegel turns to the objective mind in Section II, where he lays out the topics developed more fully in the *Philosophy of Right*: law, morality, and the ethical life. Most importantly for the present purpose, however, Hegel says at the outset of this section that "[t]he Objective Mind is the absolute Idea, but only existing *in posse* . . ." (*Enz* 3, §483; *PM* 241). That is, the moral and ethical life is rooted in finitude and historical contingency. Nevertheless, it is an anticipation of the potential truth of the Idea.

Finally, Hegel turns to the Absolute Mind, where he discusses art, revealed religion, and philosophy. Here, as in the *Aesthetics*, he reduces the presence of the Idea in art to the Idea of Beauty (*Enz* 3, §556; *PM* 293). But under religion, in Christianity, he finds that Christ's sacrificial death in negativity and "as absolute return from that negativity and as universal unity of universal and individual essentiality, has realized his being as the Idea of the spirit, eternal, but alive and present in the world" (*Enz* 3, §569; *PM* 300). The union of the Concept of God with the actuality of the incarnation has produced the reality of the living Spirit that is the absolute Idea in its full form for the first time. No longer *in posse*, the Idea is now really existent in the world. Philosophy, finally, "is the unity of Art and Religion" (*Enz* 3, §572; *PM* 302). But the task for philosophy is to bring the Idea to human self-consciousness: "philosophy is the self-thinking Idea, the truth aware of itself," such that it comprehends the relation of God and the world (*Enz* 3, §574; *PM* 313). In such self-awareness, the Idea at last comes to its fullest realization, but also for this reason philosophy cannot dispense with art or religion; they are the means of approaching the self-conscious awareness of truth.

What is of greatest significance here is that the Idea has in fact a greater role implied for itself in the arts than Hegel's treatment of it in the *Aesthetics* would indicate. For the Idea encompasses the ethical life as well as the religious life on either side of art: the former only potentially, the latter fully in actuality. This suggests that insofar as the ethical life and the religious life touch upon the domain of art, they become relevant to the Idea of Beauty Hegel identifies as the form of the Idea in art. Thus, it is not only the religiously grounded Ideal that defines the Idea for art, but the ethical life as well. Indeed, the arts form the essential link between the ethical life of the Objective Mind and the truth found in the Absolute. The Ideal, as the artistic representation of the ultimate good and the character it requires, is the sensuous manifestation of the Absolute. The ethical life of the world we live in is therefore the preparation for the truth of who we are in the Ideal.

Yet there is a tension in Hegel's thought that must be recognized: for Hegel, the ethical life and the religious Ideal are not a seamless progression from possibility to actuality. The tension between the religious Ideal and the content of the ethical life is repeated in the nature of the ethical itself. The discussion of the Ideal in the *Aesthetics* emphasizes honor, love, fidelity, self-surrender, serenity, and bliss in a way that seems much closer to the traditional concept of virtue than the discussion of the ethical life in the *Philosophy of Right*. Thus these elements of the Ideal would seem to provide a ground for the ethical life. Yet, in the *Philosophy of Right*, Hegel explicitly repudiates the religious origins of the ethical life as simply subjective; only the ethical life in the state has the requisite objectivity of spirit. To be sure, he recognizes the religious as "the most sublime of all dispositions. As intuition, feeling, representative knowledge, its task is concentrated on God as the unrestricted principle and cause on which everything depends. It thus involves the demand that everything else be seen in this light and depend on it for corroboration, justification, and verification" (*GPR* §270; *PR* 166). This includes the state, its laws, and all the duties arising therein.

Thus religion is the "groundwork of the ethical," but only a subjective one. Its subjectivity of feeling is why in the *Philosophy of Right* he expresses the gravest reservations about the moral authority of religion. If it were to become the actual authority for the state, "the state must become a prey to weakness, insecurity, and disorder. . . . " Hegel's great fear is that the religious ethic will prove ultimately antinomian, rooted in "caprice and passion, and if thereby others suffer wrong, commend them to the consolations and hopes of religion, or better still, call them irreligious and condemn them to perdition" (*GPR* §270; *PR* 166–67). That is, Hegel fears fanaticism will destroy both the state and civil society, as had happened in the religious wars of the sixteenth and seventeenth centuries. Hence, he adopts the Erastian stand of the Lutheran church in the German states: the church is subordinated to the state, and the state protects society from excesses of religious fervor. He distinguishes sharply between the state, which is the true universal, and religious faith, which is only the subjective and often merely emotional apprehension of the Absolute. In this way, in the state, the ethical life is worked out largely in the public realm. Religious virtues appear to retreat altogether from public view, subordinated to the conceptually prior duties of one's social station.

Hegel's disjunction between the ideal of character, rooted in religious faith, and the objective "ethical life" of the community poses two problems. First, it appears to make character irrelevant to civic life. Second, for the subject of ethics itself, it raises the question of whether character really matters, or whether or not we see a weakening of the classical concept of virtue of character, by which the modern world has come to disregard character as important to communal life. Thus, if character does not matter to communal life, it becomes clear that art would cease to possess much significance as a representation of the ideal of character. Indeed it would lose much of its significance altogether. It becomes imperative, then, to understand more deeply Hegel's concept of the ethical life and its relation to what may be called the civic virtues in order to understand the relation of the ethical life to art.

The Ideal and the Ethical Life

The tension in Hegel's thought between religion and the claims of the civic life is, in effect, a conflict between the Ideal and the ethical life of *Sittlichkeit*. Hegel's complete understanding of the place of religion and its contribution to the Ideal of character is not quite as simple, however, as the *Philosophy of Right* makes it seem. In *Lectures on the Philosophy of Religion*, he makes it clear that faith, as mere feeling, is the most inferior kind of knowledge of God; only as thought about God becomes explicit, founded on concrete representation, does it escape mere subjectivity (*VPR* 3, 297–98; *LPR* 150–51). What is significant for an understanding of religion's relation to the ethical life emerges in the discussion of Christianity's recognition of the trinitarian nature of God. For the Trinity makes room for an account of the community of believers in a theologically profound way, in that the Third Person of the Trinity is the Holy Spirit. But this Spirit is the spirit of love, and is precisely what is shared among the members of the faith. Hence, a community is constituted from faith, consisting in this Spirit which is love. "Thus the community itself is the existing Spirit, the Spirit in its existence, God existing as community" (*VPR* 3, 254; *LPR* 473). This is an astonishing remark, for it appears to make the Spirit of God not only immanent in, but coextensive with the church. It risks becoming a conflation of the human and divine that would constitute serious heterodoxy, far more serious than the frequent accusation that Hegel is really nothing else but a kind of pantheist. Nevertheless, Hegel is offering his own version of the traditional doctrine of the institution of the church under the article of the Holy Spirit in the Nicene Creed: "I believe one holy catholic and apostolic church." That the church was formed by the inspiration of the Holy Spirit is certainly Biblical teaching.

Moreover, Hegel goes on to say that Christianity is able to reconcile the apparently contradictory elements of religiosity and worldliness precisely in the ethical realm, *die Sittlichkeit*. This happens when the spirit of freedom, by which he means the spirit of rationality itself, penetrates the worldly realm under the influence of Christian truth, and the worldly thereby becomes "freedom that has become concrete and will that is rational." Thus, the institutions of ethical life—the family, civil society, and the state—become "divine institutions," because "the ethical is an obedience in freedom, a free and rational will, an obedience of the subject toward the ethical." By this means, the ethical life is "the reconciliation of religion with worldliness." Here, there is no conflict between religion and the ethical life (*VPR* 3, 264–65; *LPR* 483–84). But this transformation of the world by religion is accomplished most fully in the philosophical understanding of the Christian faith, arising historically from the overcoming of the antitheses of the Pietist and Enlightenment moments in the unfolding of the relation of the church to the world. Thus the fullest expression of the Holy Spirit is as a thinking spirit that knows both the form and content of God (*VPR* 3, 268; *LPR* 488). This is the origin of

Hegel's high appraisal of philosophy—but it is philosophy informed by theology.

It is now possible to call into question the hostility to religious faith which Hegel expresses in the *Philosophy of Right*. First, in his own view, the Christian faith generates a community of believers, which is the embodiment of the Holy Spirit of God. Second, it succeeds in transforming the history of both church and thought so that thinking itself, in the form of philosophy, becomes for the first time completely rational. Finally, the Christian faith so thoroughly enters into the world that it transforms the world into something rational and free: that is, it makes possible exactly the ethical life described at length in the *Philosophy of Right*. Thus, even in his religious philosophy, Hegel underscores the importance of the ethical life, but in a way that recognizes the essential contribution of the Christian faith.

As we have seen, Hegel analyzes the role of the arts in terms of an examination of the nature of the ethical life conceived as the Ideal of character. Morality (which for Hegel is the subjective aspect of personal rectitude) requires not only the inner virtues of character, but acting out of a reflective consciousness of what duty demands. This is why the ethical life of *Sittlichkeit* (the objective actuality of life within the community) is conceived in terms of the duties arising out of specific social roles. It is also why artistic didacticism is doomed to failure. For we shall not be likely to take to heart what any work of art teaches, if our social practice does not permit or require it. Indeed, it is not likely that a work of art will find any resonance if its view of the world is substantially at odds with how life is currently lived.

Nevertheless, there is such a thing as duty, and our desires and passions, the inclinations of our sensuous nature, will often enough come into conflict with what duty requires: Hegel, therefore, does not pretend that human beings automatically do whatever their social roles require of them. There is still always the need for reflective judgment. The antithesis between duty and inclination, then, requires reconciliation in the form of action that yields to the demands of duty, but also in the form of philosophical and artistic reflection on the antithesis. Hence, Hegel vigorously rejects equating the purpose of art with some utility external to art. Rather, to return again to Hegel's statement of art's purpose: "art's vocation is to unveil the truth in the form of sensuous artistic configuration, to set forth the reconciled opposition just mentioned [the antithesis of impulse and duty], and so to have its end and aim in itself, in this very setting forth and unveiling" (*VÄ* 1, 81; *A* 1, 55). The purpose of art is cognitive rather than didactic: an assistance to reflection on the nature of human existence, or rather, the occasion of just such reflection. In other words, Hegel claims that the experience of a work of art is an act of reflection on the conflicting demands of duty and passion. The acceptance of suffering and woe central to the Christian Ideal is crucial to this reconciliation of duty and passion, for without it, there is no observance of ethical duties.

The Civic Virtues of the Ethical Life

For Hegel, the essential element in the ethical life of the community is the concept of the several roles an individual fulfills: filial, educational, economic, juridical, and civic. We are members of families, associations, and estates, he argues, and these forms of social organization give us our identity, respect due from others, and loyalty to a larger whole (*GPR* §253; *PR* 153). Although it is possible to see in his specific descriptions the social landscape of early nineteenth-century Germany, his point emerges all the more forcefully in comparison with the modern world's erasure of guilds and estates in favor of individualist equality on the one hand, and in the growth of powerful bureaucratic corporations on the other. But if membership in a hierarchy of communities satisfies so many of the needs which are intrinsic to human nature, it follows that there are correlative duties, for which one develops appropriate feelings and attitudes. These might well be called virtues in the classical, Aristotelian sense, although it should be noted that Hegel distances himself from the notion of virtue. He regards the general concept of virtue as bordering on "empty rhetoric," largely because he considers virtues to be heroic qualities, unsuited to the mundane ethical characteristics of ordinary life. Hence, on this view, virtue "actually appears only in exceptional circumstances or when one obligation clashes with another" (*GPR* §150; *PR* 108). Instead of a doctrine of virtues, therefore, Hegel offers an analysis of duties.

The concept of duty arises from specific social roles, and thus will have a direct bearing on the ethical life as it is represented in the arts. In ordinary circumstances, in "an ethical community, it is easy to say what a man must do, what are the duties he has to fulfill in order to be virtuous: he has simply to follow the well-known and explicit rules of his own situation." Here, of course, Hegel does use the term "virtuous" in the Aristotelian sense rather than the heroic. But the rules are easily identified: they comprise rectitude, the life of which is the ethical life. The ethical life, then, is realized precisely when people habitually do what is customary to their social roles (*GPR* §150; *PR* 107). This is why "*die Sittlichkeit*" is the term used to discuss the entire social structure of family, civil society, and the state; the term refers to the habitual or customary (*die Sitte*), so that the forms of social and political organization are here recognized as giving rise to the customs and habits of life. But virtues are states of character arising out of habits, according to Aristotle.[5] Hence, it is absolutely appropriate for Hegel to use the term "virtuous" in the Aristotelian sense to discuss the state of character arising from habitually doing what one's situation requires, and it is also appropriate for translators to render "*die Sittlichkeit*" as "the ethical life." Nevertheless, this reduction of duty and virtue to a matter of the fulfillment of the demands of specific roles is problematic.

A closer examination shows, however, that Hegel's "ethical life" is reminiscent of much in the classical concept of virtue. The political life was central to the ancient world's conception of the ethical life: Aristotle grounded his discussion of the human good on the concept of happiness as self-sufficiency, but hastened to add that "by self-sufficiency we do not mean that which is sufficient for a man by himself, for one who lives a solitary life, but also for parents, children, wife, and in general for his friends and fellow citizens, since man is born for citizenship."[6] But Aristotle was most concerned to offer an ethic of the citizen of the classical *polis*, rather than an ethic derived from specific social roles. This is quite different from Hegel, whose concept of duty deriving from social roles is capable of greater specificity than the classical model provided. Thus, Aristotle derived his concept of virtue as the fulfillment of the function of man, conceiving this function in terms of both the exercise of the rational principle of the soul and the living of life in the contexts of family, friendship, and citizenship.[7] Cicero, more explicitly, ranked the duties arising in social and political life according to their origin: "duties are owed first to the immortal gods, secondly to one's country, thirdly to one's parents and then down the scale to the others."[8] For both Aristotle and Cicero, then, the virtues constituting the ethical life were obligations arising in large part from the necessity of living in community with others.

The individual found his life's purpose, his moral bearings, and his identity only within the context of a specific city and his own family; however great an individual's achievements, they were accomplished within the constitutive framework whose claims always transcended the individual.[9] The institutions of state and society provided the essential context for the pursuit of the good life through wisdom and the moral virtues. Virtue and the political life, therefore, were mutually dependent: together, they constituted the ethical life in the ancient world.

The appeal of the classical conception, especially of the cardinal virtues of prudence, justice, courage, and temperance, has always been their universality, their applicability to all people. The question, therefore, is whether Hegel is able to identify anything universal in his discussion of the character traits or duties required of citizens occupying particular social roles. In fact, Hegel does establish a claim for a universal obligation within any given state, and that is patriotism. By considering the state as an institutional organization of a people, he denies the Enlightenment notion of a social contract, which always risks making the state appear optional for its members. But "it is only as one of its members that the individual himself has objectivity, genuine individuality, and an ethical life" (*GPR* §258; *PR* 156). That is, one's identity is formed by the irreducible fact of living in a particular country. The continued existence of any particular state, therefore, depends on the subjective attitude of the people comprising it, rather than on any voluntary submission to a contractual realization of interests. Hence, patriotism is crucial; it is not just a spirit of sacrifice for the whole, but rather "the sentiment which, in the relationships of our daily life and under ordinary conditions, habitually recognizes that the community is one's substantive groundwork and end" (*GPR* §268; *PR* 164). The key word is "habitually": Hegel recognizes a habit of feeling as a mode of acknowledgement of a universal political obligation. But habits of feeling are precisely states of character in an Aristotelian sense: thus, the duty of patriotism is a virtue. It is both a universal obligation within any particular state and an ineliminable aspect of human nature.

The various social roles to which an individual might be attached carry with them, however, the potential to form character as well as a sense of attachment. Here, Hegel's fusion of the concept of the ethical life as customary roles and the ethical life as the life of virtue in the classical sense bears fruit. The specific roles determine the particular states of character owed out of a sense of duty. For the agricultural class, a member of it "accepts unreflectively what is given him and takes what he gets, thanking God for it and living in faith and confidence that this goodness will continue" (*GPR* Zus §203; *PR* 270). This simple virtue of gratitude and trust in divine Providence is complemented by devotion to the ties of family (*GPR* §203; *PR* 131). Together, they constitute the strength of the nobility and the peasantry.

In contrast, the business class is founded on the individual's own energy and achievement, whether as a craftsman, a manufacturer, or a tradesman. Hence the demand for law, order, and freedom in towns provides the necessary framework for individual success (*GPR* Zus §204; *PR* 270). But just such social qualities correspond to individual rectitude in matters of property, contract, and justice, topics treated at length at the outset of the *Philosophy of Right*. Thus, in one sense, these individual virtues are matters of natural law or abstract right. But their social realization occurs only as a consequence of a particular economic and political organization with their intrinsic public roles. Hence, the public realm attains the significance of shaping the behavior and characters of all the members of society. It matters greatly that it shape them for the good.

We are now in a position to understand some of the apparently puzzling aspects of Hegel's treatment of the individual arts. In particular, the prominence of the concept of the ethical life in his discussion of poetry and architecture now makes sense. In tragedy, the conflicts among various duties, as in Antigone's conflict between duty to family and duty to the state, are indeed relevant to this poetic form of art, even when the Ideal of serenity seems impossible to achieve. Moreover, the conflict between duty and passion can now be seen as the central conflict of art in general; in the epic, this takes the form of the conflict between the specific social role of the warrior and his private inclinations, as for Achilles. This conflict between duty and passion, resolved in favor of duty, goes far toward explaining why it is essential to preserve the epics that have come down to us, even though the modern age is no longer able to produce any of its own. Too narrow a focus on art as the representation of the Ideal, as Hegel originally frames his aesthetic, blinds us to the larger reality of the ethical order in both its content as the Ideal and as *Sittlichkeit*. Unless we recognize the relevance of both to art, the arts will not be fully intelligible as the beauty of the ethical order in its entirety.

Architecture's nature as the foundational art, then, also emerges more clearly as a result of understanding the centrality of the ethical life as *Sittlichkeit* to art. A building's purpose is expressed intrinsically in the classical tradition, rather than remaining external to the ornamentation, as Hegel regards it. The classical doctrine of propriety prescribes appropriate levels of ornamentation for the domestic dwelling, the institutions of public commerce and the state, and houses of worship; these are the forms of building enclosing what Hegel calls "the ethical life," together with the religious life. For that reason, the building's purpose is indeed a suitable candidate for the truth which, united with the form, would constitute the intelligible beauty of a building in Hegel's view. But aspects of the ethical and religious life answer to what he identifies as the potential and actual realization of the Idea; the Idea is therefore what is represented in the art of architecture. The absence of the Ideal in architectural aesthetics, far from a weakness of Hegel's approach, points to the most important truth about the art of building and therefore about art in general: the ethical life is the beginning of the higher modes of knowing truth as found in art and religion.

The virtues that Christianity established are even more directly relevant to the formation of the ethical life than Hegel himself indicates. For as chivalry developed the fundamental and earlier religious love of God into love, fidelity, and honor directed toward secular society, these ways of feeling became models for the virtues required in the secular world. Specifically, the chivalric love of the knight for his lady, although only a subjective passion and not the ethical relation of marriage, nevertheless became the foundation of the relation of marriage, in that love is now taken as an essential precondition for marriage (although Hegel disapproved).[10] So, too, with fidelity: originally a tie between a knight and his lord, for example, and (except between a king and his immediate vassals) "removed from the life of the state," it nevertheless became the foundation for the formation of the state, as the more abstract loyalty of patriotism replaced the earlier, more personal loyalty to one's master. Finally, the sense of honor, although originally simply a matter of seeking recognition of the "abstract inviolability of the individual person," and not a defense of either one's own rectitude or the common good, laid the foundation for these concepts, for justice, as administered in civil society, must arise in the first place from just such a recognition of the inviolability of the individual (*VÄ* 2, 171–72; *A* 1, 553–54). Thus it would be a mistake to separate the romantic Ideal too sharply from the ethical life: in each case, the feelings cultivated—as virtues in the classical sense—are what have developed into the practices and institutions of the Christianized secular world. Love, honor, and fidelity become the roots of marriage, civil society, and the patriotism felt toward one's country. The ethical life as *Sittlichkeit* is not so divorced from the religious Ideal as Hegel would have us believe; the latter is indeed the foundation of the former, so that the arts cannot be isolated from the ethical life as if the ethical life were divorced from the Ideal of art.

If the secular realm of the ethical life can itself be transformed by the Christian Ideal, then the virtues of love, honor, and fidelity become valuable not only to the individual, but to the entire society, supplying a stable ideal of character and a norm for behavior. Indeed, it is not too much to say that without such ideals and norms, no society could long exist; this affirms Hegel's claim that ultimately the religious and ethical realms have the same foundation in rational freedom and must be reconciled in the roles that individuals live in their families, civil society, and the state. This recalls Aristotle's point in discussing the virtues as the foundation not simply of personal happiness, but of friendship and citizenship. But whereas Aristotle only touches upon the ethical role of art in discussing music, Hegel makes the arts central to the articulation of the virtues comprising the Ideal. In Hegelian terms, the arts assume a high importance in sustaining the Ideal of character in the public realm as the foundation of a civil society that cannot be considered solely economic in nature. The arts take the virtues of the subjective spirit out of the subordinate realm of religious communities and establish them in the objective, public realm of the ethical life of the state.

Thus, only an aesthetic that acknowledges both the Ideal and the ethical life will succeed in making sense of art as a category of endeavor to know the truth. Hegel's original aesthetic, which sought to define art in terms of the representation of the Ideal, must be amended to include the ethical life explicitly as relevant to the content of art. To insist on this is not to be unfaithful to Hegel, for the examination of texts other than the *Aesthetics* has shown how deeply interrelated the Ideal and the ethical life really are in his thought. Moreover, by placing Hegel's consideration of the ethical life in the larger historical context of the classical conception of civic life, character, and duty, it has become clear just how similar Hegel's account is to the classical conception. Any claim for art to be fundamentally ethical in nature makes artistic representation of the ethical order a central component of the good life of the city. The modern retreat from the claims of civic life, therefore, becomes a key part of the problem of modernist aesthetics, which elevates the autonomy of art at the price of its moral and ethical nature. Indeed, the artistic movement of modernism itself must be seen as problematic on the grounds of its own participation in the disavowal of ethical function and civic good. Modernism's denial of beauty is deeply rooted in a denial of the legitimacy of the ethical.

It remains to be seen, therefore, just how an aesthetic might be reconstructed along Hegelian lines in order to allow the arts to be seen as legitimately concerned with traditional concepts of beauty, the ethical life, and the Ideal of character. After a century in which modernism has unrelentingly assaulted these concepts, it is impossible to say in what an artistic responsibility to tradition might consist. What artistic norms could possibly ground contemporary artistic practice has become, in effect, a forbidden question. Yet it is precisely the question that must be asked if the ethical nature of art that is relevant to a genuine civic life is to be realized.

Chapter 9

Normativity in the Arts and the Particularity of Tradition

We have seen that Hegel's aesthetic requires the arts to represent the ethical order, holding it up to our view as a reflection of who we truly are as human beings. The arts remind us of the totality of that ethical order: the duties arising out of the determinate communities to which we necessarily belong, as well as the Ideal of serenity that is the representation of the ideal of character. As I have argued, this is a persuasive claim. Moreover, in making this claim, Hegel has constructed an aesthetic that is responsible to the arts as they were traditionally practiced; indeed, his aesthetic enables us to make better philosophical sense of the artistic traditions than would be possible if we were to regard only the statements of various historical theories of arts as given by the leading practitioners through the centuries. Thus, implicitly, Hegel's aesthetic validates the centrality of tradition to the practice of the arts—this in spite of the fact that Hegel's progressivist sense of history does not seem a promising foundation for a vindication of tradition. The sense in which this might be true, therefore, requires attention.

To claim explicitly that tradition is or ought to be normative at some level for art is, moreover, a controversial claim today. After a century of artistic modernism, a defense of tradition seems quite impossible—and this in spite of the advent of a postmodernism that employs some elements of realism for ironic purposes in painting, and some reference to classical elements of architecture, although without a coherent syntax of classical forms. The concept of a narrative representation remains foreign to both painting and to sculpture; and music, in either the remnants of the modernist styles or the new minimalism, appears far removed from the narrative potential inherent in the traditional syntax of tonality. The question arises, therefore: to what extent, beyond the representation of the ethical order, might art require a recognition of the normativity of tradition? Does responsibility to tradition extend to style, or to syntax (as in tonality for music, or the classical orders for architecture), or to specific forms such as the sonata or the sonnet, or to the principles and purposes underlying genres such as the symphony or tragedy? More generally, does not the very concept of tradition as a source of authority for the arts risk absolutizing the historically contingent and the merely locally valid? These issues are both serious and crucial for the completion of a coherent aesthetic. Attention to both the concept of tradition and Hegel's metaphysic is necessary to address them. It is precisely the suspicion of tradition originating in the modernist movements in the early twentieth century that must be overcome in order to make sense of Hegel and the possibility of an aesthetic capable of recognizing the legitimacy of tradition.

The Arts and the Concept of Tradition

The modernist conception of artistic creativity has been the creation of something entirely new: not simply new works in existing styles and genres, but new styles, new genres, new syntaxes.[1] It must be understood as a radicalization of the concept of creativity that was already emphasized in the Romantic era of the nineteenth century as requiring the individual artist to produce an identifiably personal style. But Romantic art (after Hegel's time) remained within certain stylistic parameters; modernist art began by definitively rejecting these in a stylistic rupture that cannot be accommodated as a type of continuity.[2] Moreover, this new conception of artistic creativity is echoed in twentieth-century philosophical aesthetics. John Dewey, for example, saw the essence of art in the effort "to reach out and seize any material that stirs" the mind to create "a new experience." But this is accompanied by a "[r]efusal to acknowledge the boundaries set by convention."[3] Thus, although it is common to speak of the advent of modernist styles as another chapter in the history of styles, something far more radical is at work. What changed with the advent of modernism was the very concept of creativity, in which entirely new approaches to art resulted in completely new syntaxes. These created new styles, but the originality lay in the quest for revolutionary new artistic languages. Such a concept of artistic innovation necessitated the dismantling of all prior traditions.

Although the established art world continues to maintain the modernist hostility to the earlier traditions, there are encouraging signs that a renewed respect for tradition may be emerging, however slowly. There are in fact representational painters and neotonal composers whose work, though not widely known, is acknowledged in the nonacademic press.[4] Among academic writers, a few historians have challenged the reigning hostility to tradition in the arts, most notably Paul Oskar Kristeller and Jacques Barzun. Barzun remains pessimistic about the possibility of a genuine renewal of the arts in what he terms, accurately, "the vacuum of belief." He sees that art in the modern age, which does nothing but complain about existence, has reached a point that the only option "is the liquidation of five hundred years of civilization—the entire modern age dating from the Renaissance."[5] He expects that what will emerge from the wreckage of Renaissance culture will likely resemble Medieval art in some ways; but it will cease at least to be nihilistic.

Kristeller, however, has stated a broader case: true creativity in the arts entails respect for inherited tradition, and originality cannot be the primary aim of an artist. He notes, in particular, that historically "[e]ven the most original work of art is likely to be a new attempt within a well established genre—a novel, a play, a poem, a building, a painting, a composition. . . ."[6] This is a radical claim of the highest importance, and it raises the question of the appropriate role of tradition in the arts. For if this is true, then the well-established genre, rather than style, will be the locus of traditional norms, as Hegel's aesthetic implies.

Within the discipline of philosophy, Alasdair MacIntyre has made a serious effort to justify the importance of tradition, specifically with respect to moral matters, but by reference to artistic traditions in his *After Virtue*. Traditions, to be living and vital, embody continuity of conflict: they always, in his view, contain multiple solutions to common problems.[7] Nonetheless, there is also the dimension of practices which particular traditions transmit, and it is the concept of a practice the arts illuminate especially well. Excellence in an art—and in the perception of art—requires learning the historically existing standards of excellence; there are rules which must be obeyed and goods to be achieved. For "we cannot be initiated into a practice without accepting the authority of the best standards realized so far"—even though those standards, as well as the works of art which they help us judge, may both be disputed.[8] Thus, although these standards and the practices they inform have a history, and are never simple or unchanging, they nevertheless constitute traditions which cannot be ignored.

To repeat, this is a controversial claim after a century of modernist assault on the legitimacy of traditions, and MacIntyre develops his argument at greater length in his subsequent works: there must be an account of the rationality of moral traditions, in particular, adequate to meet the challenge of historical relativism that is often used to justify modernist presentism. This rationality consists in the development of ever greater coherence within the tradition of enquiry, so that in that sense there is progress. But he insists that it does not reach a Hegelian state of perfect or absolute knowledge; instead, there will inevitably arise "epistemological crises," which, if met successfully, will result in the finding of a solution that will both explain former as well as present inadequacies, and demonstrate the continuity of the tradition.[9] In judging between conflicting traditions, then, the best tradition will be that which is able to incorporate the best insights of the rival traditions.[10] Far from having a static view of tradition, then, MacIntyre constructs an account of the dynamic of tradition-based rationality.

If artistic traditions are conceived along similar lines, then the creative process will have to be understood as functioning best when guided by traditional standards, but still able to incorporate alternative solutions to formal problems and new perspectives on the ethical order. The collapse of the accepted understanding of the ethical order—in the legitimacy either of the family, or of civil society, or the state, or a religious perception of the world—or a sense of exhaustion of traditional forms altogether, would constitute, however, the equivalent of an epistemological crisis. These possibilities are precisely what have arisen in the twentieth century, and the response of the arts has been to jettison tradition altogether, rather than to retain those elements which would hold promise for the future. The result has been the radical transformation of artistic syntaxes.

The crisis in the arts that constitutes modernism, therefore, must be understood as not just another turning point in the history of style, but a rupture that was both aesthetic and ethical, indeed also religious in many cases. The aim was not simply to invent new styles, new forms, or new artistic languages, although these were the consequences of the crisis. Rather, the driving forces in the emergence of artistic modernism were the revolutionary transformation of society and the moral or spiritual transformation of human nature. The entire ethical and religious order was called into question, so that art was now called upon, in the view of the avant-garde, to proclaim the rejection of the old, and adopt the new worldview. The aim of modernism is not to present who we are, but what we might become after jettisoning all allegiance to the old ethical order. This entails the several dimensions of political revolution, moral revaluation, and spiritual realignment that marked the early twentieth century and accompanied the rise of artistic modernism. The crisis of modernism cannot be understood as simply the rise of a new ethical order along Hegelian lines, for the aim was the destruction of the ethical order altogether. Thus, modernism cannot be assimilated to the prior tradition.

In philosophy, political life, and the arts, therefore, it is imperative to recognize historical change and the possibility of legitimately conflicting views, but also the possibility of genuine error that must be rejected through a deepening of the traditional understanding of things, rather than assimilating it to the detriment and confusion of the tradition. The artistic traditions inherited from their genesis in the ancient Greek and Roman world and developed through the nineteenth century cannot simply be made to subsume twentieth-century modernism or the subjectivist postmodernism of more recent times. The rupture with, and rejection of even a developing tradition has been too great in all of its dimensions: political, moral, spiritual, and aesthetic. Tradition, therefore, legitimately has a claim to our attention as an alternative to the crisis posed by modernism. Hegel's metaphysics is valuable precisely for showing us how this might be so.

The Particularity of Form in Hegel's Aesthetic

For Hegel, art must be understood within the larger metaphysical construct of universality, particularity, and individuality. These are all required to complete an account of the structure of reality. The individuality of the work of art is immediately intelligible, but the relationship between universality and particularity requires elucidation. We are tempted, in a nominalist world, to think of the universal as simply a trait held in common among many individual examples, and the particular as redundant with the individual. But Hegel insists the universal is "not just something common against which the particular stands out on its own; instead the universal is what particularises (specifies) itself..."(*Enz* 1, §163, Zus 1; *EL* 240). Here Hegel rejects the temptation of nominalism: the true universal cannot be merely a shared property among the members of what is perceived to be a class; rather, it is the active, eternal source of both the particular and the individual. Thus, it can be the fusion of the transcendent Platonic Idea and an immanent Aristotelian form that is always united with matter. Put another way, it is the genus, which contains but also generates the species.

Hegel indeed conceives the universal as the totality of the species (*WL* 2, 280; *SL* 606). But, to repeat: the universal here is not the abstract universal of nominalism; it is the self-generating principle which issues in the determinate being of particularity. As Hegel insists, "a principle contains the beginning and the essential nature of its development and realization" (*WL* 2, 285; *SL* 610). Hence, the species reveal the genus: they are not differentiated from the genus, but only from one another (*WL* 2, 280; *SL* 605–6). That is, the particular is distinguished by the character of determinateness: the Concept is now determinate because it gives itself the distinguishing form of being. Hegel concludes, therefore, that the "particular has universality within it as its essential being; but in so far as the determinateness of the difference [of species] is posited and thereby has being, universality is a form assumed by the difference, and the determinateness as such is the content" (*WL* 2, 283; *SL* 608). The content of particularity, in other words, is the determinateness or differentiation, whereas the "form" is the structure of the universal in the species. In this, Hegel is faithful to Aristotle's sense of form: there is no being without form. Hence, the particular is not merely locally valid for it always contains and reveals the universal.

This relation between form and content poses great difficulties for art; it is not precisely what we might expect on the prevailing artistic understanding of these terms. It is tempting to identify the universal as the content of the arts, for example, leaving the particular arts as distinguished by their forms arising from their different material means of sensuous representation. But Hegel, on the basis of the above passages in the *Science of Logic*, might reply that the accepted sense of the relation between the form and content is a result of nominalist abstraction: it mistakes the particular as the sole locus of real being, relegating the universal to the position of a merely mental construct. Viewed with respect to the question of what determines the species of the particular, the principle of differentiation is itself the content of the species. The "form," therefore, must be understood in the Aristotelian sense of the term: the form of a thing is not principally the external shape, superficially changing according to the requirements of the species, but rather the essential nature of the genus as manifested in particular species. Hence the classical and romantic "art-forms" in Hegel's usage: these historical forms derive from the universality of the Ideal of serenity, but their particularity resides in the distinctive nature of their religious roots of the Ideal. If we are to be faithful to Hegel's conception of form and content, then, it will be necessary to return to the definition of art given in terms of the union of form and content in order to deepen our understanding of it.

Hegel defines the vocation of art as being "to unveil the truth in the form of sensuous artistic configuration . . . " (*VÄ* 1, 81; *A* 1, 55). If form were taken as the sensuous artistic shape, then the truth would become the content, and the manifold artistic forms would be left unspecified, but potentially infinite. In this view, Hegel's use of the terms "classical art-form," or "romantic art-form," would denote a curiously limited classification of historical styles rooted in religious principles. If, on the other hand, "form" is understood as the *Science of Logic* requires, then Hegel's use of "form" in the definition of the vocation of art can be seen as denoting precisely the universal element in the Aristotelian sense of the essential nature of the genus "art." That is, art is defined by having "artistic configuration," but the particulars of that configuration cannot be identified at the outset. To call the symbolic, classical, and romantic approaches "art-forms," therefore, is to see their characteristic configurations are determined by the unfolding and self-revealing of the divine. The content of the art forms, then, is not the universality of religious or moral truth, since that universality is already contained in the concept of art itself, but rather the particular species of fine art. This is why Hegel identifies the five fine arts, first of all, as belonging to one or the other of the forms, even though this tends to oversimplify the history of the arts.

In this way, he fills the historical art forms with determinate content based on the requirements of the historical spirit at each stage of human knowledge of the divine, joined together with the requirements of the sensuous material employed in each of the arts. Thus, Hegel avoids identifying the art forms as styles—although there will be stylistic implications, since there must be an appropriateness of the sensuous element to the spiritual in art. But as we have seen, art forms are larger than mere styles.

This should be regarded as only the beginning, however, of an attempt to determine the content of the genus "art." Hence, Hegel further determines the particular historical forms, distinguishing at least some of the significant approaches within each. In so doing, he does not take the approach of art historians, who might look only at the differences of style or configuration (the nominalist sense of form), but rather sees the different conceptions of the divine and of human freedom as determinative. That is, the dialectical relation of the human and the divine becomes the determining principle of the history of the arts within each particular art form.

The Normativity of Genres and Syntax

Particularity, however, is not exhausted by the art forms, the individual arts, or the historical approaches within the art forms, for it develops into what are easily understood as the different subspecies of each art: the genres, and the artistic syntaxes that make them intelligible. Here we see particularity manifest as the determinateness distinctive to particular ways of conceiving the end and aim of art. In literature, the differences between epic, dramatic, and lyric poetry arise from differences of artistic aim: the epic shows the hero establishing law of his own volition, whereas drama shows the conflict between volition and preexisting duty, or between the duties arising in a determinate social context themselves. The lyric, on the other hand, is the reflection of the individual's emotional reaction to his situation; it does not seek to resolve a conflict externally, but rather to establish an internal acceptance of the truth of the external circumstances for the individual. Within each of these, then, there arise further subdivisions, the actual genres of tragedy and comedy, or the forms of ballad and sonnet, for example, with their particular conventions. In music, the genres of the symphony, opera, art song, and so forth establish the expectation of formal structures in each case: respectively, the sequence of movements with their possible forms of sonata or rondo (for example), the articulation of recitative and aria, the dialectical relation of voice and piano in the rendering of poetry into music. Similarly, painting has its genres or types: historical narrative, landscape, still life; and architecture might be best understood in terms of the distinctions between sacred, public, and private building construed as its genres, each of which demands different ornamentation to reflect its proper purpose. The purpose of each genre determines the particular standard structure of configuration.

This means that genres are governed by structural conventions arising from their unique aims. The English sonnet, for example, has fourteen lines, so that there will be three quatrains in which to establish and develop the problem posed by the poem, followed by a couplet, set off by its own rhyme, that draws a conclusion or establishes a resolution. A classical symphony, to choose a nonverbal example, is expected to have four movements, in which the slower inner movement in a contrasting key establishes the emotional pathos to be resolved by the faster minuet (or scherzo) and finale. And a public building in the approach of classical architecture demands an elevation of ornament and at the same time a solidity of style corresponding to the dignity of the public realm itself. Thus, the conventions governing the genres provide the context for the apprehension of individual works. To be sure, individual works may deliberately violate the conventions establishing the genre, as when a symphony of Beethoven or Mahler, for example, inverts the order of the scherzo and the slow movement. But the violation is intelligible only in terms of a knowledge of the general rule, and it acquires significance only because the general rule remains intact. The norm remains valid in spite of the individual departure.

The conventions governing genres, therefore, become authoritative norms. They arise from the end each genre has as a species of the universal Idea and they assume the force they do precisely because of the universality of the Idea as the totality of actual life: this is what we have seen elaborated in the ethical and religious life. The genres, although arising contingently in historical development within the art forms as Hegel describes them, exhibit a force of compulsion thereafter because of the inherent logic of their ways of presenting the Idea. Though contingent in origin, they become necessary in operation: their local validity arises from the universal and cannot be dismissed as merely local. Their conventions, then, no longer appear arbitrary, but rather become incumbent on any artist wishing to create a work possessing intelligibility.

At the same time, as a condition of that intelligibility, the audience for any art must have a degree of familiarity with those conventions through acquaintance with earlier works. That is, just as the artist must know the governing principles of the genres of his art, so too the audience requires an artistic education so that they will know the governing principles as expectations. In this way, styles may indeed develop or change substantially, but if the configuration of the genres remains essentially unchanged, new works in a new style will nevertheless be intelligible. Hence, the existence of conventions governing genres both allows creativity to flourish within the bounds set by the genres and allows for that creativity to be understood and accepted by audiences. This indeed was the state of the arts before the twentieth century.

The genres, therefore, constitute a specific locus of artistic tradition. This normativity is justified in Hegelian terms by the particularity of artistic form at all its levels as the revelation of the universality of the Idea. That is, the ethical and religious life cannot attain representation apart from the historically constitutive art forms, individual arts, and genres. The normativity of the ethical and religious life implies the normativity of their representational traditions.

Moreover, the demands of the genres will reflect larger questions of artistic practice usually considered under the category of artistic purpose and syntax: for example, the aim of expressivity in opera and madrigal composition at the end of the Renaissance gave birth to the syntax of tonality in music. As long as such expressivity remains essential to the art of music, tonality will be required as a condition of intelligibility. Similarly, the classical style in architecture has a presumptive claim on the art of building as long as the sacred and public realms are understood to have a dignity requiring them to be distinguished from each other and from the private. It is only if the end disappears that the syntax will lapse into desuetude.

This is not to say that artistic approaches and genres will not develop and change; indeed, if the arts present the ethical good in sensuous configuration, and if the moral practice of a civilization has a degree of progress, to that extent, the arts will reflect moral progress as a progressive history of style. By the same token, if there is moral or ethical regress, then art will regress—a point the music theorist,

François-Joseph Fétis, makes in constructing the history of tonality in the nineteenth century. He saw tonality developing from the (modal) *tonalité unitonique* of the Renaissance to the *ordre transitonique* after Monteverdi. But Mozart's discovery of the potential of remote modulations initiated the *ordre pluritonique*, which permitted a much wider range of emotional expression than the Baroque period had known; for Fétis, this was the pinnacle of the development of tonality. What came after Mozart was decay: the *ordre omnitonique*, in which any tone could function as the tonic, corresponding to the nineteenth century's love of surprise and novel emotions. He diagnosed this as "one of the maladies of the human species in our time...."[11] Thus the history of tonality that is normally understood as a "progress" in the realization of the potential of tonality could also be seen as a cycle of development and decay in music as an art, because of the ethical decay of society in the emotions cultivated as central to the individual.

Of course, not all artistic change will be intelligible simply as the reflection of moral progress or regress. The potentialities inherent in each genre have their own inner development, to be revealed in history; this is the legitimate foundation of the formalist approach to art history. Nevertheless, such developments in artistic tradition frequently reflect changes in characteristics of personality and the relation to the Ideal, so that a purely formalist conception of the history of the arts will always remain ultimately inadequate. Hegel's conception of history as the unfolding of the spirit is deeper.

Moreover, because all the arts are characterized by self-conscious reflection as well as artistic creativity, so that theoretical reflection becomes an integral aspect of the total practice of the art, artistic practice can indeed become an example of a developing tradition. For such reflection is able to legitimate changes in a practice, broadening the scope of styles or forms available to an art. For example, the development of architectural practice in the nineteenth century reflected not just the return to the medieval Gothic as a legitimate style in combination with the still dominant classical tradition; it also witnessed the discovery of "picturesque styles" for domestic architecture based largely on vernacular English and Italian models from the sixteenth and seventeenth centuries. Nevertheless, this recovery of earlier styles under the category of "the picturesque" did not occur accidentally. It was accompanied by a theoretical reflection, as in Andrew Jackson Downing's treatises, that started from the premises of

Vitruvian classicism and then broadened the category of beauty to include the picturesque as expressing more of "the beauty of sentiment" than "the beauty of form."[12] The essential characteristic of the picturesque styles was their asymmetry, in contrast to the more strict symmetry of traditional classical architecture; the need for balance of masses around a central axis did not, on Downing's view, require mirror image symmetry. The development of a practice in this manner would be unimaginable without such theoretical reflection to make sense of the possibilities opened up by the discovery of styles and approaches not formerly considered part of mainstream classical architecture. As a result, therefore, the aesthetic of the picturesque remained the dominant approach to domestic architecture in America throughout the nineteenth century after 1830, giving the American domestic landscape a unified look in spite of its many individual styles.

The development of new styles of architecture in the nineteenth century illustrates a second important point: style is not in itself normative. Although the Gothic, Italianate, Second Empire, and Queen Anne were all in some sense revivals of earlier styles, they were not associated with the specifically American heritage. Their introduction was at the cost of Palladian-inspired classicism inherited from the eighteenth century, and their success was eventually at the expense of the severely classical Greek Revival. Thus a self-conscious recovery of older models that frequently had only minimal relation to the classical principles of architecture was successful. This means that styles could change fairly substantially and still be perceived and justified according to classical principles. Ultimately, the elements employed and their disposition were more important than specific stylistic appearances.

Overarching the category of artistic genre, therefore, lies the matter of syntax: for instance, tonality in music or the orders in classical architecture. For the genres of architecture—the private, civic, and sacred—would be indistinguishable without the differences in kind and degree of ornamentation made possible by the syntax of the orders, and the success of sonata form from the late eighteenth century to the early twentieth must be traced to the capacity of tonality to allow different key levels to be perceived as structural components. Similarly, what may be called the syntax of perspective developed in the fifteenth century allowed the development of the different genres of painting. The depiction of narrative, for example, was crucially dependent on the ability to depict foreground, middle ground, and background elements to order meaning embodied in the depicted moment of the story.[13] Finally, perhaps in poetry the matter of syntax is subsumed in the ordinary centrality of syntax to any language, but here the concept must be broadened to include figures of speech that are key components of poetic construction, distinguishing poetry from prose as much as the use of meter as another element of poetic syntax. Thus, both syntax and genres are normative within the arts, but in different ways: syntax provides only the broadest of principles governing artistic representation, whereas genres develop the potentialities of syntax to more specific expressive and representational purposes.

Syntax and the genres, therefore, are the loci of normativity in the arts. Style is not: styles are defined by individual artists' conceptions of the Ideal, their currency changing more frequently than the traditions defining the genres, due to contingencies of social practice and philosophical reflection. Style is essentially personal, although it also usually has many elements shared in common among contemporaries. Thus, within the romantic art form, as Hegel defines it, we find medieval romance, Elizabethan drama, the epic poetry of John Milton, and the quite different poetic sensibilities of Wordsworth, Keats, and Lord Byron within the Romantic movement properly so-called. All have different styles; although the three Romantic poets just mentioned have much more in common with each other than they do with either Shakespeare or Milton. Such pluralism of style is to be expected as characteristic of the metaxological realm.[14]

Moreover, even when we see the same genre being cultivated at different times, both the artistic form (Hegel's configuration) and the thought expressed are usually radically different. Both Shakespeare and Wordsworth wrote sonnets, but the English sonnet form Shakespeare favored has a different structure from the Italian sonnet form Wordsworth generally employed. Nevertheless, the structures of the English and Italian sonnets constitute normative forms. They remain viable models for the presentation of serious ideas concerning love, life, and death. This is true of genres in general: they set before us who we are, so that both the ethical nature of art and the artistic form are mutually fitting and manifest artistic beauty. The history of a genre, then, will necessarily be the history of a tradition as it has been developed through the creative efforts of its practitioners. Hegel's aesthetic permits us to understand the particularity of artistic traditions as species of the universal ethical nature of art.

The Normativity of Artistic Tradition in the Hegelian Perspective

So far, Hegel's understanding of the nature of art as the representation of the full Idea, embracing both the ethical life and the religious Ideal, appears persuasive in its own right. We have also seen that the normativity of particular artistic forms (historical art forms, artistic syntax, and genres) are justified by the universality of the genus of art. Yet the concept of the universal may still appear unable in itself to ground the normativity of artistic particularity; simply to call the genus of art a universal does not in itself appear to imply an immediate content, much less one that is capable of binding the practice of the arts to definite norms. Indeed, Hegel concedes that the universal is absolutely infinite, unconditioned self-identity; that as "the utterly simple determination," it has no explanation (*WL* 2, 275; *SL* 601). On the other hand, as the genus, the universal Concept has the quality of determinateness, although we are so accustomed to regarding the genus as simply a nominalist abstraction of common properties that Hegel's point always threatens to be lost. The way in which universality establishes the normativity of particular Concepts requires a deeper examination.

To be sure, Hegel gives examples of universals as genera: life, spirit, free power, and boundless blessedness (*WL* 2, 277; *SL* 603). But more concretely, Hegel insists that the universal is the totality of the Concept, that is, the totality of the species and individuals which the universal generates (*WL* 2, 278; *SL* 604). This is the content of the universal that as determinate is neither nominalist nor utterly simple. Applied to artistic traditions, this means that the universal, in the determinate sense, consists in the totality of those particular genres and syntaxes which constitute artistic traditions. Their normativity follows from their comprising the totality of artistic universality. As Hegel gives it, the universal "is also the substance of its determinations; but in such wise that what was a contingency for substance, is the Notion's [Concept's] own self-mediation, its own immanent reflection" (*WL* 2, 276–77; *SL* 603). Thus contingency is raised to necessity, and for the arts the historical contingency of particular genres and the discovery of appropriate syntaxes become necessary for all further artistic endeavors having a similar purpose. There simply is no intelligible artistic creation apart from the particularity of such traditions.

The existence of genuine norms in developing artistic traditions, therefore, has the capacity to prevent art from succumbing to radical historicism that sees tradition as purely accidental. For history, although contingent, bears witness to the universal Idea that determines the particular traditions of syntax and genre. But such norms also preclude the radical presentism that is the essence of artistic modernism, and by which all tradition is banished from consideration in the name of justifying whatever happens to be considered the current artistic style and syntax. A Hegelian perspective on aesthetics demands a critique of the assumptions of modernism and postmodernism: there just is an ethical content that art requires to be represented, together with the historical forms of the Ideal and the ethical life that engender particular traditions. The purpose of art generates, through historical processes, genres whose structures and syntax constitute normative traditions supervening the merely locally valid and historically contingent. Hegel's metaphysic, therefore, succeeds in explaining what was always taken for granted before the advent of modernism: the authority of past practice in establishing standards for the arts.

Chapter 10

Art and the Beauty of the Absolute

If Hegelian historicism indeed succeeds in vindicating the role of tradition as a source of norms for art, then it becomes important to return to the question of what prevents such historicism from degenerating into mere presentism: and that, as we have seen, is the concept of the divine. Yet it has proven difficult to understand Hegel on the divine, precisely because of his own ambiguities as well as the rival interpretations of scholars seeking to make sense of those ambiguities. It is clear, however, that Hegel's concept of the divine entails both transcendence and immanence, or to put it more consistently with his own terminology, absoluteness and contingency. For he does not simply equate God with the world; there is a residue of transcendence in his concept of God. But while this level of understanding might suffice for placing the Ideal in both the absolute and contingent realms, it is crucial for justifying the Ideal that the divine not remain at the level of an assumption derived from faith or even revelation. For Hegel's entire philosophy seeks to place our understanding of the Absolute on a firmer, more rational foundation than religion as faith by itself would customarily allow. It is necessary, then, to follow Hegel in his quest for the justification of the Absolute in order to ground the aim of art philosophically in categories that transcend the historicity even of divine revelation.

The Absolute and the Idea of the Good

Hegel's claim that "art has above all to make the Divine the centre of its representations" makes it appear that art springs from and thus has responsibility to religious conceptions of the Divine, as if art were entirely subordinate to religion in its purpose. Yet closer attention to Hegel's description of the relation of art and religion shows a substantially different argument. For he says in the same passage that since "the Divine is nevertheless essentially determinate in itself, and since it therefore disencumbers itself of abstractness, it resigns itself to pictorial representation and visualization" (*VÄ* 1, 231; *A* 1, 175). That is, artistic representation is the inevitable consequence of all religious perception: hence the centrality of the arts to Christian worship in its historical forms. But it is also for this reason that the arts develop within the purely secular sphere as the absolutely proper and inevitable consequence of the Christian understanding of the world in its relation to God.

Hegel concludes, therefore, that although the Divine is pure spirit, and thus "an object of intellectual reflection alone," yet "the spirit embodied in activity, because it always reverberates only in the human breast, belongs to art" (*VÄ* 1, 231; *A* 1, 176). Art is the inherent consequence of the realization of divine activity. It will be recalled, however, that the Ideal is specifically artistic: it is never simply an intellectual construct, because it is the goal of human activity and not a purely intellectual contemplation of the Divine as pure spirit. Thus art has always been the key to making the Divine appear to be real in this world. In this sense, only art can make religious truth real. Although Hegel sees the Protestant Reformation's devaluation of visual respresentation as being more spiritual than earlier traditions, the importance of art in general to Protestant worship was not abandoned. Both music and poetry, in the form of hymns, continued to be cultivated as central to Protestant worship, and it is significant that both these arts, as the most spiritual in nature, rank among the highest artistic achievements of the Protestant parts of Germany. Perhaps, however, Hegel's iconoclastic Protestantism needs to be questioned as not lying entirely in line with the logic of his own argument, for it is difficult to consign the splendors of Baroque and Rococo Roman Catholic churches to a kind of historical purgatory, as if the visual arts are not really spiritual enough for Christian worship. Thus Hegel's original point remains valid: art is central to making the Ideal actual in this world. The arts are not simply servants of religion; they create the actuality of the ultimate good of life by holding it up to our contemplation, both sensuous and intellectual, in representation.

The problem, then, is how to conceive the ultimate good of life in a way that is not simply sectarian. For Hegel, this takes the form of the Absolute Idea. In Hegelian language, the Idea is the union of the Concept with its actualization; the Absolute Idea is the totality of conceptual truth as it is realized in actuality (*Enz* 1, §213; *EL* 287). The Absolute Idea thus occupies the same position in Hegel's philosophy as the Idea of the Good does in Plato's metaphysical system: it is the ultimate reality. Yet it also answers to the philosophical need to understand the Whole, and to make the Whole ultimate is a problem. This Absolute Idea Hegel calls being, life, and self-knowing truth in its totality (*WL* 2, 549; *SL* 824). It has an historical actuality from the fact that life is necessarily temporal, not merely theoretical in character. But because it is historical in nature, it is essentially process, so that the totality of truth contained in the Absolute Idea must be the totality of historical development towards the goal of the complete theoretical knowledge and practical realization of the Good. But for Hegel, the Absolute Idea appears to lack the transcendence of Plato's Idea of the Good; once again, the ultimate Hegelian *telos* appears merely immanent within the temporal realm.

The Absolute Idea, however, includes all its predecessor forms: the Idea of life, and the Idea of cognition (including both truth and the good). It is the Idea of the Good which particularly merits our attention here for its suggestive connections with classical philosophy. What matters for Hegel regarding the Good is the universality of moral categories in judgments expressed as predications. "This action is good" is a judgment comparing the singular act to its concept, to what it ought to be (*Enz* 1, §171, Zus; *EL* 249). Hegel is clear that judgments are not subjectivist, for goodness is fundamentally a moral universal. Recalling Plato's language, the Idea of the Good appears in the *Science of Logic* as the consummation of the Idea of cognition in general, so that, as for Plato, the Good is the source of cognition of all truth (*Rep* 508e). But following Aristotle, Hegel conceives of the Good as the object of willing or desire. The Idea in this mode of being is practical, that is, moral, having the character of "an ought-to-be" (*WL* 2, 544; *SL* 820). Its character as the object of an ought-to-be removes it from the realm of the purely subjective: "The subject has here vindicated objectivity for itself; its immanent determinateness is the objective, for it is the universality that is just as much absolutely determined ..." (*WL* 2, 542; *SL* 818). The Good, therefore, is an absolute universal and, at the same time, a particular end, apprehensible and realizable by individual subjects. But because the Good is explicitly to be realized in actuality, its realization is subject to the contingencies of externality, so that its external existence is "not a realization corresponding to its Idea" (*WL* 2, 544; *SL* 820). That is, the Good must be conceived as a goal, which operates as a final cause in the world, but is not fully realized in the world. Its nature as a universal is what makes it absolute.

Hegel recognizes both that the contingency of actual life creates conflicts for the realization of the good, and the possibility of conflict among the several particular kinds of good: "good in its concrete existence is not only subject to destruction by external contingency and by evil, but by the collision and conflict of the good itself" (*WL* 2, 544; *SL* 820). The latter, inner conflict is the origin of his perception of the tragically conflicting duties in *Antigone*; even if his reading of that tragedy stretched the point too far, it remains true that different partial goods may well conflict. But more fundamentally, there are worlds in opposition: the good, in which thought finds its true being, and the realm of actuality. The realm of the Good just is what Plato would call a transcendent realm. But the Idea of the Good is the ultimate form of the Idea of cognition, the penultimate form partially constitutive of the Absolute Idea. The Absolute Idea, therefore, contains an element that is irreducibly transcendent. It simply cannot be reckoned as purely immanent.

Thus, although we can understand the Ideal and the ethical life, as Hegel describes them, in terms of the actuality and potentiality of the Absolute Idea, this hierarchy within the truth of who we are as human beings, while suggesting their continuity, does not state their relationship clearly. For in another respect, they constitute two apparently opposite poles: the Ideal, of transcendent origin, and the ethical life, of purely temporal origin. Yet we have seen that the former is the foundation of the latter, in spite of Hegel's own suspicions of the claims of religious priority for ethical categories. Moreover, Hegel holds that the arts decline into ugliness and irrelevancy once the Ideal is totally forgotten, as he saw that it was in the realist and subjectivist literature of his own day. Again, in spite of Hegel's own historicism, his argument rather points to the necessity of holding both the transcendent and the temporal poles together in a dialectical relationship centered on the Good. Art flourishes only in the middle, between pure transcendence and mere historicism: the metaxological is the realm of the ethical life informed by the Ideal of bliss as the ultimate good. But it is essential to reject the confusion in Hegel's Absolute Idea between the ultimate truth and the Whole. The transcendent cannot be allowed to disappear into the Whole without a trace.

The Goodness of the World

What is at stake may be put more clearly by turning to the metaphysical language of Saint Thomas Aquinas. The issue here is the goodness of being itself. Saint Thomas considers the concept of the good as a "transcendental." Goodness is first of all characteristic of all being: "goodness" names the characteristic of desirableness inherent in existence, for as Aristotle says, "goodness is what all desire."[1] Certainly all beings aim at continuing in existence: "The very act of existing (*ipsum esse*) thus has the character of goodness."[2] Saint Thomas expands the concept of the good, however, in identifying how it is extended beyond the category of being:

> So first and foremost then a good is something that perfects something else by being its goal, though secondarily we call goods things that lead to a goal—namely, useful goods—and things that are natural consequences of a goal. . . . "[3]

Hence God alone is good in being the final cause or end of all His creation, but goodness is a quality found in all created beings first by virtue of their existence, and secondarily to the extent that they serve God and are creations of God. It is for this reason that Saint Thomas describes the transcendentals of unity, truth, and goodness as names which add something to the concept of all being.[4] The transcendental "good" has its origin in God, but is also applicable in the created world.

This goodness is insisted upon repeatedly in the first chapter of Genesis, where after each day of creation the refrain occurs: "And God saw that it was good." Both Jewish and Christian liturgies take Isaiah 6:3 as central to their glorification of God: "Holy, holy, holy is the Lord of hosts; the whole earth is full of his glory"—in which "the earth" is to be understood as the entire created world, "heaven and earth" in the Christian *Sanctus*. For the modern nihilist, however, the world is perceived as a prison, an evil to be endured, however it came into being. The point of contention is the perception of the goodness or badness of the world, which is largely a matter of the perception or not of a providential order in the world. Yet the choice between the two perspectives is not an arbitrary one: only the conviction that the created order is ultimately and originally good allows for even the approximate realization of the Ideal in this world. The nihilist perception precludes it. Thus whether any kind of reconciliation to the Ideal is possible depends on a belief in the fundamental goodness of the world, however informed by sin human nature has become after its original creation.

The possibility of reconciliation to the Ideal, in even its most general sense simply as serenity or bliss, has a profound influence on the nature of art. For representation of the reconciliation to the Ideal of repose as the good of life is possible only on an understanding of the good of the Ideal being a true possibility in this world. Such an understanding is the essential characteristic of Christianity, which acknowledges the existence of sin and woe, but insists that reconciliation to the Ideal has already been accomplished in Jesus Christ, and therefore is the object of all believers' faith and the object of their own lives. The lives of the saints reveal the reality of the redemption from sin beginning in this world and fulfilled in the next, and the arts represent both the original Ideal in Christ and the subsequent achievements of the saints. This does not detract in any way from the conviction that a complete reconciliation of the individual to the Ideal of serenity and bliss is possible only in heaven. Nor does the Christian perspective depart from the structure of the Jewish perspective that such reconciliation (still to use Hegel's language) will be possible only after the coming of the Messiah and the resurrection of the dead. For both religions regard the continuity of this life and the next as part of the order of God's creation.

In contrast, the metaphysic that has so deeply influenced artistic modernism has been deeply hostile to the goodness of the world; we have already traced the hostility to the concept of beauty. The aesthetic theories characteristic of modern philosophy have often muted this, although the alienation of Adorno makes the rejection of both beauty and goodness explicit. But the formative influences on the twentieth-century avant-garde itself now require some elucidation, and that must begin with Friedrich Nietzsche, who identified the main problem of modernity and provided a possible artistic solution. Nietzsche enables us to understand in turn the appeal of yet more radical thinkers, whose reconception of art was crucial to the emergence of abstraction and the rejection of the entire representational tradition.

The complexity of Nietzsche's philosophy has made him the prophetic voice of much that transpired in the twentieth century. His emphatic rejection of religion, conventional morality, and the philosophical tradition, together with what he perceived as the decadence of the nineteenth century, made his thought a decisive turning point in all areas of philosophy, with important implications for the arts. His search for "new values" founded on the recognition of human nature as the "will to power" marks his philosophy as both a significant insight into psychological pathology and a dangerous prescription for tyrants. He connected the need for new values to the decline of the old into nihilism, the condition in which there is no perception of a clear aim or purpose to existence. In his view, it was impossible to continue to posit a transcendent realm, or a Kantian "in itself," or the divinity of any god.[5] There is no meaning in history (Hegel's error) or individual existence (religion's delusion). The result is despair, but also the opportunity to begin again, to create new values based on all that is left—the value of power (*WP* §14, 14). Thus, Nietzsche's thought has been linked to the totalitarianism of both the Nazi and fascist Right and the Marxist Left.[6] Yet for art, Nietzsche is much more ambiguous and his influence more complex.

From his first major work, *The Birth of Tragedy*, to his final collection of notes later published by his sister as *The Will to Power*, Nietzsche cast his discussion of the arts in terms taken from the classical world. In contrasting the Apollonian and the Dionysian impulses of dreams and terror respectively, Nietzsche saw both at work in ancient Greece, with their union decisive for that highest dramatic art, tragedy. Hence he saw art as the great stimulus of life, countering the denial of life he thought intrinsic to both Christianity and the Buddhist philosophy of negation, which had been recreated by Arthur Schopenhauer (*WP* §853, 452). Art seeks beauty, which is itself life-enhancing: the ugly is harmful in just the degree that it negates beauty (*WP* §804, 423). Finally, Nietzsche insists that all great art relies on convention; art cannot succeed without it (*WP* §809, 428). Thus, it is possible to see in Nietzsche's aesthetic an almost traditional understanding of art, which then appears to be considerably at odds with the rest of his philosophy.

Yet this conclusion would be far too simple. For Nietzsche sees art's connection with life solely in physical terms: it reflects and enhances "animal vigor," specifically in terms of sexuality, intoxication, and (significantly) cruelty (*WP* §§801–2, 421–22). Its origins lie in merely physical longing, its sensuous nature emerging not from our senses, but from our own sensuality. It enhances life by exercising the muscles as well as the senses, increasing strength, desire, and our recollections of intoxication (*WP* §809, 427). Great art has the ability, to increase severity—hence the centrality of cruelty—and to take one out of one's normal contact with reality into the substitute for transcendence, namely, intoxication. It is solely an animal vigor that Nietzsche sees in art: his apparently traditionalist language serves as a cover for, once again, a complete rejection of tradition. The spirituality and ethical substance of art have been eviscerated, and the connection of art with the ethical order rejected.

An art for modern times, then, avoids the moral and religious themes characteristic of the tradition Hegel vindicates. Nietzsche praises the art of Homer, the epic poetry of heroes who are not afraid of death; he castigates the dissatisfaction with reality that he sees as characteristic of nineteenth-century romanticism (*WP* §845, 445). What is needed for modern times is the celebration of nihilism: the nihilistic artist is concerned with situations in which there is no justice, where there is indeed the perfection of evil (*WP* §850, 448). For art, in being the stimulus to life, must celebrate the tragic life, in which he sees suffering as willed and exalted. Existence is affirmed precisely when "the highest degree of pain cannot be excluded." This is the secret of the Dionysian impulse (*WP* §853, 452–53). This recalls Nietzsche's acceptance of pain and woe in *Thus Spoke Zarathustra*: the love of fate and the embrace of the doctrine of eternal recurrence—willing that everything should repeat itself just as it was, without any diminution of suffering—become the source of his peculiar joy.[7] The solution to nihilism, therefore, is to embrace suffering, and much like Schopenhauer, whom Nietzsche came to reject, he sees in art the representation of the will, but now a will to suffer, not a willing that needs to be escaped or denied.

This aesthetic, then, is the key to understanding much of modernist art. The Expressionists embraced it ardently; the representation of pain was frequently the content of their art. The aesthetic of expressivism was often in fact simply the aesthetic of the expression of pain and despair—taken, however, as the norm of life, rather than its antithesis. The message that artists of the first modernist generation absorbed from Nietzsche was that art had tremendous power:

and by focusing on sexuality, cruelty, despair, and the unreality of intoxication, the world as they knew it could be destroyed through art. Such destruction constituted the "beauty" and "creativity" of art, and through such destruction, a new world with new values founded on the will to power could be brought into existence.[8] It was an apocalyptic vision, but although it is often considered as regenerative, it is really instead only a celebration of what Nietzsche himself calls "barbarism." For power of this kind can be exercised only as destruction.

The celebration of nihilism, however, is suitable only for souls like Nietzsche's, who are strong in their weakness of not being able to see a way out of the prison their own psychology has created. Instead, Nietzschean nihilism was only the first step in the road taken by modernism. The second step, still crucial to the Expressionists, but taking them from representational to abstract art, was to add to the nihilism of Nietzsche the spiritual trappings of a revived gnosticism. This is the position of Kandinsky and Schoenberg, which was based largely upon the modern theosophy of Rudolf Steiner, and which itself derived from the theosophy of Madame Blavatsky.[9] This modern gnosticism rested on the perception of the cosmos as evil, owing to its materiality; this was shared in common with ancient gnostic systems.[10] But there was now added a measure of spirituality missing from Nietzsche's nihilism. For the ancient gnostic, the evil of materiality was explained by the world's creation by demonic gods, whereas for the modern theosophy of Rudolf Steiner, there was no creation of the universe, only a cosmic evolution of matter from spirit. "Luciferic beings" were what he credited with giving humans their freedom—in a way that both accounts for the introduction of evil and the progress of the cosmos.[11] The imprisonment of the spark of the divine spirit in the material body constituted the evil from which both the ancient and modern gnostic sought escape by means of the secret knowledge imparted by spiritual teachers.[12] But for modern theosophy there is no ultimate salvation in heaven, only an endless round of reincarnation as the form taken by the justice of an impersonal spirit.[13] Thus two of the most influential creators of artistic and musical modernism found their inspiration in a system of thought that considered human existence fundamentally untenable yet subject to a strict justice that offered little solace; their art sought to express the emotional suffering of such a worldview. As in Nietzsche's case, the only solution was to embrace despair, but now considered as a spiritual salvation.

This same view of the untenability of human existence may also describe the more politicized revolutionary views of art. The modernist aspiration to destroy inherited traditions has been motivated by a sense that these aspects of historical contingency are the particular manifestations of our material condition; in this sense, it is parallel to the gnostic hatred of materiality. The projection of a utopian solution onto the future, then, is less a transposition of heaven onto earth than a product of the hatred of present existence born out of a sense of justice that knows no mercy for human failings. Thus the radical Left's rejection of "bourgeois" ornament in architecture is not simply a product of class war, but a rejection of the material charm of the dominant architectural tradition under the mask of an antibourgeois ideology. Indeed, the Futurist movement reveals more purely the fundamental hostility to tradition as a condition of existence, so that its links to Fascism become the revealing of a kind of political gnosticism.[14] The project of a violent overthrow of the world always rests upon a denial of the worth of this world as we know it. Hence it is with good reason that the fundamental character of modernity is sometimes noted as gnosticism.[15]

In contrast, Hegel's Idea, although always risking a historicist justification of whatever the contingencies of history have produced, has the merit of endowing the temporal world with the dignity of being. If this dignity of being is understood as exactly what is most at stake, the rejection of which has produced the crisis of modernism, then finding ways to express this dignity of being, without risking the dangers of either historicism or determinism, is essential. To insist on the fundamental goodness of the world is of the utmost importance, and to call it, after the manner of Saint Thomas, a "transcendental," seems the surest terminology. As a correction of and supplement to Hegel, this would expand the insight that in Hegel's terms is expressed by saying that the Idea of the Good is part of the Absolute Idea. What is at stake is not just moral duty, the ethical good, or the Ideal of serenity, important as those are. Rather, it is the goodness of existence itself.

The importance for art of the Absolute Idea in its totality for Hegel's aesthetic may now emerge clearly. For it is precisely the Idea which guarantees the universality of ethical substance he postulates for art through its inclusion of the Idea of the Good. Moreover, the Idea accounts for the complexity of content represented in the arts, as Hegel's initial conception of art as the representation of the Ideal of human life appears far too narrow to accommodate even his own discussion of architecture, painting, and poetry. Instead, as we have seen, the Idea in its totality is necessary to account for the traditional styles and contents of these arts, architecture requiring the dimension of the ethical life of civil and political society as well as the dimension of religious worship crucial to the apprehension of the Absolute Idea. Finally, the paintings of the Renaissance and Baroque show the goodness of the world as well as God's providential order of justice and mercy. Indeed the sense of divine justice and mercy is vital to the drama and epic literature of both the classical and Christian eras. The Ideal of life as spiritual freedom and bliss that Hegel initally provides as the content of art proves insufficient for understanding the history of any of the arts. Rather, it is the ideals of character and moral action, rooted in the relationship of humanity to the divine, as well as the sense of the goodness and beauty of this world, which more meaningfully describe the aims of painters, composers, and poets alike. Thus, Hegel's definition of art as the sensuous representation of the truth, or the Idea in its totality, is closer to the mark than his particular conception of art as the representation of the Ideal. The Idea comprises all the essential subject matter of the fine arts. For goodness and truth are genuine universals, and Hegel's concept of the Idea, with its relation to the Good, embraces all their dimensions and justifies their claim to universality as transcendentals.

Art, therefore, presents this transcendental goodness as a fact about the world for human apprehension. Art is humanity's attempt, literally, to re-present this truth about the world in a sensuous fashion, because goodness is perceived least abstractly by means of the sensuous. Goodness is in the first place an intuitive apprehension, and as such is best perceived by the most direct representation, by the sensuous in art. Thus, the value of art is not diminished at all by Hegel's placement of religion and philosophy as "higher" activities of the Spirit; rather, the essential nature of art as the foundation for both religious worship and philosophical cognition is vindicated. For without a prior apprehension of the goodness of the world, it is little likely that anyone will be led to worship God as the Providence of the world, or to speculate as to the nature of the transcendent Good in itself. Art is one of the significant means for such an apprehension. As Alberti claimed in the Renaissance, there is nothing which does not gain in beauty by being associated with painting. In general, it is true that art collects what fragments of beauty and goodness we perceive in life and displays them in a more concentrated and congenial form for all to see or hear. Art, therefore, turns out to be of vital importance. Its beauty, as the being of goodness, is normative because therein lies its claim to universality. In this sense art depicting the ethical substance of life offers us a vision of the beauty of the Absolute.

Conclusion

Just as Hegel was able to criticize artistic developments in his day, it is time that we return to an aesthetic that permits us to do the same in our day. We have lived too long with the legacy of Kantian metaphysics and aesthetics. For Kant, it was impossible to say in what freedom of the will consists, what the soul essentially is, or what God might mean concretely in terms of divine revelation—concepts that Kant had asserted were his express aim to defend at the outset of the *Critique of Pure Reason*. The consequence, however, is to leave the freedom of the will conceived as pure spontaneity—or as the will to power, in Nietzsche's later formulation. The traditional conception of the soul and its freedom of will lay, however, in its rationality, and this is the concept Hegel defends. If it is denied, then, as in Kantian philosophy, it leads inevitably to a perception that we are not at home in the world, that the determinism of the physical world of appearances is the shape of our prison. A God who cannot be regarded as either the Creator or Redeemer will cease to matter, and there will be no salvation from the prison of our existence: this is the origin of the nihilism that has so deeply affected the West in the past one hundred years, and against which the existentialist revolt of Nietzsche, Heidegger, and their pupils seems both understandable and futile.

In a Kantian world, the arts have little place and only a formal significance; they do not reflect the dignity of the ethical order, because there is no validity to the larger, deterministic world in which we are thought to live according to this barren philosophy. Hegel reminds us, however, that this is not the only, and certainly not the best, way of conceiving the world. For him, humanity is at home in a world shaped fundamentally by custom and the ethical life, and molded by religious conviction resting on philosophically defensible instances of divine revelation. The arts have the task of reflecting this ethical world because it is the true understanding of the world.

Moreover, the arts in general have a necessarily public nature precisely because the truth they represent is shared in common (whether it is recognized as common today or not). If art is the representation of the Ideal and the ethical life, then the fact that much art does this publicly means that these truths—the ideals of character and our place within family life and civil society—are appropriately put on public display. Thus, while the public nature of art requires a sense of the validity of the public realm itself in order to be justified, at the same time it contributes to the importance of the public realm by its additional function of displaying the truth of who we are as human beings. This means that art, when it is true to its vocation, transforms the apparently private virtues of the subjective spirit into publicly held ideals. But equally, through its sensuous nature, art transforms the physical world in which we live into one of beauty and nobility. In such a manner, we come to feel at home in the world.

Therefore, Hegel turns out to offer a persuasive corrective to the prevailing modernist and postmodernist accounts of the arts. To be sure, it is necessary to supplement what he says explicitly in the *Aesthetics* about the Ideal with what remains implicit in his treatment of the individual arts concerning the ethical life of customary duties, just as it is necessary to turn to other sources in his philosophical corpus to understand the legitimacy of his arguments regarding the ethical life, the existence of artistic norms, and the claims for the universality of artistic beauty. But Hegel is faithful to the tradition of theoretical reflection on the arts as well as to the primacy that tradition has accorded to beauty as a first principle of the arts. His faithfulness to the tradition, moreover, is not merely an accident of history, but is justified by his metaphysic of universality and particularity. It is all the more possible to see the power of his arguments now, perhaps, knowing the deficiencies of modernist approaches to the arts and the failings of contemporary aesthetic theories which try to accommodate them. Art must be representation, with an ethical content that is both individual and communal, in a way that respects traditional genres and artistic syntaxes. It gives rise to a beauty that lends dignity to our shared life in common with others.

If this seems to be an indictment of some of the most cherished assumptions about art today, then perhaps it is time to reconsider those assumptions and take the Hegelian perspective to heart as the beginning of a reconstruction of the role of art. As Hegel recognized, art is not the supreme object of importance in human endeavor, but it is the foundation for both religious perception and philosophical understanding. Together, art, religion, and philosophy are the modes of Absolute knowing; they define our civilization's highest achievements. The good life depends on acknowledging them in the contexts of tradition and transcendence.

Notes

Notes to Introduction

1. See Christopher Menke, *The Sovereignty of Art: Aesthetic Negativity in Adorno and Derrida*, trans. Neil Solomon (Cambridge, MA and London: MIT Press, 1998), 252.

2. Modernism as an artistic movement therefore shares in the definition of modernity in general, by which to be modern is the absolutely fundamental value: see Gianni Vattimo, *The End of Modernity: Nihilism and Hermeneutics in Postmodern Culture*, trans. Jon R. Snyder (Baltimore, MD: Johns Hopkins University Press, 1991), 99. Cf. the remarks of Jürgen Habermas, "Modernity Versus Postmodernity," in Howard Risatti, ed., *Postmodern Perspectives: Issues in Contemporary Art*, 2nd ed. (Upper Saddle River, NJ: Prentice Hall, 1998), 55.

3. See Werner Koepsel, *Die Rezeption der Hegelschen Ästhetik im 20. Jahrhundert* (Bonn: Bouvier Verlag Herbert Grundmann, 1975) for the history of Hegel's influence in the twentieth century, and especially for Adorno (269 ff.).

4. Martin Heidegger, *Being and Time*, trans. Joan Stambaugh (Albany: State University of New York Press, 1996), 18 on the historical nature of Dasein, 391 on the authenticity of the future for Dasein. Only the future holds the possibility of authentic life.

5. Plato makes this distinction in the *Timaeus*, 27–28; the two worlds are also referred to as the intelligible and the sensible.

6. See the discussion in Augustine, *On Free Choice of the Will*, Book 3, §15, trans. and ed. Thomas Williams (Indianapolis and Cambridge: Hackett Publishing, 1993), 24–25.

7. Stanley Rosen emphasizes this in his *G. W. F. Hegel: An Introduction to the Science of Wisdom* (New Haven and London: Yale University Press, 1974), 33.

8. Emil L. Fackenheim, *The Religious Dimension in Hegel's Thought* (Bloomington and London: Indiana University Press, 1967).

9. Bernard M. G. Reardon, *Hegel's Philosophy of Religion* (London: Macmillan, 1977), recognizes the ambiguity of Hegel's language (103) and the unity of God and the world in Hegel's conception, but insists that "God is not simply the world" (102).

10. Quentin Lauer, *Hegel's Concept of God* (Albany: State University of New York Press, 1982), emphasizes that the disjunction in nature between God as Absolute Spirit and both the material condition of the created world and the finite nature of human spirit means that there cannot be any risk of reduction of God to the finitude of creation (139).

11. Charles Taylor, *Hegel and Modern Society* (Cambridge and New York: Cambridge University Press, 1979), 37–40.

12. Cyril O'Regan, *The Heterodox Hegel* (Albany: State University of New York Press, 1994), 45, 73.

13. Stephen Houlgate, in *Freedom, Truth and History*, emphasizes Hegel's rejection of supernaturalism (189), but also God's difference from humanity, even as humanity "is itself an integral part of the life of God" (197). William Desmond is much more critical, calling Hegel's God an idol in his recent *Hegel's God: A Counterfeit Double?* (Aldershot: Ashgate, 2003); he argues that Hegel's concept of God is equivocal, involving at least a reconfiguration of authentic divine transcendence in the language of "holistic immanence" by which God becomes the self-generating Whole of wholes 13).

14. The concept of "the ethical" requires some preliminary clarification. In the classical Aristotelian sense, it refers to character, whereas in Hegel's usage, it refers to the life of customary duties. But abstract duty itself, in the Kantian sense, he calls "moral" in nature. Of course, today, ethical is likely to mean those specific public obligations attendant on a particular profession, while moral refers to the arena of private action. What is lost, in other words, is both the primacy of character and the sense of custom and tradition in ethics, and the concern with duty that must be done just because that is what is right. However, the ethical will mean, throughout the discussion that follows, both the classical sense of virtue in character and the life of customary duties; the context will make clear which is intended. When moral is used, in general it should be understood in the broadest possible sense, unless Kant is the specific object of discussion.

Notes to Chapter 1

1. Lest it be thought that this is a purely personal and idiosyncratic observation, a leading textbook on art history calls postmodernist paint-

ing "barren" and "gutted of all significance"—an honest assessment that is all too rare in the field: see H. W. Janson and Anthony F. Janson, *History of Art: The Western Tradition*, 6th ed. (New York: Harry N. Abrams, 2001), 921.

2. Arthur C. Danto, *After the End of Art: Contemporary Art and the Pale of History* (Princeton and Chichester: Princeton University Press, 1997), 5.

3. For example, see Friedrich Nietzsche, *Beyond Good and Evil*, trans. R. J. Hollingdale, ed. Michael Tanner (London: Penguin, 1990), §260, 195, where he redefines nobility in the moral sense as consisting in the knowledge of creating values, so that there are no fixed moral absolutes; also Martin Heidegger, *Being and Time*, trans. Joan Stambaugh (Albany: State University of New York Press, 1996), 208 for the rejection of eternal truths.

4. Gianni Vattimo, *The End of Modernity*, 56.

5. T. M. Knox, Introduction to Hegel, *Aesthetics: Lectures on Fine Art*, vi.

6. Martin Heidegger, *Being and Time*, 169, 176.

7. For a thorough survey of recent analytical aesthetics, see Stephen Davies, *Definitions of Art* (Ithaca, NY and London: Cornell University Press, 1991).

8. There are, of course, other ways of characterizing the modern conception of art: see, for example, Preben Mortensen, *Art in the Social Order: The Making of the Modern Conception of Art* (Albany: State University of New York Press, 1997) 1, where the author identifies the five fine arts Hegel also treats, the doctrine of autonomy from didactic or cognitive ends, the creation of art by genius, and the presentation of subjective truth as constitutive of the modern conception. He traces the emergence of these to the eighteenth century. But autonomy and subjectivity are the most important elements for our purposes, and they are joined in the twentieth century to other ways of conceiving the purposes of art.

9. See the discussion in Harold Osborne, *Aesthetics and Art Theory: An Historical Introduction* (New York: Dutton, 1970), 262–72.

10. Alan H. Goldman, *Aesthetic Value* (Boulder, CO: Westview Press, 1995), 8.

11. Monroe Beardsley, *Aesthetics: Problems in the Philosophy of Criticism*, 2nd ed. (Indianapolis and Cambridge: Hackett Publishing, 1981), 466.

12. Beardsley, *Aesthetics*, 511.

13. Beardsley, *Aesthetics*, 566.

14. Malcolm Budd, *Values of Art: Pictures, Poetry and Music* (London: Penguin, 1995), 44.

15. Budd, *Values of Art*, 154–55.

16. As in John Passmore, *Serious Art* (La Salle, IL: Open Court, 1991).

17. Immanuel Kant, *Kritik der Urteilskraft*, ed. Karl Vorländer (Hamburg: Felix Meiner, 1990), §16; *Critique of Judgement*, trans. J. H. Bernard (New York and London: Collier Macmillan Publishers, 1951), 66. Hereafter abbreviated *CJ*.

18. John Dewey, *Art as Experience* (1934; repr., New York: Berkley Publishing Group, 1980), 46–47, 53.

19. Dewey, *Art as Experience*, 57.

20. Dewey, *Art as Experience*, 61. Dewey appears indebted here to Leo Tolstoy's expressionist theory.

21. Dewey, *Art as Experience*, 65.

22. Alasdair MacIntyre, *After Virtue: A Study in Moral Theory*, 2nd ed. (Notre Dame, IN: University of Notre Dame Press, 1984),13ff.

23. MacIntyre, *After Virtue*, 86.

24. Dewey, *Art as Experience*, 189.

25. Monroe Beardsley, *Aesthetics*, 574–76. The values of aesthetic experience he cites include relief of tension, promotion of inner harmony, refinement of perception, development of the imagination, fostering of mutual sympathy, and the unique discovery of an ideal of completion and perfection otherwise missing in life. These benefits, it must be emphasized, accrue to the individual: the value of art remains entirely subjective.

26. Martin Heidegger, "On the Origin of the Work of Art," in *Poetry, Language, Thought*, trans. Albert Hofstadter (1971; repr., New York: HarperCollins, 2001), 38. Hereafter abbreviated *PLT*.

27. Heidegger makes "the world" fundamentally "innerworldly" or subjective, *Being and Time*, 94ff. He insists on the subjectivity of all interpretation, 141, and on the relativism of all truth to individual perception, 208.

28. See Vincent Van Gogh's letter of April 1888 to Emile Bernard, reprinted in Herschel B. Chipp, *Theories of Modern Art: A Source Book by Artists and Critics* (Berkeley and London: University of California Press, 1968), 32.

29. Theodor W. Adorno, *Aesthetic Theory*, ed. Gretel Adorno and Rolf Tiedemann, trans. Robert Hullot-Kentor (Minneapolis: University of Minnesota Press, 1997), 1, 8.

30. Adorno, *Quasi una fantasia: Essays on Modern Music*, trans. Rodney Livingstone (London and New York: Verso, 1992), 257.

31. Gianni Vattimo, *The End of Modernity*, 53.

32. Vattimo, *The End of Modernity*, 53–54.

33. Chantal Georgel, "The Museum as Metaphor in Nineteenth-Century France," in Daniel J. Sherman and Irit Rogoff, *Museum Culture: Histories, Discourses, Spectacles* (Minneapolis: University of Minnesota Press, 1994), 119.

34. Adorno, *Philosophy of Modern Music*, trans. Anne G. Mitchell and Wesley V. Blomster (New York: Seabury Press, 1973), 9–10, calls the concert an empty ritual that must be destroyed. Cf. Lydia Goehr, *The Imaginary Museum of Musical Works: An Essay in the Philosophy of Music* (Oxford: Clarendon Press, 1992), 271–72.

35. See Richard Leppert and Susan McClary, eds., *Music and Society: The Politics of Composition, Performance and Reception* (Cambridge: Cambridge University Press, 1987), xviii; also the essays by Thelma Golden, Eleanor Heartney, and Jennie Klein in Howard Risati, *Postmodern Perspectives: Issues in Contemporary Art*, 265 ff.

36. Christoph Menke, *The Sovereignty of Art: Aesthetic Negativity in Adorno and Derrida*, trans. Neil Solomon (Cambridge, MA and London: MIT Press, 1998) 252–54. On the theme of alienation in Heidegger, Adorno, and Derrida, see J. M. Bernstein, *The Fate of Art: Aesthetic Alienation from Kant to Derrida and Adorno* (University Park: Pennsylvania State University Press, 1992).

37. Cf. Jacques Barzun, *The Use and Abuse of Art* (Princeton, NJ and London: Princeton University Press, 1974).

38. See, for example, Suzanne Marchand, "The Quarrel of the Ancients and the Moderns in the German Museums," in Susan A. Crane, ed., *Museums and Memory* (Stanford, CA: Stanford University Press, 2000), 179–199.

39. The term "public realm" is used by James Howard Kunstler, in *Home from Nowhere: Remaking Our Everyday World for the Twenty-First Century* (New York: Simon & Schuster, 1996), who uses it specifically to refer to the public environment created by architectural facades: see 36. But I have broadened the concept considerably throughout this discussion.

Notes to Chapter 2

1. Wassily Kandinsky, *Concerning the Spiritual in Art*, trans. M. T. H. Sadler (1914; repr., New York: Dover, 1977), 52.

2. Kandinsky, "On the Question of Form," in *The Blaue Reiter Almanac*, rev. ed., ed. Wassily Kandinsky and Franz Marc, trans. Klaus Lankheit (1974; repr., New York: Da Capo Press, 1989), 161.

3. Arnold Schoenberg, "Problems of Harmony," in *Style and Idea*, rev. ed., ed. Leonard Stein, trans. Leo Black (1934; Berkeley: University of California Press), 280.

4. Le Corbusier [Charles-Edouard Jeanneret], *Towards a New Architecture*, trans. Frederick Etchells (1931; repr., New York: Dover, 1986), 114–22, 143.

5. Only recently do we find serious defenses of beauty in art, as in John Lane, *Timeless Beauty in the Arts and Everyday Life* (Dartington Totnes, England: Green Books, 2003), and Stephen D. Ross, *The Gift of Beauty: The Good as Art* (Albany: State University of New York Press, 1996). Both are general treatments of the subject, but Lane's approach is refreshingly discriminating—and critical of the modernist abandonment of beauty.

6. As given by J. L. Ackrill and J. O. Urmson in their notes to Aristotle's *Nichomachean Ethics*, trans. W. D. Ross (1925; repr., Oxford: Oxford University Press, 1980), xxviii.

7. See Stephen Bungay, *Beauty and Truth: A Study of Hegel's Aesthetics* (Oxford: Oxford University Press, 1984), and William Desmond, *Art and the Absolute: A Study of Hegel's Aesthetics* (Albany: State University of New York Press, 1986), in both of which the titles point to the concern with truth. Bungay refers briefly to what he also calls "ethical substance" in art (66), and Desmond emphasizes the religious nature of the Ideal (35ff.), but it remains true that the ethical has not received the emphasis that would place Hegel within the tradition of aesthetics that posited a natural link between truth, beauty, and moral goodness in artistic representation. Richard Dien Winfield, however, has more recently advocated returning to the inspiration of Hegel to reconceive aesthetics, and has emphasized the connection between truth, beauty, and ethical conduct in the arts: *Systematic Aesthetics* (Gainesville: University Press of Florida, 1995), esp. 134ff. The neo-Kantian Hans-Georg Gadamer is more typical of non-Hegelian philosophers in criticizing the identification of beauty and truth in Hegel: see *The Relevance of the Beautiful and Other Essays*, trans. Nicholas Walker, ed. Robert Bernasconi (Cambridge and New York: Cambridge University Press, 1986), 37. For a history of the relation between intellectual content and artistic beauty, see Frederick Will, *Intelligible Beauty: Aesthetic in Thought from Winckelmann to Victor Cousin* (Tübingen, Germany: 1955); Hegel is treated briefly, together with Schelling, 180–96.

8. See St. Augustine, *On Free Choice of the Will*.

9. Compare Hegel's *Enz.* 3, §481; this is the key to Hegel's philosophy of history, in which Christianity brings the realization of freedom to universality for the first time (§482).

10. Stephen Houlgate makes freedom the key to his analysis of Hegel's thought in his *Freedom, Truth and History: An Introduction to*

Hegel's Philosophy (London and New York: Routledge, 1991). Merold Westphal explores the tensions between freedom realized in political and religious communities in his *Hegel, Freedom, and Modernity* (Albany: State University of New York Press, 1992).

11. Cf., for example, Leon Battista Alberti, *On Painting*, trans. Cecil Grayson, ed. Martin Kemp (1972; London: Penguin, 1999), 90–91. This doctrine of selection was always important in the visual arts.

12. See Stephen Bungay, *Beauty and Truth*, 62–65.

13. Most modern philosophers of aesthetics are suspicious of claims that art communicates knowledge, as is Etienne Gilson in *The Arts of the Beautiful* (1965; n.p.: Dalkey Archive Press, 2000), 142–43; yet Gilson comes close to Hegel's position in recognizing that art is most true to its mission when it serves religion (182).

14. Aristotle, *Metaphysics*, trans. Richard Hope (Ann Arbor: University of Michigan Press, 1960), 1078b, 276.

15. Aristotle distinguished three good motives of choice: the noble, the advantageous, and the pleasant: *Nichomachean Ethics* 1104b26ff.; in the *Eudemian Ethics*, 1248b34–37, the ultimate goal is the "fine-and-good," where "Fine things are the virtues and the deeds resulting from virtue." *Eudemian Ethics, Books I, II, and VIII*, trans. and ed. Michael Woods, 2nd ed. (Oxford: Clarendon Press, 1992), 41.

16. *Symposium*, 204c, in Plato, *Lysis, Symposium, Gorgias*, trans. W. R. M. Lamb, vol. 166 of the Loeb Classical Library (Cambridge, MA: Harvard University Press, 1925).

17. *Phaedrus* 250, in Plato, *Phaedrus and the Seventh and Eighth Letters*, trans. Walter Hamilton (London: Penguin, 1973) 56–57.

18. *Phaedrus* 251, 57.

19. Plato, *Republic*, 508.

20. Plotinus, *Enneads* I.6; cf. Marsilio Ficino, *Commentary on Plato's Symposium on Love*, trans. and ed. Sears Jayne (Woodstock, CT: Spring Publications, 1985), 49.

21. *Timaeus* 87, in Plato, *Timaeus and Critias*, trans. Desmond Lee, rev. ed. (London: Penguin, 1977), 118–19.

22. Cf. *Philebus* 66, where Plato captures the good in terms first of measure, and secondly in terms of proportion, beauty, and perfection. Here beauty is linked with something that goes beyond order.

23. William Desmond, *Being and the Between* (Albany: State University of New York Press, 1995).

Notes to Chapter 3

1. Burke, *A Philosophical Enquiry into the Origin of our Ideas of the Sublime and Beautiful*, ed. Adam Phillips (Oxford and New York: Oxford University Press, 1990), 53.

2. See Friedrich Schiller, "On the Sublime," and "Concerning the Sublime," in *Essays*, ed. Walter Hinderer and Daniel O. Dahlstrom (New York: Continuum, 1993), 22–44, 70–85. Schiller here extends Kant's concept of the sublime as the "absolutely great" in the *Critique of Judgement*, §25, trans. J. H. Bernard (New York: Macmillan, 1951), 86.

3. Beat Wyss, *Hegel's Art History and the Critique of Modernity*, trans. Caroline D. Saltzwedel (Cambridge and New York: Cambridge University Press, 1999), 1; also Arthur C. Danto, *The Philosophical Disenfranchisement of Art* (New York: Columbia University Press, 1986), 107.

4. For Hegel's conception of the history of philosophy as a developing tradition, which issues in a pronounced doctrine of progress and (effectively) philosophical presentism, see *Hegel's Introduction to the Lectures on the History of Philosophy*, trans. T. M. Knox and A. V. Miller (Oxford: Clarendon Press, 1985), 47–51 (from the Berlin Introduction of 1820). I have discussed the origin of Hegel's historicist presentism in more detail in "Hegel's Aesthetic and the Possibility of Art Criticism," in *Hegel and Aesthetics*, ed. William Maker (Albany: State University of New York Press, 2000), 35–37. Yet it is important to emphasize that Hegel's is not a radical historicism or presentism: his dialectic of transcendence and immanence remains metaxological. See also Carl Rapp, *Fleeing the Universal: The Critic of Post-Rational Criticism* (Albany: State University of New York Press, 1998).

5. The Spirit is embodied in the state, which is necessarily historical: Hegel, *VPG*, 30ff.; *PH*, 17ff. But the Spirit is also the Third Person of the Holy Trinity, manifest in the community of the church: *VPR*3, 254; *LPR*, 473. The *VPG* is much more secularist than the *VPR*.

Notes to Chapter 4

1. Only Jack Kaminsky, *Hegel on Art: An Interpretation of Hegel's Aesthetics* (Albany: State University of New York Press, 1962), discusses the individual arts in detail.

2. Malcolm Budd, *Values of Art: Pictures, Poetry and Music*, 48.

3. Richard Wollheim, *Painting as an Art* (Princeton, NJ: Princeton University Press, 1987), 89; cf. Roger Scruton, *The Aesthetic Understanding: Essays in the Philosophy of Art and Culture* (London and New York: Methuen, 1983), 102ff.

4. Hegel's aesthetic of the fine arts has not fared well among commentators: Konrad Schüttauf, for example, is quite critical of his system in *Die Kunst und die bildenden Künste: Eine Auseinandersetzung mit Hegel's Ästhetik* (Bonn, Germany: Bouvier Verlag, 1984).

5. Johann Joachim Winckelmann, *Reflections on the Imitation of Greek Works in Painting and Sculpture*, trans. Elfriede Heyer and Roger C. Norton (La Salle, IL: Open Court, 1987), 33.

6. Winckelmann, *Reflections*, 21.

7. Winckelmann, *Reflections*, 17.

8. Winckelmann, *Reflections*, 91.

9. Winckelmann, *Reflections*, 90.

10. Sir Joshua Reynolds, *Discourses*, from Edward Malone, *The Works of Sir Joshua Reynolds* (London, 1797), quoted in Holt, *A Documentary History of Art*, vol. 2, 274, 276.

11. Victor Cousin, *Lectures on the True, the Beautiful, and the Good*, trans. O. W. Wight (New York: Appleton, 1875), 149.

12. Leon Battista Alberti, *On Painting*, trans. Cecil Grayson, ed. Martin Kemp (1972; London and New York: Penguin, 1991), 93; cf. 71.

13. Alberti, *On Painting*, 71.

14. Alberti, *On Painting*, 75, 76, 80.

15. Alberti, *On Painting*, 76.

16. Giovanni Paolo Lomazzo, *The Idea of the Temple of Painting*, trans. and ed. in Elizabeth Gilmore Holt, *A Documentary History of Art*, vol. 2, rev. ed. (Princeton, NJ: Princeton University Press, 1982), 84. The passage is borrowed entirely from Marsilio Ficino, *Sopra lo amore o ver Convito di Platone*, vol. 4.

17. Lomazzo, *The Idea of the Temple of Painting*, in Holt, *A Documentary History of Art*, 2: 85.

18. Cf. Giovanni Pietro Bellori, "The Lives of Modern Painters, Sculptors and Architects" (1672), trans. Kenneth Donahue, in Elizabeth Gilmore Holt, *A Documentary History of Art*, 2: 94–106.

19. Nicolas Poussin, "Observations on Painting," from Charles Jouanny, *Correspondance de Nicolas Poussin* (Paris, 1911), trans. and ed. in Elizabeth Gilmore Holt, *A Documentary History of Art*, 2: 142–45.

20. Charles Alphonse Du Fresnoy, *The Art of Painting*, trans. John Dryden, 2nd ed. (London, 1716), quoted in Holt, *A Documentary History of Art*, 2: 166–67.

Notes to Chapter 5

1. See Stephen Bungay, *Beauty and Truth: A Study of Hegel's Aesthetics*, 133 and 141, on the inadequacies of Hegel's aesthetic of music; also Julian Johnson, "Music in Hegel's Aesthetics: A Re-Evaluation," *British Journal of Aesthetics* 31 (1991): 152.

2. For a thorough discussion of Hegel's musical background, see Adolf Nowak, *Hegels Musikaesthetik* (Regensburg: Bosse, 1971), 16–24.

3. Bungay, *Beauty and Truth*, 136; Carl Dahlhaus, *Esthetics of Music*, trans. William Austin (Cambridge: Cambridge University Press, 1982), 57. Such a criticism rests on a misinterpretation of Hegel's position on instrumental music, however.

4. Bungay, *Beauty and Truth*, 136.

5. Eduard Hanslick, *On the Musically Beautiful: A Contribution towards the Revision of the Aesthetics of Music*, trans. and ed. Geoffrey Payzant (Indianapolis, IN: Hackett, 1986), 14–18.

6. Bungay argues that "the treatment of music is peculiar in that there is no sustained attempt to locate the ideal": *Beauty and Truth*, 133. Dahlhaus also finds this mysterious in his *Esthetics of Music*, 48–49.

7. This was not as unusual as it might seem for the nineteenth century, as other writers also spoke of a religious mood in sacred music, for example, Wilhelm August Ambros, *The Boundaries of Music and Poetry: A Study in Musical Aesthetics*, trans. J. H. Cornell (New York: Schirmer, 1893), 62.

8. Hegel's position is more sophisticated than this, as we shall see. Nevertheless, he was certainly not alone in claiming the relevance of thought and feeling to the sense of profundity in music (953–54): cf. Christian Gottfried Körner against the Kantian reduction of music to a merely formal play in "Über Charakterdarstellung in der Musik," excerpts translated in *Music and Aesthetics in the Eighteenth and Early Nineteenth Centuries*, ed. Peter Le Huray and James Day (Cambridge: Cambridge University Press, 1981), 236–39.

9. The charge of "logocentrism" against Hegel's musical aesthetic is common. See Bungay, *Beauty and Truth*, 137; Johnson, "Music in Hegel's Aesthetics," 152. What lies behind this complaint is the conviction that music must be *sui generis*—that there cannot be a reduction of this particular art to a significance expressible in words, or else music would become a species of poetry. But, of course, music was a part of poetry in the classical position of Aristotle's *Poetics*.

10. The ideology of the historically necessary development of a new musical language has dominated the avant-garde since Arnold Schoenberg: see his argument for necessity in "Composition with Twelve Tones (1), (1941)," in *Style and Idea: Selected Writings of Arnold Schoenberg*, ed. Leonard Stein, trans. Leo Black (Berkeley, CA: University of California Press, 1984), 216. Anton Webern had emphasized the historical necessity even more strongly in a 1933 essay: see *The Path to the New Music*, ed. Willi Reich, trans. Leo Black (London: Universal, 1975), 32–33. The assertion that any sound (or lack thereof) can be considered music is associated most famously with John Cage. For relevant excerpts from Cage's writings, see Edward A. Lippman, ed., *Musical Aesthetics: A Historical Reader*, 3 vols. (Stuyvesant, NY: Pendragon Press, 1990), 3: 421–36.

11. It should be recalled from chapter 1 that Hegel implicitly made feeling at home in the world one of the results of art that was true to its aim. Cf. Roger Scruton on the deprivation of order in functionalist architecture, with the resulting inhospitableness of the built environment, in his *Aesthetics of Architecture* (Princeton, NJ: Princeton University Press, 1979), 249.

12. Cf. the theory of intervals and tones of attraction and repose in François-Joseph Fétis, *Traité complet de la théorie et de la pratique de l'harmonie, contenant la doctrine de la science et de l'art*, 4th ed. (Paris: Brandus, 1849), 21-22.

13. See, for example, Arnold Schoenberg, "Problems of Harmony" (1934), in *Style and Idea*, 280–84.

14. See William Thomson, *Schoenberg's Error* (Philadelphia: University of Pennsylvania Press, 1991).

15. I have argued this at length in *From Classicism to Modernism: Western Musical Culture and the Metaphysics of Order* (Aldershot: Ashgate, 2001), 49–67.

16. Hanslick, *On the Musically Beautiful*, 31.

17. Jean-Philippe Rameau, *Treatise on Harmony*, trans. Philip Gossett (New York: Dover Publications, 1971), 155.

18. Christian F. D. Schubart, *Ideen zu einer Ästhetik der Tonkunst* (Leipzig: Reclam, 1977), 284–87. Schubart's discussion was by no means an isolated phenomenon, and it was widely influential: see Rita Steblin, *A History of Key Characteristics in the Eighteenth and Early Nineteenth Centuries* (Ann Arbor, MI: UMI Research Press, 1983).

19. Again, I have argued this at length in *From Classicism to Modernism*, 92–115.

20. The problem of meaning and profundity in music, especially instrumental music, is a matter of considerable debate today: see David A. White, "Toward a Theory of Profundity in Music," *Journal of Aesthetics and Art Criticism* 50 (1992): 23–34; also Peter Kivy, *Music Alone: Philosophical Reflections on the Purely Musical Experience* (Ithaca and London: Cornell University Press, 1990), 202ff. Kivy confesses on 216 that he has no clear idea what makes music sound profound.

21. See Nowak, *Hegels Musikaesthetik*, 156, for a brief illustration of this point.

22. The musical error of formalist aesthetics lies in the refusal to recognize the way that Western art music has been written and perceived historically. Hanslick's discussion of Beethoven's *Egmont Overture* is simply perverse in denying the character of the music and its clear relationship to the character of Egmont in Goethe's drama: see Hanslick, *On the Musically Beautiful*, 74–75.

23. Carl Dahlhaus discusses Hegel's relation to his musical contemporaries in his *Klassische und romantische Musikästhetik* (Laaber: Laaber-Verlag, 1988), 230–248.

24. See Bungay, *Beauty and Truth*, 71–89; also William Desmond, *Art and the Absolute: A Study of Hegel's Aesthetics*, 103–65.

Notes to Chapter 6

1. See, for example, Howard Risatti, ed., *Postmodern Perspectives*, in which half of the chapters in this compilation of essays concern ideology, feminism, or marginality.

2. Budd, *Values of Art*, 83–84.

3. John Gardner, *On Moral Fiction* (New York: Basic Books, 1978), 5.

4. *Iliad* VII, lines 90–102. See Homer, *The Iliad*, trans. Richmond Lattimore (Chicago and London: University of Chicago Press, 1951).

5. Hegel develops the concept of the ethical life for advanced societies in much greater detail in his *Philosophy of Right*, §§142–360. There, however, the emphasis in on the relations to family, civil society, and the state.

6. Aristotle, *Poetics* 1462a–b, in *On Poetry and Style*, trans. and ed. G. M. A. Grube (1958; repr., Indianapolis and Cambridge: Hackett, 1989), 61–62.

7. Michael Schulte traces the origin of Hegel's theory of tragic conflict to the *Phenomenology of Spirit* of 1807 in his *Die "Tragödie im Sittlichen": Zur Dramentheorie Hegels* (Munich: Wilhelm Fink Verlag, 1992).

8. *Poetics* 1454a, in *On Poetry and Style*, 29–30. Grube justifies the translation of the Greek *spoudaios* in the definition of tragedy as morally good: xxi–xxii.

9. Walter Kaufmann discusses these interpretations in his *Tragedy and Philosophy* (Princeton, NJ: Princeton University Press, 1968), 56, dismissing Gerald F. Else's *Aristotle's Poetics: The Argument* (Cambridge, MA: Harvard University Press, 1957). Kaufmann's own poetics of tragedy, presented with great erudition (87–117), seems ultimately wrongheaded when it insists on explaining catharsis by awakening forgotten and repressed sorrows and in claiming "that fates worse than ours can be experienced as exhilarating" (98). In fact, Else has not been completely alone; cf. Dorothea Krook, *Elements of Tragedy* (New Haven, CT: Yale University Press, 1969), 8–17, where she argues that tragic suffering is the expiation of the original violation of the moral order.

10. Sophocles, *Antigone*, lines 1393–1400, in *The Three Theban Plays: Antigone, Oedipus the King, Oedipus at Colonus*, trans. Robert Fagles, ed. Bernard Knox (New York and London: Penguin, 1982), 124.

11. *Antigone*, lines 1468–1470, in *The Three Theban Plays*, 128.

12. This passage begins with line 913; when the Furies assemble, they dance around Athena as their leader: see Aeschylus, *The Oresteia: Agamemnon, The Libation Bearers, The Eumenides*, trans. Robert Fagles, ed. Fagles and W. B. Stanford (New York and London: Penguin, 1975), 271–76.

13. *Oedipus at Colonus*, line 1098, in *The Three Theban Plays*, 344.

14. To be sure, Hegel remarks that Oedipus illustrates a second type of tragic collision, between fate obeyed unconsciously and unintentionally, and "wide-awake consciousness": *VÄ* 3, 545; *A* 2, 1214. But Hegel does not dwell on this as he does on Antigone's conflict with Creon.

15. These lines from *Antigone*, lines 499–505, in *The Three Theban Plays*, 82.

16. Plato confirms the order of honors owed to the gods cited by Hegel: first to the gods of Olympus, "the patron-gods of the state," then to the gods of the underworld, next the spirits, heroes, and ancestral gods, followed by one's living parents: *The Laws*, Book IV, trans. and ed. Trevor J. Saunders (London and New York: Penguin, 1970), 176. But although Creon invokes Zeus as his witness (*Antigone*, line 205), he does not forbid the burial of Polyneices in order to honor Zeus; his sole concern is the priority of the state over friendship (line 203). Thus Antigone is on the mark in saying that Zeus did not forbid the burial of Polyneices, and certainly not the gods of the underworld, either. Creon's irrationality and concern for his own power emerge clearly a bit later, in lines 328–56.

17. *Antigone*, line 823, in *The Three Theban Plays*, 97.

18. Cf. Aristotle, *The Nichomachean Ethics* 1160b, Book VIII.10.

19. Sophocles, *Oedipus the King*, lines 433–59 and 698–703, in *The Three Theban Plays*, 182, 194–95.

20. *Oedipus the King*, lines 884–98, in *The Three Theban Plays*, 206.

21. Significantly, Kierkegaard later agreed with Hegel on this point: "Our age has lost all the substantial categories of family, state, kindred; it must turn the single individual over to himself completely . . . [so that] he becomes his own creation." But then compassion, and with it, the sense of the tragic, is lost. Søren Kierkegaard, *Either/Or*, 2 vols., ed. and trans. Howard V. Hong and Edna H. Hong (Princeton, NJ and Oxford: Princeton University Press, 1987), 1: 149.

22. Shakespeare, *Hamlet*, III.i, lines 57–60. Cited from William Shakespeare, *Tragedies* (London: J. M. Dent & Sons, 1906), 482–574.

23. *Hamlet*, III.i, lines 71, 76–82.

24. Johann Wolfgang von Goethe, *Faust, Erster und Zweiter Teil*, ed. Sybille Demmer (Munich: Deutscher Taschenbuch Verlag, 1997), Part I, lines 430–509.

25. *Faust*, Part I, lines 1765–75.

26. Friedrich Schiller, *The Piccolomini*, II.v, in *The Robbers and Wallenstein*, trans. and ed. F. J. Lamport (London and New York: Penguin, 1979), 249–50.

27. *The Piccolomini*, II.iii, 246.

28. As reported by his wife, the Duchess of Friedland, in *Wallenstein's Death*, III.iii, 373.

29. *Wallenstein's Death*, III.xv, 397.

30. *Wallenstein's Death*, III.xviii, 402.

31. *The Eustace Diamonds*, 2 vols. in one, ed. W. J. McCormack (Oxford and New York: Oxford University Press, 1982), 1: 320.

Notes to Chapter 7

1. Pollio Vitruvius, *De architectura libri decem* I, iii, §2; *The Ten Books on Architecture*, trans. Morris H. Morgan (1914; repr., New York: Dover 1960), 17.

2. Leon Battista Alberti, *De re aedificatoria* VI, 2; *On the Art of Building in Ten Books*, trans. Joseph Rykwert, Neil Leach, and Robert Tavernor (Cambridge, MA: MIT Press, 1988), 155.

3. Andrea Palladio, *I Quattro libri dell'architettura* I, i; *The Four Books of Architecture*, trans. Isaac Ware (1738; repr., New York: Dover, 1965), 1.

4. See Stephen Bungay, *Beauty and Truth: A Study of Hegel's Aesthetics*, 99–108, on Hegel's architectural aesthetic. Jack Kaminsky's treatment of Hegel on architecture emphasizes the Symbolic phase as the appropriate birthplace of the art, but pays little attention to the classical phase, and only modest attention to the Gothic: see *Hegel on Art: An Interpretation of Hegel's Aesthetics*, 42–64.

5. On the translation history of Alberti's *De re aedificatoria*, see Rykwert, Leach, and Tavernor, xxii–xxiii. On Palladio's influence in Germany, especially in Berlin under Frederick the Great, see David Watkin and Tilman Mellinghoff, *German Architecture and the Classical Ideal* (Cambridge, MA.: MIT Press, 1987), 19.

6. Indeed, modernist architects have openly rejected ornamentation; see, for example, Le Corbusier [Charles-Edouard Jeanneret-Gris], *Towards a New Architecture*, trans. Frederick Etchells (1931; repr., New York: Dover, 1986), esp. 142–43. Karsten Harries criticizes the modern aesthetic attitude toward decoration, in *The Ethical Function of Architecture* (Cambridge, MA: MIT Press, 1997),28ff.

7. *The Ten Books of Architecture*, I, iii, §2, 17.

8. *The Ten Books of Architecture*, I, ii, §4, 14. On this, see Alexander Tzonis and Liane Lefaivre, *Classical Architecture: The Poetics of Order* (Cambridge, MA: MIT Press, 1986), 117ff.

9. *The Ten Books of Architecture*, I, ii, §5, 14.

10. *The Ten Books of Architecture*, I, ii, §§5–9, 15–16: Vitruvius considers the latter kind of propriety a species of Economy.

11. *On the Art of Building*, VI, §2, 156.

12. *On the Art of Building*, IX, §5, 301–3.

13. *On the Art of Building*, VI, §13, 183–84.

14. *On the Art of Building*, VII, §3, 194. Alberti emphasizes the psychological effect of ornament in a temple, as inspiring awe and admiration, thus making it worthy of God.

15. *On the Art of Building*, IX, §8, 312.

16. *On the Art of Building*, VII, §3, 195.

17. *On the Art of Building*, IX, §1, 292. Cf. Aristotle, *The Nichomachean Ethics* IV, §2, 1123a: the virtue of magnificence requires expenditure in one's house suitable to one's wealth, for a house is also a public ornament.

18. *The Four Books of Architecture*, I, §1; Ware, 1.

19. On Renaissance theory and practice, see Rudolf Wittkower, *Architectural Principles in the Age of Humanism*, 3rd ed. (1962; repr. New York: Norton, 1971). For a pictorial catalogue of Palladio's buildings, see Henry Hope Reed, *Palladio's Architecture and Its Influence* (New York: Dover, 1980).

20. *The Four Books of Architecture*, IV, Preface, 79. I have modernized Ware's spelling, and have corrected his translation of the Italian "*con la soavissima armonia del temperato. . . .*"

21. Alberti, *On the Art of Building*, VII, §3, 195; Palladio, *The Four Books of Architecture*, IV, §2, 81.

22. John Onians, *Bearers of Meaning: The Classical Orders in Antiquity, the Middle Ages, and the Renaissance* (Princeton, NJ: Princeton University Press, 1988), 313–14. The trend is plainly visible in Palladio's own work, as shown in Reed, *Palladio's Architecture*.

23. Indeed, proportion is often taken to have been the heart of the traditional concept of beauty: see W. Tatarkiewicz, "The Great Theory of Beauty and Its Decline," *Journal of Aesthetics and Art Criticism* 31 (1972–1973), 167.

24. See Onians, *Bearers of Meaning*, 40-41.

25. This is not to imply that Hegel was the first to question the code of proportionality; Claude Perrault had done so in the Baroque era already: see his *Ordonnance for the Five Kinds of Columns After the Method of the Ancients*, trans. Indra Kagis McEwen, ed. Alberto Perez-Gomez (Santa Monica: Getty Center for the History of Art and the

Humanities, 1993), esp. 49–51, where he calls proportion an example of arbitrary beauty. Thus, Hegel shares in this new skepticism of proportions.

26. Roger Scruton echoes Hegel's arguments regarding the importance of ornamentation for making proportions visible, and for the necessity of terminations and moldings in *The Aesthetics of Architecture* (Princeton, NJ: Princeton University Press, 1979), 67–69, 253.

27. See especially Plato, *Republic* 441c–444d.

28. On the importance of light to the Gothic style, see Otto von Simson, *The Gothic Cathedral: Origins of Gothic Architecture and the Medieval Concept of Order*, 3rd ed. (Princeton, NJ: Princeton University Press, 1988), 50–55.

29. In fact, the "mystical meaning" of proportions was vital to Gothic builders: see Otto von Simson, *The Gothic Cathedral*, 21–50.

30. Cf. St. Thomas Aquinas on beauty as consisting in integrity, harmony, and brightness: *Summa theologica*, 5 vols., trans. Fathers of the English Dominican Province, rev.ed. (1911; 1948 ed. repr.: Westminster, MD Christian Classics, 1981), Pt.1, Q. 39, Art. 8 Answer, vol.1: 201.

31. Onians, *Bearers of Meaning*, 128.

32. Otto von Simson, *The Gothic Cathedral*, 56–58.

33. See Otto von Simson, *The Gothic Cathedral*, 8, and for Notre Dame of Paris and the Cathedral of Chartres in particular, 221.

34. As Georges Duby shows, sculpted forms representing the powers of evil can be found even within the sanctuaries of medieval Gothic churches: see *The Age of the Cathedrals: Art and Society, 980–1420*, trans. Eleanor Levieux and Barbara Thompson (Chicago, IL: University of Chicago Press, 1981), 276–77.

35. See Wittkower, *Architectural Principles in the Age of Humanism*, 21.

36. David Watkin, *A History of Western Architecture* (New York: Thames and Hudson, 1986), 240.

37. Harries loses hope for the ethical life of the community in the modern world, undermining his wish for a restoration of architecture: *The Ethical Function of Architecture*, 352ff.

Notes to Chapter 8

1. *Politics* 1337b; all quotations are from the Benjamin Jowett translation, ed. Stephen Everson (Cambridge: Cambridge University Press, 1988).

2. Martin Heidegger, *Being and Time*, trans. Joan Stambaugh (Albany: State University of New York Press, 1996), 164, 166.

3. See his essay, "Building Dwelling Thinking," from a lecture of 1951, in *Poetry, Language, Thought*, trans. and ed. Albert Hofstadter (1975; repr. New York: HarperCollins, 2001), 141–59.

4. The literature on Heidegger's political guilt is large, but particularly insightful is Karl Löwith's *Martin Heidegger and European Nihilism*, ed. Richard Wolin, trans. Gary Steiner (New York: Columbia University Press, 1995), especially 211ff.

5. Aristotle, *The Nichomachean Ethics*, trans. David Ross (Oxford: Oxford University Press, 1925), II, §1, 1103a.

6. *NE*, I, §7, 1097b.

7. *NE*, I, §7, 1098a; Books VIII and IX concern friendship, a topic which Ross oddly thinks is misplaced in the *NE*. In fact, it follows directly from Aristotle's first premise regarding citizenship.

8. Cicero, *On Duties*, ed. M.T. Griffin and E. M. Atkins (Cambridge: Cambridge University Press, 1991), I, §160, 62.

9. Indeed, Alasdair MacIntyre has made the same point regarding the constitutive nature of specific communities for the moral life in general: see his *After Virtue: A Study in Moral Theory*, 2nd ed. (Notre Dame, IN: University of Notre Dame Press, 1984), 220.

10. Hegel felt that it is more ethical to resolve upon marriage first, so that the inclination to love comes afterward: *GPR*, §162; *PR*, 111–12.

Notes to Chapter 9

1. For the consequence of modernist art turning on itself, rejecting not only the prior traditions but the predecessor modernist movements, see Renato Poggioli, *The Theory of the Avant-Garde*, trans. Gerald Fitzgerald (Cambridge, MA and London: Harvard University Press, 1968).

2. I have explored this discontinuity for the case of music in Part 2 of *From Classicism to Modernism: Western Musical Culture and the Metaphysics of Order*, 121ff.

3. John Dewey, *Art as Experience*, 189.

4. *The American Arts Quarterly* has been particularly active in championing traditionalist artists; see especially the Spring 2001 and Winter 2002 issues, which focus on the architecture and sculpture appropriate to public spaces.

5. Barzun, *The Use and Abuse of Art*, 9ff., 141, 149–50. The origin of his pessimism lies in his initial consideration, "Why art must be challenged": the movements since World War II, such as Abstract

Expressionism, Pop Art, Aleatory Art, and Minimalist Art, reduce art to the merely interesting, destroying its claim to be taken seriously by any observer or the larger society (14–17).

6. Paul Oskar Kristeller, "Afterword: 'Creativity' and 'Tradition,'" reprinted from the *Journal of the History of Ideas* 44 (1983), 105–113, in *Renaissance Thought and the Arts: Collected Essays*, rev. ed. (Princeton, NJ and Chichester: Princeton University Press, 1990), 257, 255, and (for the quotation) 253.

7. Alasdair MacIntyre, *After Virtue: A Study in Moral Theory*, 2nd ed. (Notre Dame, IN: University of Notre Dame Press, 1984), 222. His conception of dynamic tradition, like that of Jaroslav Pelikan, owes much to John Henry Newman: Jaroslav Pelikan conceives the history of Christian doctrine and worship as a developing tradition, and he defends tradition for its essentially dynamic nature, after the manner of John Henry Newman in the nineteenth century. See Jaroslav Pelikan, *The Vindication of Tradition* (New Haven, CT and London: Yale University Press, 1984); see also his magisterial five volume *The Christian Tradition: A History of the Development of Doctrine* (Chicago, IL and London: University of Chicago Press, 1971–1989).

8. MacIntyre, *After Virtue*, 190.

9. Alasdair MacIntyre, *Whose Justice? Which Rationality?* (Notre Dame, IN: University of Notre Dame Press, 1988), 361–62.

10. Alasdair MacIntyre, *Three Rival Versions of Moral Enquiry: Encyclopaedia, Genealogy, and Tradition* (Notre Dame, IN: University of Notre Dame Press, 1990), 125: he argues that Thomist-Aristotelian philosophy is an illustration of this principle.

11. François-Joseph Fétis: See his *Triaté complet de la théorie et de la pratique de l'harmonie, contenant la doctrine de la science et de l'art*, 4th ed. (Paris: Brandus, 1849), 165–83. Fétis coined the term "tonality."

12. Andrew Jackson Downing, *Victorian Cottage Residences* (1842; repr. from the 1873 ed.; New York: Dover Publications, 1981), 1–25. See also Downing's *The Architecture of Country Houses* (1850; repr. New York: Dover Publications, 1969), 1–38, in which the picturesque styles are characterized as expressing personal character through the aesthetic category of the sublime. This shift is significant in employing more traditional terminology than the earlier treatise, but does not alter the underlying meaning attached to the picturesque as the goal of country architecture in the emerging suburbs of New York City.

13. See the discussion of Poussin's *The Ashes of Phocian Collected by his Widow* in Richard Wollheim, *Painting as an Art* (Princeton, NJ: Princeton University Press, 1987), 215–20, in which the woman gathering the ashes occupies the central position in the foreground, the city of Megara in the middle ground, and Nature, in the form of a mountain and

a forest, in the background. Wollheim argues, persuasively, that the moral act in the foreground, by which the ashes of a man falsely accused of treason against Athens are gathered up by his widow, echoes the strength of Nature depicted in the background: the connection between Nature and moral law was the essence of the Stoic teaching to which Poussin subscribed. But the city is in complete contrast to these two settings in the painting; Wollheim concludes (220): "In her stubborn act of piety the woman has placed herself beyond the world of custom and civic obligation; complacent *sittlichkeit* has nothing to offer her."

14. On plurivocity in the metaxological realm, see William Desmond, *Being and the Between* (Albany: State University of New York Press, 1995), 177ff.

Notes to Chapter 10

1. St. Thomas Aquinas, *Summa Theologica*, 5 vols., trans. Fathers of the English Dominican Province, rev. ed. (1911; repr. Westminster, MD: Christian Classics, 1981), Part I, Question 5, Article1; the quotation from Aristotle is from the beginning of the *Nichomachean Ethics* I, i, as rendered in the translation of the *Summa*.

2. St. Thomas Aquinas, *Quaestiones Disputatae de Veritate*, Question 21, Article 2 (Reply), in James F. Anderson, trans., *An Introduction to the Metaphysics of St. Thomas Aquinas* (Washington, DC: Regnery Gateway, 1953), 83. Cf. ST I, Q.5, Art. 2 (Reply), in which he states that every being, considered in itself, is good.

3. St. Thomas Aquinas, *Quaestiones Disputatae de Veritate*, Question 21, Article 1 (Reply), in Thomas Aquinas, *Selected Philosophical Writings*, trans. and ed. Timothy McDermott (Oxford and New York: Oxford University Press, 1993), 63.

4. See the excerpts from *De Veritate* in Anderson, *An Introduction to the Metaphysics of St. Thomas Aquinas*, and the remarks on the relation of beauty and goodness in the *Summa Theologica* I, Q. 5, Art. 4.

5. Friedrich Nietzsche, *The Will to Power*, trans. Walter Kaufmann and R. J. Hollingdale (New York: Random House, 1967), §3, 9. Hereafter abbreviated *WP*.

6. See Bruce Detwiler, *Nietzsche and the Politics of Aristocratic Radicalism* (Chicago: University of Chicago Press, 1990).

7. This is the burden of "The Drunken Song" in the Fourth Part of *Thus Spoke Zarathustra*, as given in Walter Kaufmann, trans. and ed., *The Portable Nietzsche* (Harmondsworth and New York: Penguin, 1954), 429–36.

8. See the discussion of Nietzsche's influence on both German and French modernist art of the early twentieth century in Donald E. Gordon, *Expressionism: Art and Idea* (New Haven, CT and London: Yale University Press, 1987), 14–19.

9. See Sixten Ringbom, *The Sounding Cosmos: A Study in the Spiritualism of Kandinsky and the Genesis of Abstract Painting* (Åbo: Åbo Akademi, 1970); on Schoenberg, see Etter, *From Classicism to Modernism: Western Musical Culture and the Metaphysics of Order*, chapters 6 and 7, 144–205.

10. For a good summary of ancient gnostic systems, see Hans Jonas, *The Gnostic Religion: The Message of the Alien God and the Beginnings of Christianity*, 2nd ed. (Boston: Beacon Press, 1963), 42–47. A more recent study by Kurt Rudolph, *Gnosis: The Nature and History of Gnosticism*, trans. Robert M. Wilson (New York: HarperCollins, 1987), 53ff., although taking into account the Nag Hammadi corpus, does not differ in substantial detail from Jonas's earlier account. Ascribing a general gnostic sense to the diversity of specific intellectual systems from late antiquity is possible due to the striking similarity of the broad outlines of these systems.

11. Rudolf Steiner, *An Outline of Occult Science*, trans. Maud Monges and Henry B. Monges, rev. ed. by Lisa D. Monges (Spring Valley, NY: Anthroposophic Press, 1972), 103, 206. Madame Helena P. Blavatsky also taught that there was no creation of the universe, only instead a perpetual cycle of appearance and disappearance of the universe, an alternation of its subjective and objective being; its appearance may be called evolution or emanation. See her account in *The Key to Theosophy: A Simple Exposition Based on the Wisdom-Religion of All Ages* (1889; repr. Pasadena, CA: Theosophical University Press, 1995), 83–84.

12. Rudolf Steiner, *Theosophy: An Introduction to the Supersensible Knowledge of the World and the Destination of Man*, trans. E. D. S. (Chicago, IL: Rand McNally, 1910), 46. Cf. Blavatsky, *Theosophy*, 29, where she identifies the divine spark in man with the Universal Spirit.

13. Steiner, *Theosophy*, 78, 83; cf. Blavatsky, who rejects explicitly the idea of divine forgiveness, *The Key to Theosophy*, 110, 225.

14. Hans Jonas remarks on the close parallels between the modernist philosophy of Martin Heidegger and ancient gnosticism in his Epilogue to *The Gnostic Religion*, 320–40, so that the enthusiasm Heidegger manifested for Nazism becomes intelligible not only as a direct outgrowth of his existentialism in *Being and Time*, but also as a political consequence of a fundamentally gnostic attitude. On the relation of modernity to the hatred of existence, see also Modris Eksteins, *Rites of Spring: The Great War and the Birth of the Modern Age* (Boston:

Houghton Mifflin, 1989). Finally, on the concept of political gnosticism, see Eric Voegelin, *Science, Politics and Gnosticism: Two Essays* (Washington, DC: Regnery Gateway, 1968).

15. See the preparatory discussion of this in Cyril O'Regan, *Gnostic Return in Modernity* (Albany: State University of New York Press, 2001).

Bibliography

Adorno, Theodor W. *Aesthetic Theory*. Edited by Gretel Adorno and Rolf Tiedemann. Translated by Robert Hullot-Kantor. Minneapolis: University of Minnesota Press, 1997.

———. *Philosophy of Modern Music*. Translated by Anne G. Mitchell and Wesley V. Blomster. New York: Seabury Press, 1973.

———. *Quasi una Fantasia: Essays on Modern Music*. Translated by Rodney Livingstone. London: Verso, 1994.

Aeschylus. *The Oresteia: Agamemnon, The Libation Bearers, The Eumenides*. Translated by Robert Fagles. Edited by R. Fagles and W. B. Stanford. New York and London: Penguin, 1975.

Alberti, Leon Battista. *On Painting*. Translated by Cecil Grayson. Edited by Martin Kemp. London: Penguin, 1991.

———. *On the Art of Building in Ten Books [De re aedificatorio]*. Translated by Joseph Rykwert, Neil Leach, and Robert Tavernor. Cambridge, MA: MIT Press, 1988.

Ambros, Wilhelm August. *The Boundaries of Music and Poetry: A Study in Musical Aesthetics*. Translated by J. H. Cornell. New York: Schirmer, 1893.

Aquinas, Thomas. *An Introduction to the Metaphysics of St. Thomas Aquinas*. Edited and translated by James F. Anderson. Washington, DC: Regnery Gateway, 1953.

———. *Selected Philosophical Writings*. Translated and edited by Timothy McDermott. Oxford and New York: Oxford University Press, 1993.

———. *Summa Theologica*. 5 vols. Translated by Fathers of the Dominican Province. Rev. ed. 1911. Westminster, MD: Christian Classics, 1981.

Aristotle. *Eudemian Ethics: Books I, II, and VIII*. Translated and edited by Michael Woods. 2nd ed. Oxford: Clarendon Press, 1992.

———. *Metaphysics*. Translated by Richard Hope. 1952. Ann Arbor: University of Michigan Press, 1960.

———. *Nichomachean Ethics*. Translated by W. D. Ross. Edited by J. L. Ackrill and J. O. Urmson. 1925. Oxford: Oxford University Press, 1980.

———. *Poetics*. Translated and edited by G. M. A. Grube. *On Poetry and Style*. 1958. Indianapolis, IN: Hackett, 1989.

———. *The Politics*. Translated by Benjamin Jowett. Edited by Stephen Everson. Cambridge: Cambridge University Press, 1988.

Augustine. *The Enchiridion on Faith, Hope and Love*. Translated by J. F. Shaw. Edited by Henry Paolucci. Chicago: Regnery Gateway, 1961.

———. *On Free Choice of the Will*. Translated by Thomas Williams. Indianapolis, IN and Cambridge: Hackett, 1993.

Barzun, Jacques. *The Use and Abuse of Art*. Princeton, NJ and London: Princeton University Press, 1974.

Beardsley, Monroe. *Aesthetics: Problems in the Philosophy of Criticism*. 2nd ed. Indianapolis, IN and Cambridge: Hackett, 1981.

Bernstein, J. M. *The Fate of Art: Aesthetic Alienation from Kant to Derrida and Adorno*. University Park: Pennsylvania State University Press, 1992.

Blavatsky, Helena Petrovna. *The Key to Theosophy: A Simple Exposition Based on the Wisdom-Religion of All Ages*. 1889. Pasadena, CA: Theosophical University Press, 1995.

Budd, Malcolm. *Values of Art: Pictures, Poetry and Music*. London: Penguin, 1995.

Bungay, Stephen. *Beauty and Truth: A Study of Hegel's Aesthetics*. Oxford: Oxford University Press, 1984.

Bürger, Peter. *Theory of the Avant-Garde*. Translated by Michael Shaw. Minneapolis: University of Minnesota Press, 1984.

Burke, Edmund. *Philosophical Enquiry into the Origin of Our Ideas of the Sublime and Beautiful*. Edited by Adam Phillips. Oxford and New York: Oxford University Press, 1990.

Chipp, Herschel B., ed. *Theories of Modern Art: A Source Book by Artists and Critics*. Berkeley: University of California Press, 1968.

Cicero, Marcus Tullius. *On Duties*. Translated and edited by M. T. Griffin and E. M. Atkins. Cambridge: Cambridge University Press, 1991.

Crane, Susan A., ed. *Museums and Memory*. Stanford, CA: Stanford University Press, 2000.

Dahlhaus, Carl. *Esthetics of Music*. Translated by William Austin. Cambridge: Cambridge University Press, 1982.

———. *Klassicsche und romantische Musikästhetik*. Laaber, Germany: Laaber-Verlag, 1988.

Danto, Arthur C. *After the End of Art: Contemporary Art and the Pale of History*. Princeton, NJ and Chichester, UK: Princeton University Press, 1997.

———. *The Philosophical Disenfranchisement of Art*. New York: Columbia University Press, 1986.

Davies, Stephen. *Definitions of Art*. Ithaca, NY and London: Cornell University Press, 1991.

Desmond, William. *Art and the Absolute: A Study of Hegel's Aesthetics*. Albany: State University of New York Press, 1986.

———. *Being and the Between*. Albany: State University of New York Press, 1995.

———. *Hegel's God: A Counterfeit Double?* Aldershot, UK: Ashgate, 2003.

Detwiler, Bruce. *Nietzsche and the Politics of Aristocratic Radicalism*. Chicago: University of Chicago Press, 1990.

Dewey, John. *Art as Experience*. 1934. New York: Berkley Publishing Group, 1980.

Downing, Andrew Jackson. *The Architecture of Country Houses*. 1850. New York: Dover, 1969.

———. *Victorian Cottage Residences*. 1842. New York: Dover, 1981.

Duby, Georges. *The Age of the Cathedrals: Art and Society, 980–1420*. Translated by Eleanor Levieux and Barbara Thompson. Chicago: University of Chicago Press, 1981.

Eksteins, Modris. *Rites of Spring: The Great War and the Birth of the Modern Age*. Boston: Houghton Mifflin, 1989.

Etter, Brian K. *From Classicism to Modernism: Western Musical Culture and the Metaphysics of Order*. Aldershot, UK: Ashgate, 2001.

Fackenheim, Emil L. *The Religious Dimension in Hegel's Thought*. Bloomington and London: Indiana University Press, 1967.

Fétis, François Joseph. *Traité complet de la théorie et de la pratique de l'harmonie*. 4th ed. Paris: Brandus, 1849.

Ficino, Marsilio. *Commentary on Plato's Symposium on Love*. Translated and edited by Sears Jayne. Woodstock, CT: Spring Publications, 1985.

Fine, Gail. *On Ideas: Aristotle's Criticism of Plato's Theory of Forms*. Oxford: Clarendon Press, 1993.

Gadamer, Hans-Georg. *The Relevance of the Beautiful and Other Essays*. Translated by Nicholas Walker. Edited by Robert Bernasconi. Cambridge and New York: Cambridge University Press, 1986.

Gardner, John. *On Moral Fiction*. New York: Basic Books, 1978.

Gilson, Etienne. *The Arts of the Beautiful*. 1965. Dalkey Archive, 2000.

Goehr, Lydia. *The Imaginary Museum of Musical Works: An Essay in the Philosophy of Music*. Oxford: Clarendon Press, 1992.

Goethe, Johann Wolfgang. *Faust, Erster und Zweiter Teil*. Edited by Sybille Demmer. Munich: Deutscher Taschenbuch Verlag, 1997.

Goldman, Alan. *Aesthetic Value*. Boulder, CO: Westview Press, 1995.

Gordon, Donald E. *Expressionism: Art and Idea*. New Haven, CT and London: Yale University Press, 1987.

Hanslick, Eduard. *On the Musically Beautiful*. Translated by Geoffrey Payzant. Indianapolis, IN: Hackett, 1986.

Harries, Karsten. *The Ethical Function of Architecture*. Cambridge, MA: MIT Press, 1997.

Hegel, Georg Wilhelm Friedrich. *Aesthetics: Lectures on the Fine Arts*. Translated by T. M. Knox. 2 vols. Oxford: Clarendon Press, 1975.

———. *The Encyclopaedia Logic*. Translated by T. F. Geraets, W. A. Suchting, and H. S. Harris. Indianapolis, IN: Hackett, 1991.

———. *Enzyklopädie der philosophischen Wissenschaften im Grundrisse (1830)*. Edited by E. Moldenhauer and K. Michel. Vols 8–10, *Sämtliche Werke*. Frankfurt am Main: Suhrkamp, 1970.

———. *Grundlinien der Philosophie des Rechts oder Naturrecht und Staatswissenschaft im Grundrisse*. Edited by E. Moldenhauer and K. Michel. Vol. 7, *Sämtliche Werke*. Frankfurt am Main: Suhrkamp, 1970.

———. *Introduction to the Lectures on the History of Philosophy*. Translated by T. M. Knox and A. V. Miller. Oxford: Clarendon Press, 1985.

———. *Lectures on the Philosophy of Religion: The Lectures of 1827*. Translated by R. F. Brown, P. C. Hodgson, J. M. Stewart, and H. S. Harris. Edited by P. C. Hodgson. Berkeley and London: University of California Press, 1988.

———. *The Philosophy of History*. Translated by J. Sibree. New York: Dover, 1956.

———. *Philosophy of Mind: Part Three of the Encyclopaedia of the Philosophical Sciences (1830)*. Translated by William Wallace and A. V. Miller. Oxford: Clarendon Press, 1971.

———. *Philosophy of Right*. Translated by T. M. Knox. Oxford: Oxford University Press, 1952.

———. *The Science of Logic*. Translated by A. V. Miller. Edited by H. D. Lewis. 1969. Atlantic Highlands, NJ: Humanities Press International, 1989.

———. *Vorlesungen über die Ästhetik*. Edited by E. Moldenhauer and K. Michel. Vols. 13–15, *Sämtliche Werke*. Frankfurt am Main: Suhrkamp Verlag, 1970.

———. *Vorlesungen über die Geschichte der Philosophie*. Edited by E. Moldenhauer and K. Michel. Vols. 18–20, *Sämtliche Werke*. Frankfurt am Main: Suhrkamp, 1971.

———. *Vorlesungen über die Philosophie der Geschichte*. Edited by E. Moldenhauer and K. Michel. Vol 12, *Sämtliche Werke*. Frankfurt am Main: Suhrkamp, 1970.

———. *Vorlesungen über die Philosophie der Religion*. Edited by Walter Jaeschke. Vols. 3, 4a, 5, *Vorlesungen, Ausgewählte Nachschriften und Manuskripte*. Hamburg: Felix Meiner Verlag, 1984.

———. *Wissenschaft der Logik*. Edited by E. Moldenhauer and K. Michel. Vols. 5–6, *Sämtliche Werke*. Frankfurt am Main: Suhrkamp, 1969.

Heidegger, Martin. *Being and Time: A Translation of 'Sein und Zeit'*. Translated by Joan Stambaugh. Albany: State University of New York Press, 1996.

———. *Poetry, Language, Thought*. Translated by Albert Hofstadter. 1971. New York: HarperCollins, 2001.

Holt, Elizabeth G. *A Documentary History of Art*. 2 vols. Rev. ed. Princeton, NJ: Princeton University Press, 1982.

Homer. *The Iliad*. Translated by Richmond Lattimore. Chicago and London: University of Chicago Press, 1951.

Houlgate, Stephen. *Freedom, Truth and History: An Introduction to Hegel's Philosophy*. London and New York: Routledge, 1991.

Janson, H. W., and Anthony F. Janson. *History of Art: The Western Tradition*. 6th ed. New York: Harry N. Abrams, 2001.

Jeanneret-Gris, Charles-Edouard. *Towards a New Architecture*. Translated by Frederick Etchells. 1931. New York: Dover, 1986.

Johnson, Julian. "Music in Hegel's Aesthetics: A Re-Evaluation." *British Journal of Aesthetics* 31 (1991): 152–62.

Jonas, Hans. *The Gnostic Religion: The Message of an Alien God and the Beginnings of Christianity*. 2nd ed. Boston: Beacon Press, 1963.

Kaminsky, Jack. *Hegel on Art: An Interpretation of Hegel's Aesthetics*. Albany: State University of New York Press, 1962.

Kant, Immanuel. *Critique of Judgement*. Translated by J. H. Bernard. New York: Macmillan, 1951.

———. *Kritik der Urteilskraft*. Edited by Karl Vorländer. Hamburg: Felix Meiner, 1990.

Kaufmann, Walter. *Tragedy and Philosophy*. Princeton, NJ: Princeton University Press, 1968.

Kierkegaard, Søren. *Either/Or*. Translated and edited by Howard V. Hong and Edna H. Hong. 2 vols. Princeton, NJ and Oxford: Princeton University Press, 1987.

Kivy, Peter. *Music Alone: Philosophical Reflections on the Purely Musical Experience*. Ithaca, NY and London: Cornell University Press, 1990.

Koepsel, Von Werner. *Die Rezeption der Hegelschen Ästhetik im 20. Jahrhundert*. Bonn: Bouvier Verlag, 1975.

Kristeller, Paul Oskar. *Renaissance Thought and the Arts: Collected Essays*. Rev. ed. Princeton, NJ and Chichester, UK: Princeton University Press, 1990.

Krook, Dorothea. *Elements of Tragedy*. New Haven, CT: Yale University Press, 1969.

Kunstler, James Howard. *Home from Nowhere: Remaking Our Everyday World for the Twenty-First Century*. New York: Simon & Schuster, 1996.

Lane, John. *Timeless Beauty in the Arts and Everyday Life*. Dartington Totnes, UK: Green Books, 2003.

Lauer, Quentin. *Hegel's Concept of God*. Albany: State University of New York Press, 1982.

Le Huray, Peter, and James Day, eds. *Music and Aesthetics in the Eighteenth and Early Nineteenth Centuries*. Cambridge: Cambridge University Press, 1981.

Leppert, Richard, and Susan McClary, eds. *Music and Society: The Politics of Composition, Performance and Reception*. Cambridge: Cambridge University Press, 1987.

Lippman, Edward A., ed. *Musical Aesthetics: A Historical Reader*. 3 vols. Stuyvesant, NY: Pendragon Press, 1990.

Löwith, Karl. *Martin Heidegger and European Nihilism*. Translated by Gary Steiner. Edited by Richard Wolin. New York: Columbia University Press, 1995.

MacIntyre, Alasdair. *After Virtue: A Study in Moral Theory*. 2nd ed. Notre Dame, IN: University of Notre Dame Press, 1984.

———. *Three Rival Versions of Moral Enquiry: Encyclopaedia, Genealogy, and Tradition*. Notre Dame, IN: University of Notre Dame Press, 1990.

———. *Whose Justice? Which Rationality?* Notre Dame, IN: University of Notre Dame Press, 1988.

Menke, Christopher. *The Sovereignty of Art: Aesthetic Negativity in Adorno and Derrida*. Translated by Neil Solomon. Cambridge, MA and London: MIT Press, 1998.

Mortensen, Preben. *Art in the Social Order: The Making of the Modern Concept of Art*. Albany: State University of New York Press, 1997.

Nietzsche, Friedrich. *Beyond Good and Evil*. Translated by R. J. Hollingdale. Rev. ed. by Michael Tanner. London: Penguin, 1990.

———. *Thus Spoke Zarathustra*. Translated and edited by Walter Kaufmann. *The Portable Nietzsche*. New York: Penguin, 1954.

———. *The Will to Power*. Translated by Walter Kaufmann and R. J. Hollingdale. New York: Random House, 1967.

Nowak, Adolf. *Hegels Musikaesthetik*. Regensburg, Germany: Bosse, 1971.

Onians, John. *Bearers of Meaning: The Classical Orders in Antiquity, the Middle Ages, and the Renaissance*. Princeton, NJ: Princeton University Press, 1988.

O'Regan, Cyril. *Gnostic Return in Modernity*. Albany: State University of New York Press, 2001.

———. *The Heterodox Hegel*. Albany: State University of New York Press, 1994.

Osborne, Harold. *Aesthetics and Art Theory: An Historical Introduction*. New York: Dutton, 1970.

Palladio, Andrea. *The Four Books of Architecture [I Quattro libri dell'architettura*]. Translated by Isaac Ware. 1738. New York: Dover, 1965.

Passmore, John. *Serious Art*. La Salle, IL: Open Court, 1991.

Pelikan, Jaroslav. *The Christian Tradition: A History of the Development of Doctrine*. 5 vols. Chicago and London: University of Chicago Press, 1971–1989.

———. *The Vindication of Tradition*. New Haven, CT and London: Yale University Press, 1984.

Perrault, Claude. *Ordonnance for the Five Kinds of Columns after the Method of the Ancients*. Translated by Indra K. McEwen. Edited by Alberto Perez-Gomez. Santa Monica, CA: Getty Center for the History of Art and the Humanities, 1993.

Plato. *The Laws*. Translated and edited by Trevor J. Saunders. London and New York: Penguin, 1970.

———. *Lysis, Symposium, Gorgias*. Translated by W. R. M. Lamb. Vol. 166 of the Loeb Classical Library. Cambridge, MA: Harvard University Press, 1925.

———. *Phaedrus and the Seventh and Eighth Letters*. Translated by Walter Hamilton. London: Penguin, 1973.

———. *Statesman, Philebus, Ion*. Translated by Harold N. Fowler and W. R. M. Lamb. Vol. 164 of the Loeb Classical Library. Cambridge, MA: Harvard University Press, 1925.

———. *Timaeus and Critias*. Translated by Desmond Lee. Rev. ed. London: Penguin, 1977.

Plotinus. *Enneads*. Translated by A. H. Armstrong. 2nd ed. Vols. 440–46 of the Loeb Classical Library. Cambridge, MA: Harvard University Press, 1989.

Poggioli, Renato. *The Theory of the Avant-Garde*. Translated by Gerald Fitzgerald. 1968. Cambridge, MA: Harvard University Press, 1996.

Rameau, Jean Philippe. *Treatise on Harmony*. Translated by Philip Gossett. New York: Dover, 1971.

Rapp, Carl. *Fleeing the Universal: The Critique of Post-Rational Criticism*. Albany: State University of New York Press, 1998.

Reardon, Bernard M. G. *Hegel's Philosophy of Religion*. London: Macmillan, 1977.

Reed, Henry Hope. *Palladio's Architecture and Its Influence*. New York: Dover, 1980.

Ringbom, Sixten. *The Sounding Cosmos: A Study in the Spiritualism of Kandinsky and the Genesis of Abstract Painting*. Åbo: Åbo Akademi, 1970.

Risatti, Howard, ed. *Postmodern Perspectives: Issues in Contemporary Art*. 2nd ed. Upper Saddle River, NJ: Prentice Hall, 1998.

Rosen, Stanley. *G. W. F. Hegel: An Introduction to the Science of Wisdom*. New Haven, CT and London: Yale University Press, 1974.

Ross, Stephen David. *The Gift of Beauty: The Good as Art*. Albany: State University of New York Press, 1996.

Rudolph, Kurt. *Gnosis: The Nature and History of Gnosticism*. Translated by Robert M. Wilson. San Francisco: HarperCollins, 1987.

Schiller, Friedrich. *Essays*. Edited by Walter Hinderer and Daniel O. Dahlstrom. New York: Continuum, 1993.

———. *The Robbers and Wallenstein*. Translated and edited by F. J. Lamport. London and New York: Penguin, 1979.

Schoenberg, Arnold. *Style and Idea: Selected Writings*. Translated by Leo Black. Rev. ed. by Leo Stein. Berkeley: University of California Press, 1984.

Schubart, Christian F. D. *Ideen zu einer Ästhetik der Tonkunst*. 1806. Leipzig: Reclam, 1977.

Schulte, Michael. *Die "Tragödie im Sittlichen": Zur Dramentheorie Hegels*. Munich: Wilhelm Fink Verlag, 1992.

Schüttauf, Konrad. *Die Kunst und die bildenden Künste: Eine Auseinandersetzung mit Hegels Ästhetik*. Bonn: Bouvier Verlag, 1984.

Scruton, Roger. *Aesthetics of Architecture*. Princeton, NJ: Princeton University Press, 1979.

Shakespeare, William. *The Tragedy of Hamlet, Prince of Denmark. Tragedies*. London: J. M. Dent & Sons, 1906.

Sherman, Daniel J., and Irit Rogoff. *Museum Culture: Histories, Discoveries, Spectacles*. Minneapolis: University of Minnesota Press, 1994.

Simson, Otto von. *The Gothic Cathedral: Origins of Gothic Architecture and the Medieval Concept of Order*. 3rd ed. Princeton, NJ: Princeton University Press, 1988.

Sophocles. *The Three Theban Plays: Antigone, Oedipus the King, Oedipus at Colonus*. Translated by Robert Fagles. Edited by Bernard Knox. New York: Viking Penguin, 1982.

Steblin, Rita. *A History of Key Characteristics in the Eighteenth and Early Nineteenth Centuries*. Ann Arbor: UMI Research Press, 1983.

Steiner, Rudolf. *An Outline of Occult Science*. Translated by Maud Monges and Henry B. Monges. Rev. ed. by Lisa D. Monges. Spring Valley, NY: Anthroposophic Press, 1972.

———. *Theosophy: An Introduction to the Supersensible Knowledge of the World and the Destination of Man*. Translated by E. D. S. Chicago: Rand McNally, 1910.

Tatarkiewicz, Wladyslaw. "The Great Theory of Beauty and Its Decline." *Journal of Aesthetics and Art Criticism* 31 (1972–1973): 165–80.

Taylor, Charles. *Hegel and Modern Society*. Cambridge and New York: Cambridge University Press, 1979.

Thomson, William. *Schoenberg's Error*. Philadelphia: University of Pennsylvania Press, 1991.

Trollope, Anthony. *The Eustace Diamonds*. 2 vols. in one. Edited by W. J. McCormack. Oxford and New York: Oxford University Press, 1982.

Tzonis, Alexander, and Liane Lefaivre. *Classical Architecture: The Poetics of Order*. Cambridge, MA: MIT Press, 1986.

Vattimo, Gianni. *The End of Modernity: Nihilism and Hermeneutics in Postmodern Culture*. Translated by Jon R. Snyder. Baltimore: Johns Hopkins University Press, 1991.

Vitruvius, Pollio. *The Ten Books on Architecture* [*De architectura libri decem*]. Translated by Morris H. Morgan. 1914. New York: Dover, 1960.

Voegelin, Eric. *Science, Politics and Gnosticism*. Washington, DC: Regnery Gateway, 1968.

Watkin, David. *A History of Western Architecture*. New York: Thames and Hudson, 1986.

Watkin, David, and Tilman Mellinghof. *German Architecture and the Classical Ideal*. Cambridge, MA: MIT Press, 1987.

Webern, Anton. *The Path to the New Music*. Translated by Leo Black. Edited by Willi Reich. 1963. London: Universal Edition, 1975.

Westphal, Maurice. *Hegel, Freedom, and Modernity*. Albany: State University of New York Press, 1992.

White, David A. "Toward a Theory of Profundity in Music." *Journal of Aesthetics and Art Criticism* 50 (1992): 23–34.

Will, Frederick. *Intelligible Beauty: Aesthetic Thought from Winckelmann to Victor Cousin*. Tübingen: M. Niemeyer, 1958.

Winckelmann, Johann Joachim. *Reflections on the Imitation of Greek Works in Painting and Sculpture*. Translated by Elfriede Heyer and Roger C. Norton. La Salle, IL: Open Court, 1987.

Winfield, Richard Dien. *Systematic Aesthetics*. Gainesville: University Press of Florida, 1995.

Wittkower, Rudolf. *Architectural Principles in the Age of Humanism*. 3rd ed. 1962. New York: Norton, 1971.

Wollheim, Richard. *Painting as an Art*. Princeton, NJ: Princeton University Press, 1987.

Wyss, Beat. *Hegel's Art History and the Critique of Modernity*. Translated by Caroline D. Saltzwedel. Cambridge and New York: Cambridge University Press, 1999.

Index